POSTMARKED BOMBAY

TRUE TALES OF A TEXAN IN BRITISH COLONIAL INDIA, 1937–1945

Harriet Claiborne
3/10/24

HARRIET CLAIBORNE

WESTBOW
PRESS
A DIVISION OF THOMAS NELSON
& ZONDERVAN

Copyright © 2023 Harriet Claiborne.

All rights reserved. No part of this book may be used or reproduced by any means, graphic, electronic, or mechanical, including photocopying, recording, taping or by any information storage retrieval system without the written permission of the author except in the case of brief quotations embodied in critical articles and reviews.

WestBow Press books may be ordered through booksellers or by contacting:

WestBow Press
A Division of Thomas Nelson & Zondervan
1663 Liberty Drive
Bloomington, IN 47403
www.westbowpress.com
844-714-3454

Because of the dynamic nature of the Internet, any web addresses or links contained in this book may have changed since publication and may no longer be valid. The views expressed in this work are solely those of the author and do not necessarily reflect the views of the publisher, and the publisher hereby disclaims any responsibility for them.

Any people depicted in stock imagery provided by Getty Images are models, and such images are being used for illustrative purposes only.
Certain stock imagery © Getty Images.

Photographs, maps, and illustrations contained in this book are the sole property of the author unless otherwise credited.

Scriptures are taken from King James version of the Bible, public domain.

ISBN: 979-8-3850-0651-9 (sc)
ISBN: 979-8-3850-0652-6 (hc)
ISBN: 979-8-3850-0650-2 (e)

Library of Congress Control Number: 2023916603

Print information available on the last page.

WestBow Press rev. date: 10/02/2023

In thanksgiving for my son, John, who was intent on discovering the hidden story behind his Grandpa's tall tales.

CONTENTS

Acknowledgments vii
Preface ix
Introduction xi

Part I. Waiting for a Train

Chapter 1   Adventure, Ho! 1
Chapter 2   The Bombay Office 7
Chapter 3   Trains and Motorcycles 25
Chapter 4   Umarkhed 35
Chapter 5   Classing Cotton 46
Chapter 6   Monsoon 52
Chapter 7   Rugger 56
Chapter 8   Theoretically, It Ought to Work 65
Chapter 9   Christmas and the Tiger 76
Chapter 10   Dreamboat In 86

Part II. Getting to Know Her

Chapter 11   Bombay at Last! 95
Chapter 12   The Wedding 99
Chapter 13   Honeymoon Bliss? 106
Chapter 14   Housekeeping in Bombay 133
Chapter 15   Karachi Stories 140

Part III. The War Years 1942–1945

Chapter 16 Unnecessary Persons 165
Chapter 17 Strategic Materials 175
Chapter 18 Back to India 191
Chapter 19 Kashmir Adventures 207
Chapter 20 New Beginnings 215

Part IV. War's End

Chapter 21 VJ Day Joy 231
Chapter 22 An Extraordinary Birthday Bash 234
Chapter 23 White Men in Nepal? 243
Chapter 24 Home at Last and Away Again 276

Afterword 281

ACKNOWLEDGMENTS

How do I say, "Thank you!" to patient, forgiving people who asked for a book and never gave up hope, over a span of several years, that they might see one? Begun in love, written, and edited in joy and in hope, working on "The Book" has become a parable of life itself, frequented with laughs and tears.

Pat Walsh was instrumental, in the early days, in sharing her vision of starting a writing group and reading my first pages. Without her continuing encouragement, this book would never have been written.

A writing group materialized to help, in the persons of Linda Jewel, John Barringer, and Larry Quinlan. They gave their honest but kind critique when most needed. Their own pages were amazing and set a high bar for me to reach.

So many friends kept asking, "When will you be finished with the book?" I could not quit; I had to persevere. Annilee Quinlan—close friend who never gave up; Kathi Frelk—my faithful team editor, par excellence. Bless her patience! Sharon Veenker and Alvin Johnson who stepped in as readers when it was most needed. Barbra Vogen brought an insistent, yet gracious push to finish what I had started and not to give up.

A special thank-you to all my family, especially Elizabeth Burbage, Harry and Idie's granddaughter, who wanted a romance. She and her family listened to many rewrites and signed me up for an online course, Pitch to Published, which was very helpful!

More thanks go to Noah Kazek, Harry and Idie's great grandson, and to Noah's mom, Tasha. Their family took turns reading chapters at every Christmas visit for years.

Jerry Jenkins's nonfiction class was amazing, As a Christian and a bestselling author, he has chosen to share his writing and publishing insights over the internet, a real ministry to new authors.

Wynne Brown shared her time and talent with me via the Pima County Library program in Tucson. Generous and helpful, she introduced me to Charlie McKee, who made all the difference as I tried to comprehend producing a book for family and a book for general readers. She is a fierce editor and kind guide extraordinaire!

Daniel Edwards, from Colorado and Nepal, was working on his own book about railroads in Nepal when he called me about Harry's reports to the State Department and encouraged me to keep writing and editing,

The people at WestBow Press did a great job of leading me through the many steps of publishing. I appreciated the good work of the editing team and look forward to working with the design team. Being able to correspond with a person made a huge difference!

I hope I have not forgotten anyone! Please know that your encouragement on airplanes, at lunch, even in rejection letters, helped me to grow as a writer and focus on the next steps. May you be blessed, and may you see the Lord's hand in Idie's and Harry's India story and claim that grace for your own.

PREFACE

What do you do when you inherit a wonderful house, filled to overflowing with beautiful things from around the world? Dad died first, in 2003, and then Mom, in 2009. My sister and I were their only children, and we had no idea what memorabilia hid in the closets, so long overlooked.

My sister and I went exploring. The treasure we found was not in the exquisite Chinese porcelains or the minerals from Brazil or even the Japanese woodblock prints but in small boxes tucked safely away in a back closet. They were handwritten letters between our parents, Harry and Idie Witt, from 1937 to 1945. Harry's letters to Idie were postmarked Bombay, India, and Idie's to Harry, Houston, Texas.

The letters were full of love and longing, adventure, and faith. They also told a story about a twenty-four-year-old Texan's impressions of a culture once powerful and now defunct—British Colonial India. Harry took a job overseas in 1937, leaving his family and sweetheart, for three years without home leave. His descriptive tales of traveling in the interior (up-country) of India and of learning how to do business with Hindus, Muslims, and British merchants helped his sweetheart, Idie, feel as if she were with him.

In February 1939, rumors of war spread throughout Europe and the British Empire. Idie showed her courage when she boarded a ship to marry Harry in Bombay. They honeymooned in Kashmir, where grand adventures began.

Later letters recall their separation during World War II, when Idie, along with other American wives, was evacuated from India. Harry stayed, loaned to the US government by his employer to procure strategic materials for the war effort—mica for military radios and beryl ore for the atomic bomb.

My sister and I grew up hearing their stories, sharing them with children, grandchildren, and friends, who clamored for a book. As I read and collated their letters, notes, and journals, I felt history come alive. I worked, for years, on a narrative account of this refreshing glimpse into a time now gone, but I could not write with the same passion Harry felt for Idie, for India, and for the Lord.

"Why not let Harry tell the story?" a friend suggested. And so, I did. What follows is Harry's true story, told in the first person.

Some of Harry's attitudes might disturb modern readers; I hope they will accept them within the context of the time in which he lived.

Harry did not speak of his work during the war, and little of it appears in his letters. I obtained that information from the National Archives and from an article in the *National Geographic Magazine,* January 1946, which mentions Harry by name.

This is Harry and Idie's story of their India days and of a love they kept burning across a vast ocean and throughout a world war. May it inspire you, while giving you a good laugh or two along the way.

INTRODUCTION

Howdy! My name is Harry Witt, a country boy from Texas. I set out for Bombay, India, in November 1937, with my business associate, Gene Graves. We were bright-eyed and eager to begin overseas careers in the international business world. That others might look upon us as small-town country boys had not occurred to either of us, but the message came through loud and clear when Gene sent his sister a pair of gloves from a Fifth Avenue store in New York. "To Lorena, Texas," giggled the salesgirl as she filled in the address.

Gene and I worked for Anderson Clayton and Company (ACCO), headquartered in Houston, Texas, with offices overseas, including India, South America, Europe, Egypt, and China. ACCO had expanded to meet the demands for cotton during World War I, and by 1936, Indian cotton production had reached a new height of productivity.

We were on our way because ACCO's Bombay office had asked for two new men; young and willing to stay three years without home leave, remaining single for that time. They wanted someone with talent for administration. That was Gene. They also needed a man with a strong back, not necessarily one with brains, to live and work in the remote villages of up-country India. That was me.

My boss began describing the job in terms calculated to eliminate future disappointment: enduring a hot, dirty country, perhaps living in a mud hut, boiling all drinking water, and eating only tinned food. As Mr. Whittington talked, dazzling visions of adventure in a strange land, accumulation of wealth, and a chance for heroic deeds flew through my mind. I knew next to nothing about India but almost shouted *yes* the moment he paused for breath.

The call of the mysterious East was loud and irresistible. It had to be because the entire family rebelled at little brother going to that "heathen country." The company had given me ten days to prepare. However, knowing the family crisis this news would provoke, I did not inform them until three days before the departure date. My mother cried copiously, convinced I was going to my death in "Dark India." Dad said nothing, but I saw his eyes light up, as if he, too, would like to explore faraway places.

Then I needed to tell my sweetheart, Idie Lacy. Her many friends thought I was deserting her, but she seemed to revel in my good fortune, cheering me on, just as she had done at my Rice Institute football games.

We met at a dance at Rice on March 3, 1933. Idie enchanted me with her sparkling smile and twinkling eyes. Next to my six-foot-three frame, she was petite, barely five feet tall, but with a zest for adventure that matched my own. I asked her if she would like to get a bite to eat. We drove to the local hot-dog stand and started a long conversation that never ended. March third became our special day; one we celebrated every year afterwards.

Idie had grown up in a comfortable part of Houston, while I lived across town in a less affluent neighborhood. She took a teaching job at George Washington Junior High in Houston upon graduating from Rice and lived with her widowed mother, Ruby, and younger brother, Ernest.

Idie and I wanted to get married when and if the two of us could earn enough money to do so. I hoped the opportunity in India could make it happen, but a wide ocean would separate us at least for three years, maybe more.

Our strength rested in a love greater than ours: "Let not your heart be troubled; ye believe in God, believe also in me" (John 14:1).

PART I
WAITING FOR A TRAIN

Waiting for a Train

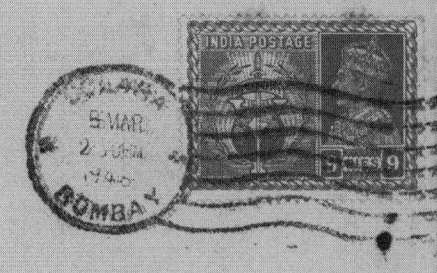

ONE

ADVENTURE, HO!

November 1937 — New York Harbor

Mountainous waves pounded the SS *Rex* as she headed out to sea. It was my first time on a ship, negotiating the pitch and roll of the Atlantic. I pulled my jacket around me and hung on to the deck railing. To me, the sleek ship represented a bridge to another world.

What have I gotten myself into? I have left all I know: my family, my job, My beloved sweetheart, Idie, and my hometown.

The *Rex* rolled from side to side, disturbing my thoughts. I could see Gene Graves struggling toward me. *At least I have a friend traveling with me.*

I grimaced against the spray pummeling my face when Gene suggested we go inside. Once in the salon, I watched heavy furniture slide past and wondered about the travel brochure's promise of "swimming and lounging on the pleasant Lido Deck."

A little guy with a gong walked in, as if he were climbing a steep hill. He announced dinner was served. Gene looked pale and left for the cabin.

I staggered to the dining room and sat across from a corpulent Italian man attacking a steaming plateful of spaghetti covered with blood-red sauce. I felt my stomach swirl as I surveyed the swaying pasta. The purser stepped up and said, "Go forward to an upper deck, and let the mist hit you in the face. It will keep you from getting seasick."

I did as the purser suggested and told Gene later, "Being peppered with saltwater and crushed ice was exhilarating. It felt as if tiny, cold needles were slapping my face, hard. Couldn't take much, but it did the job. I am not seasick."

After several stormy days, the sea calmed, and passengers left their bunks. The dining room filled with guests, and life on board began anew.

Gene and I had met Mrs. Waddell, another passenger, before we got on the ship. She was the mother of our soon-to-be boss in Bombay and was on her way to visit him and his wife. After dinner one night, the three of us took a comprehensive tour of our floating palace. I couldn't wait to write to Idie afterward.

> November 15, 1937 — SS *Rex*
>
> Darling Idie: there is a nice library, several attractive shops, two swimming pools, many large sitting rooms, a beautiful writing room, and more, but the promenade deck is my favorite. I watched the churning sea for hours one day; we rolled over so far that it seemed we would go down to Davy Jones's locker. Then, over the other way, so only the sky was visible. The significance of the Ancient Mariner's "Water, water, everywhere ..." was impressed upon me.
>
> A theater, with up-to-date projecting equipment and a large stage, provides many enjoyable hours. There is a movie every afternoon with American and Italian productions shown on alternate days. Gene and I thought the Italian film, *Scipio Africanis*, most interesting. Hannibal, Carthage, and the glory that was Rome paraded before our eyes with no comedy relief. It was an indication of what the Italians are thinking, as troops marched in every scene while legion after legion practiced the Fascist salute.
>
> Most days are given over to eating, sleeping, and reading. Incidents crop up just as we begin to feel like a couple of

gentlemen and remind us we are just a couple of green country boys.

Gene wanted some pepper the first morning in the dining room, and we carefully examined everything on the table, not finding it. Long-faced stewards stood around, and they must have known what we were searching for, but not one offered to help. We had to ask. The chief steward, with a severely straight face, picked up what we thought was a decorative wooden cask and began to twist the bottom. Pepper! Bewildered lads, we laughed at the "sold out" expression on each other's faces. The steward kept his poker face.

One night, we quietly sailed into calmer waters, and the great bulk of Gibraltar loomed before us. We arrived about midnight, and the old Rock was gaily lit. Gene, and I took a swim in the Mediterranean, but as we are late, there is no time to sightsee. You and I will have to do it sometime. Only waiting until I can return to you.

Be sweet. I do adore you, Harry

Harry and Gene

A little destroyer from the base greeted the SS *Rex* as we entered the Naples harbor. Whistles blew. Bands played. Tugboats streamed toward us. People sang and yelled greetings to friends. Troops in colorful uniforms marched past. The Italian Fascist Blackshirts stood idly by as *Rex* docked. *Rex* was a full day late, and our next ride, the nearby MN *Victoria*, impatiently let off steam. Gene and I strode a hundred yards on Italian soil and then climbed the gangway to our new home.

Standing by the rail, watching the thousand and one lights fade into the distance, I thought of Idie. I missed her! I'd received a letter she had mailed to my New York hotel the day I left Houston by train. Her sweet words said:

> By this time, you are speeding to New York. This morning will always be stamped indelibly on my heart as a delightful farewell. When you said, "I love you," it seemed to have come from the bottom of your heart. That love, my dearest one, has kept me happy and satisfied. I am anxiously waiting to hear about your trip and see if my imagination will coincide in some small degree with your actual experience.
>
> Good luck, my dear! Love you,
>
> Idie

* * *

The MN *Victoria* did not compare well, in my opinion, with the SS *Rex*. It was about one-third the size, with smaller cabins and inferior common rooms. Of interest, however, was the passenger list of many nationalities and professions: Chinese doctor and Brahmin priest, Indian raja and Italian farmer, Czech businessman and British diamond merchant, American banker and English army officer, Indian maharani and New York debutante, and German Jewish girl and boyfriend. Plus, two country boys from Texas.

All day long, and sometimes into the night, the swimming pool was crowded. At first, Gene and I were not eager to mix with our yellow and black brothers, but after a day or two, the Chinese doctor was teaching us to turn somersaults off the diving board. Meanwhile, the dark-skinned Indians in the water laughed at our miserable belly flops.

Port Said, Egypt, was the next port of call, and several of us went ashore, sure of finding treasure. Disappointment loomed, however, as hawkers, guides, and taxi drivers hounded us the moment we stepped through customs' wire barricade. Street merchants pulled at our sleeves, chattered wildly, and shoved vile postcards in our faces. Visions of a wonderful Bombay became a little fuzzy around the edges.

The ship moved into the Suez Canal and then Djibouti, the last port of call before Bombay and the last opportunity to take on water. The temperature was well over a hundred degrees. Gene and I decided to try sightseeing, choosing a taxi from the queue at the dock. We drove through a European residential district that looked livable, but other areas revealed houses built of old kerosene tins and sunbaked mud and sticks. I covered my nose as we went through the block-long fish market with sellers shooing away the flies. Less than an after we had started, Gene said, "Let's go back to the ship."

Africa faded away. As every mile brought us closer to India, I toyed with the thought that India might be like Africa and wondered if I had traveled twelve thousand miles to find a home in a mud hut.

Mrs. Waddell seemed to sense Gene's and my worry about what we would find in India. She made a point of talking to us at dinner, telling us stories of India's modern cities; of her son, Eddie, who would be our boss; and the adventures waiting for us. The next four days moved slowly as I waited to see Bombay.

* * *

November 30, 1937 — Ballard Pier, Bombay

I wiped my brow as I stood in a shed, watching a customs official begin an education on things Indian. The top of the official's head barely reached my chin.

Rummaging through my meager possessions, finding nothing on which to charge duty, the official latched onto a handful of ballpoint pens. They were hard to find in Bombay. "Expensive," he said. "You did not declare."

"No, not expensive. Cost only a few cents each."

Keeping the pens in his hand and giving me a "gotcha" smile, he continued to rummage while I sweated under the tin roof. Finally, he asked, "Do you have any beer bottles?"

What in the world would I do with beer bottles?

Another "gotcha" smile. "You must pay duty on fountain pens."

I sized him up for about ten seconds. Yes, he was serious. He meant to charge duty on my ballpoint pens. But I sure wasn't going to let him do that.

"Give me the pens," I said.

He did.

I turned and threw them off the pier into the water. Looking like I had slapped his face, which in his culture I had done, he gaped at me.

I don't know what might have happened next if another man had not joined us at that moment. He jabbered loudly with the customs man in their lingo, arms waving. It didn't last long. The customs man cleared my baggage and walked away.

Our office had sent someone to help us clear customs. He did that!

"What was the argument about?" I asked.

"Ah, you don't understand our customs," he said. "'Beer bottles' means *baksheesh* (bribe). I promised to give him five rupees."

I had met the East.

TWO

THE BOMBAY OFFICE

November 30, 1937 — Bombay

here was so much to see and experience as Gene and I got off the ship that I could hardly wait to tell Idie all about it.

Darling girl. At last, we have arrived—and I mean you and me when I say *we*. You must know you are with me every hour of the day. I hope you feel my presence too. And now, I realize how much I need your guidance and your strength. Never in my life have I felt the need, but tonight I did. You are a very vital part of my life.

We docked among a seething mass of humanity. Some passengers were important people who someday might control the destiny of India.

We were met on the boat by Mr. Waddell (Boss), Mr. Schilling (Boss), and Mr. Clayton (Mr. Boss), who is visiting from Houston. We went to the office where Gene was given a desk. They told me I'd be traveling so much I wouldn't need one. How do you like that?

We report at nine in the morning. I know whatever shall come, shall be right. My prayer is for guidance and strength, or as you would say: "Dear Lord, guide and direct him, and me."

Ever Yours, Harry

* * *

Guy Schilling took Gene and me to a nearby hotel, and after dinner there, he showed us another route to the office. "Only a couple of blocks," he said. It should have been an easy stroll, but it was one I shall never forget.

The office was in Ballard Estate, a high-rent area of British-looking brownstones. A wide paved street ran through it, dimly lit by old-fashioned stone lampposts. Something on the sidewalk made me flinch—bodies, stretched out under what resembled white sheets. We had to step over or walk around them. I lifted my feet as high as I could in the dim light.

"Dead bodies?" I asked.

"Not dead people," Guy snickered. "Only men who came outside, where it's cooler, to sleep in their *dhotis*"—traditional men's garment; a piece of stitched cloth, knotted at the waist.

It's no fun, stepping over bodies, in the dark—dead or alive.

The office building was closed for the night. The outside elevator was an out-of-this-world contraption. Nothing but a wire cage open on all sides, big enough for two people. Guy called it a "lift." I thought it didn't look strong enough to lift much.

Wooden plaques with names on them were on the wall next to it, indicating what businesses were in the building. "Ed Waddell" topped Anderson Clayton's list. Guy told Gene and me our names would be added.

The next week felt like a surrealistic movie. It began with the "lift." Gene and I got in and pushed a button. The contraption hesitated, then moved like a cranky old man needing help. We moved at less than a priest's pace, and after that, I took the stairs.

When we exited, twenty or thirty men in the bullpen stopped whatever they were doing and seemingly sized us up. "Well, come on in," a white face said. The owner of it belonged to Rene Argos, the office manager.

Bombay must have a bullpen of clerks like the Houston office was what I was thinking until I looked around for tall, slow Texans and didn't find any. Short men, the tallest of them reaching my chin, had tan, black, brown, and yellow faces. They were all fluent in English that didn't sound like English.

Several men wore western-style trousers with white cotton shirts and black shoes. Others wore dhotis, leaving their legs largely uncovered. Suspenders held up socks, clearly visible, worn with open-toed sandals. Those men were Hindus.

I walked around, getting my bearings, while listening to a ticker tape machine come to life at various times during the day. It copied messages on paper tape that snaked down into a large basket on the floor. It was a Reuters News Service machine. Those willing to pay could get the news all day long. ACCO subscribed only to market (mostly cotton) and weather reports. Cotton was our heart and soul. Weather affected cotton, whether for good or bad, and could send markets up or down. Movement on the New York or Liverpool exchange guided buying or selling cotton in India.

An Indian merchant came into the office wearing a turban, coat, and a wraparound skirt of what looked like mosquito netting. He resembled a beggar, yet he was known to sell fifty thousand bales of cotton at a time, worth approximately five million dollars in American value.

I learned a lot in a few days. The office hired a few workers to do menial jobs, such as running errands, bringing in the mail and serving tea. Office hours were supposed to be 9:30 a.m. until 6:30 p.m., but I discovered they were really 9:00 a.m. until 7:00 p.m.

Coca-Cola always seemed to be available, and tea was served at five p.m. It arrived on a tray, with a pitcher of milk and some wafers, but horrors, no lemons! Business automatically suspended during tea. I drank my tea uncertainly at first but then decided it was quite stimulating.

As each day progressed, I hopefully checked the mailbag when it arrived. Two days passed without news from Idie. I fretted. *I don't even know who won what football game. I think I am being mistreated.* Then someone told me mail could take a month or more to cross the ocean, and sometimes letters were lost.

* * *

December 2, 1937 — Bombay

Dearest Idie: I think there is another airmail letter leaving today on the same plane as this one, but I'll make another attempt. If I don't hear from you soon, I don't think I'll ever write again.

Neither Gene nor I have done any work yet. Mr. Clayton is still here, so we are hardly noticed. It sounds as if Gene will be third in charge, with great possibilities. I will live nine tenths of my time on the road and in the jungles. Sounds fascinating, but I don't know anything more.

They have told me one definite thing: learn cotton well. Mr. Whittington said almost the same thing in Houston. I'll have to learn to class Indian cotton, which is harder to do than the American type. Most of it is rather low-grade with hundreds of types and only slight differences. I don't believe I am self-sufficient to do what is before me, but I am not discouraged. You will help me with your prayers, I know.

I have seen nothing of Bombay and have no hope of doing so until Mr. Clayton leaves. Living conditions are very expensive. Everything livable is full. We are now in a second-rate hotel. The food is good, the bed not so good, but passable. While on the road, I will need to live on tin cans. I might ask you to send some of our good American-made delicious flavors.

Tell me about yourself and what you are doing. I wish you were here. Lovingly, Harry

* * *

Gene and I attended a tea in Mr. Clayton's honor the day before he returned to Houston. Noticing that the sandwiches contained ingredients I did not recognize, I ate sparingly. The frozen peaches and cream dessert, however, put a smile on my face.

The tea was held at a club, built by a maharaja, about five miles from our hotel. It was the one club that admitted both European and Indians as members, sporting the only golf course in town. The swimming pool was beautiful and the spacious verandah very comfortable. Beautiful flowers surrounded the grounds, and members who paid a small added tax could take flowers home three times a week.

While at the tea, Mr. Waddell found time to tell me a few things. I could expect to be in Bombay on an average of ten days each month; I would take lessons in Hindustani, the generally accepted language. My job would be supervising rural agents. I was to buy in the agent's territory when the agent himself could not and, likewise, sell.

Unlike transactions in the United States, much of the cotton was bought in the seed, unginned. I would have to estimate how many bales would gin out of a certain pile of cotton, plus what quality and staple it would become.

Also, quite different from the American way, Mr. Waddell told me most up-country transactions were done with cash. If an error of even five cents was detected, the merchants would write ten letters to argue about it. In short, my work would be to carry on the functions of the office outside of the office, from beginning to end.

Someone at the party asked when I would go into the interior (up-country). Mr. Waddell replied, "In about ten days."

"He must be broken in slowly," a clerk said.

"We'll see." Mr. Waddell responded.

* * *

The "bearer thing" came up during my first week at the office. Guy told me I had to have one. I wanted to say, "I don't need one," but Guy was one of my bosses.

Guy said a fella named Chand would meet me at the hotel after work. If I hired him, I would have to pay him forty rupees per month. I wasn't sure how much that was in American money, but I was sure it was too much. Neither did I want a stranger hanging around.

When I arrived at the hotel that evening, I saw a man standing by the door to my room. "Salaam, Sahib, I am Chand."

He was thirty-something, wearing a long white uniform and a white turban covering almost all of his jet-black hair. He was clean-shaven and bright eyed, straight, and slim, almost as tall as me.

I stuck out my hand and said, "Howdy."

Chand stepped back a foot or two, and again said, "Salaam." There was no handshake. Not knowing what to do, I hired Chand.

I woke up the next morning with an uneasy feeling, sensing someone was there. It was Chand, standing beside the bed, holding a wooden tray with a metal teapot and other fixings on it, including a short, fat banana.

"Good morning, Sahib," he said. "Will you take *chota hazri* in bed or at the table?"

"Chota hazri? What's that?"

"Small breakfast, Sahib."

Peeling the banana, I looked at Chand. *What am I supposed to do with him?*

No problem: Chand seemed to know. He had drawn my bath. I went into the bathroom, and Chand followed. "I will wash Sahib's back," he said.

"No, you won't."

"But it is my duty," said Chand.

Chand's duty or not, I got that straight pretty quick. Coming out and toweling off, I saw Chand holding my shirt in one hand and drawers in the other. I told him I didn't need help putting on my shirt and especially not my drawers.

When I returned to the hotel that night, Chand was sitting barefoot, in front of my door. He scrambled up, gesturing salaam, and followed me into the room. Not knowing what to do next, I said, "Good night," and Chand left. Then I noticed the room was shipshape. *Sahibs sure do live a hard life.*

* * *

Interesting things happened every day. I wrote to Idie again, even though I had not yet heard from her.

December 5, 1937 — Bombay

Sweetheart: Gene and I went to our first Bombay movie, *One Hundred Men, and a Girl*. I don't think I saw the picture, just dreamed of the time I saw it with you. At the end, they played the British national anthem. The Indians walked out, we stood. Americans sit upstairs and pay about ninety cents for a seat.

This morning, the American Colony (social group for Americans overseas) played baseball. Gene and I joined them and welcomed news from home. After the game, we went to that swanky club I told you about and watched two American swimmers do their diving tricks. They were wonderful!

It's now eleven p.m. I must turn in because I become a busy man tomorrow.

Be sweet, my darling—take care of yourself for me, Harry

* * *

A cable arrived for me at the office the next day. Hooray! It was from Idie and Bill Hanks, my mentor and good friend. The Rice Owls football team had just won the Southwest Conference, and everyone at home was celebrating. I immediately sat down to write Idie.

December 6, 1937 — Bombay

My darling Idie. Ten million thanks for the wire: "Won Conference—IdaBill" How much those few words mean; you will never know. I am so happy for Coach Jimmy and Assistant Lou and the boys. Please congratulate them for me. It means more than they won the conference, as those are the only words I have had from you since leaving N.Y!

Went down to the cotton market today, the only one of its kind in the world. There are small rooms which line the hallway; on one side are the buyers and on the other, the sellers. The seller takes samples of his cotton to the buyer and tries to sell them. They have worked out a system of prices, a code, in which no word is spoken. You merely shake hands and the number of fingers you press and the way you press them gives the price—-only the two of you know the price that is being asked for the cotton.

Don't believe I have told you about the hotel. It is built in the form of a triangle with the middle portion left open as a patio all the way up from the second floor. Gene and I usually eat dinner at the hotel restaurant. Once in a while, the fish is good; it was tonight. The meat course is usually very good, the vegetables, just so-so. The raisin pudding is excellent. This routine is followed every night. Hate to admit it, but I ate some of everything on the menu. We never know what's coming, we just let them bring it.

Love you, miss you, Harry

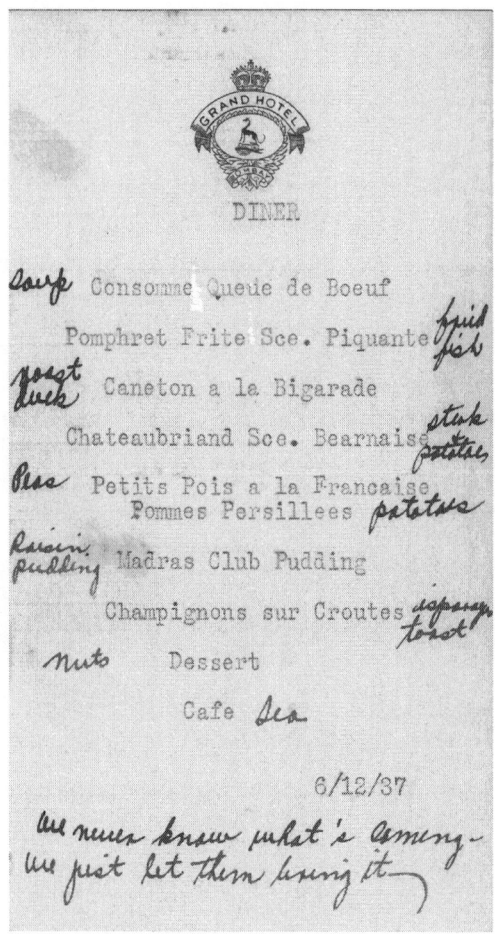

Hotel Menu

* * *

I learned combining business with pleasure was integral to the fabric of the Bombay community. One night, Gene and I were invited to a cocktail party, held for the American Express vice president, and afterward, we went to Ed Waddell's for dinner and bridge.

As dinner was finishing, Mr. Waddell said to me, "I notice you and Gene have been calling me Mr. Waddell. Our organization is a small one, and for the sake of convenience, it is perfectly all right to call me Ed. In fact, I would prefer it."

Gene then asked Ed if he could tell us something about the *Raj*.

"Sure. Raj is a Hindu word, meaning 'rule.' British rule in India had its beginnings in the 1600s with a royal charter for the East India Company (EIC). It enabled them to trade for spices, cotton, silk, indigo, and saltpeter with the Muslim (Moghul) dynasty in India. As Moghul authority began to disintegrate, the EIC evolved from a trading company to a territorial ruler. The company gradually lost commercial and political control, and the British government took possession of it in 1858, imposing direct rule over India."

One other evening, Guy took Gene and me to a show and then to his apartment for dinner. I was amazed as I counted the number of knives, forks, and spoons on the table, plus the finger bowl. Gene and I decided to try to get an apartment like Guy's. It operated like a hotel and was more spacious at about half the cost we were paying.

* * *

Struggling in my new environment, I remarked to Gene, "Sometimes I feel as if I might be learning something; then at other times I feel I know nothing. I had a lesson in Hindustani this morning. It seems difficult, but I hope to learn it fairly well."

While reading through up-country files, I discovered some interesting facts: the natives who clerked in the Bombay office and up-country were paid 125 rupees or ninety dollars a month, while the low-level worker, who put in a day of hard labor from early morning until seven at night, got twenty-five rupees a month—a little less than ten dollars.

I picked up one file to study when I saw that up-country agents never seemed to send correct information. That would be my job, to find out what they meant and why.

Writing to Idie gave me a confidante with whom I could share my adventures and also my fears of thinking I might not be up to the job before me.

December 7, 1937 — Bombay

My sweet Idie: Ed had us over again, this time for Chinese food with nothing but chopsticks with which to eat. Ed spent several years in China and became an expert on Chinese food. He has a very good Chinese cook.

The table was set with a medium bowl of rice at each place, with eight or ten larger bowls arranged around the table, holding other ingredients. I say ingredients because that is all I knew about what I was eating: meat balls, chicken, shrimp, vermicelli, and I don't know what else. The dishes were passed around and some of each was placed on top of our rice. Everyone had quite a bowl full before the passing ended.

Lesson one then began! Gene and I were immediately the cause of many laughs but before the meal was finished, we had both whipped the rather large bowl of food and even had seconds. Really was enjoyable.

I learned the cook is caring for a young fellow who needs a job; perhaps we can hire him if we can afford it.

I am going up-country Friday night with Ed for a couple of days. When you get this, I'll probably be well broken in. Hope to get some pictures for you. Bought some shorts and a topee (head covering), so I've gone completely native.

Love you, Harry

Harry's Signature in Urdu

P.S. Now that I am back at the hotel, I want to be with you a few minutes longer. Sometimes, I wonder how long three years are. Maybe time will not drag so much when there is a definite job to do. Don't be so stingy; break a rule now and then and write to me in the middle of the week, even if it is only to say hello—feeling well—goodbye.

* * *

After Ed and I returned from my first trip to the up-country, I went through the little bit of mail I had received. There it was, a letter from Idie. Hallelujah!

December 8, 1937 — Houston

Harry, my dearest. What a thrill it was to receive your sea letter! I was practicing the piano when it came, and I got so excited I missed all the notes. We had a lovely Thanksgiving. Ate dinner with Aunt Nettie and our cousins. Then, I had nothing but Teachers Convention all weekend at school.

I have had such joy in my heart since I gave you to the Lord. He has greatly supplied me with peace, contentment, and happiness. I know he is caring for you and me.

We anxiously waited for the letters from Italy. Ritch, from the office, called when the cable you sent affirmed you had arrived in Bombay. It was good news. I am sure by now you have received the cable. Hope you know IdaBill was Idie and Bill, short for cent's sake. Rice won the conference and will play New Year's Day in the Cotton Bowl.

Your letters from Italy were a little visit with you. Somehow, you are so close I can feel your presence; your soul is with mine regardless of the miles that separate us.

I send my love with a prayer. May this coming year bring health, success, joy, and the fulfillment of your heart's desires. Idie

* * *

Ed came looking for me one day, holding an invitation delivered to the ACCO office:

**Don't forget the ball game on Sunday December 12
On the Willingdon Maidan at 11 o'clock.
This may be the last chance before Christmas
To razz your favorite umpire.
Beer and hamburgers in bulk. Better come early.
H.G. Robertson, Chairman, Sports Committee.**

Willingdon Maidan was a big grassy field across from the swank Willingdon Club, rendezvous of the Bombay elite. A fringe of trees around one side made welcome shade for resting between innings. The far side had palm trees waving in the breeze.

Indians played cricket, hockey, and football (soccer) there. Europeans practiced golf and rode horses. Americans used the grassy field for baseball games.

We played two seven-inning games of softball. Sides were picked in the usual way. Hamburgers and beer were served at the end of both games by the ladies, assisted by a couple of Chinese house servants. The hamburgers tasted mighty good, our first since leaving the States.

A large enough crowd turned out for two teams with several substitutes and sideline players who knew how to do it better. What an excellent way to become acquainted with a great number of people in the shortest possible time! As might be expected at a baseball game, arguments and derogatory comments soon had first names flying about freely.

Since I was pitching, "Glass-arm Harry" resounded around the field. When I threw one away, the "just a flash in the pan" was dusted out for my embarrassment. Gene got the usual back chat every time he went to bat.

We gave back just as much as was given. "Doc" replaced Mr. Palmer. His "Hi, Pal" upon first introductions let the barriers down. Robbie, Eddie, Carter, and Dutch became familiar before the first game was over. We settled into old-fashioned razzing from the start of the second game.

These games were a little bit of the United States tucked away in India. Except for the scenery and dhotied natives, Willingdon Maidan might have been any American sandlot. Spectators yelled, "Kill the umpire!" with just as much gusto from a backless wicker seat as in the Houston bleachers. Players made the same kinds of errors and did the same type of bragging, having just as much fun.

Sometimes there were special games, such as married men versus single. Most popular was the North/South game. Many turned out to play or to see the fun. Sides were picked as carefully as possible. On several occasions it looked as if the war would be refought, but when the game ended, peace resumed.

* * *

December 25, 1938 — Bombay

Christmas Day! My first in India. I had been there less than one full month. I might as well have been on some other sizzling hot planet. I didn't like any part of that day! Ed and Faye had gone to a place called a hill station. Guy Schilling's wife and young son were in the States. So, Guy took Gene and me to high-rise apartment hopping, calling on his friends.

The temperature was pushing an unchristian one hundred degrees, as we walked into an apartment where a stranger said, "Merry Christmas," and handed me a drink. No Christmas tree, no tinsel, no children, no carols on a gramophone. We could shoot craps on the floor in a hallway if we wanted. "Spirits" abounded, but Father Christmas was absent. That's how it was all afternoon.

Gene and I dined alone in an almost empty hotel dining room. No turkey, no apple pie, no Christmas trappings. Both of us were down in the dumps.

I had been writing notes for Idie but didn't send them. I wished she could have been there or that I was "back there" to ride a bus to her place like I used to every night after work. We would sit outside and talk until the last bus came at nine. Then I rode two buses to get back home. It was always worth it.

Mr. Harmon Whittington said I would have to stay three years without home leave. It didn't mean anything at first, but later it rang in my ears like the boom of doom. I felt like I was in a three-year-long tunnel with no light at the end.

December 25, 1937 — Bombay

Dearest Idie: A Merry Christmas to you. The sun is sinking into the great beyond, and thus ends my first Christmas in India. Long shall I remember, my sweet, not the things I have done today, but the things I should have liked to have done. I can truthfully say to you, and to myself, my body and soul belong to no other but you.

Today, like never before, have I missed you. To have taken you in my arms and said, "I love you," would have been life itself, well worth the price of anything. Christmas out here isn't anything to brag about. This is just a little miss-you note, a little heart drop straight from my heart to yours.

Be sweet, I love you, Harry

* * *

I was hoping Idie was thinking of me, just as I was thinking of her. It was January before I received her letter of Christmas Day, but how I enjoyed reading and rereading it, keeping her close in my heart.

December 25, 1937 — Houston

My sweet Harry. Merry Christmas to you! I wish I could say it in person. Your two letters have been real Christmas presents! I really did not expect them.

I am heartsick you did not have a letter waiting for you when you first arrived in Bombay. I wrote you two airmails that should have arrived before the cable. Bill has also written every Sunday.

I shall always cherish your first letter. My prayers have been answered. It took going to India for you to see the

Lord must come first. All else will follow. Your precious words are indelibly stamped on my heart. I want to hear about the country, but I also want to hear about you. The most precious words in the world are "I love you."

I, too, feel your presence. We have often said that nothing can separate our love. It is just as much alive now as when we spent our evenings together. I want you to participate in everything you enjoy. By doing so, you will love me even more, if possible. Your love is such a vital part of me that I am not pining and lonesome.

You will succeed because "I can do all things through Christ which strengtheneth me." (Philippians 4:13) Remember, "all things work together for good to them that love God." (Romans 8:28)

My brother has moved to Tucson, Arizona, to go to the university there. His allergies seem much better. Ruby and I are in Fort Worth for Xmas. Your second Bombay letter came just as we were leaving. Was I thrilled! Everyone here sends their love. Cousin Arthur is sorry you are not playing with Rice for the Cotton Bowl game, so he can have a ticket.

All my love, Idie

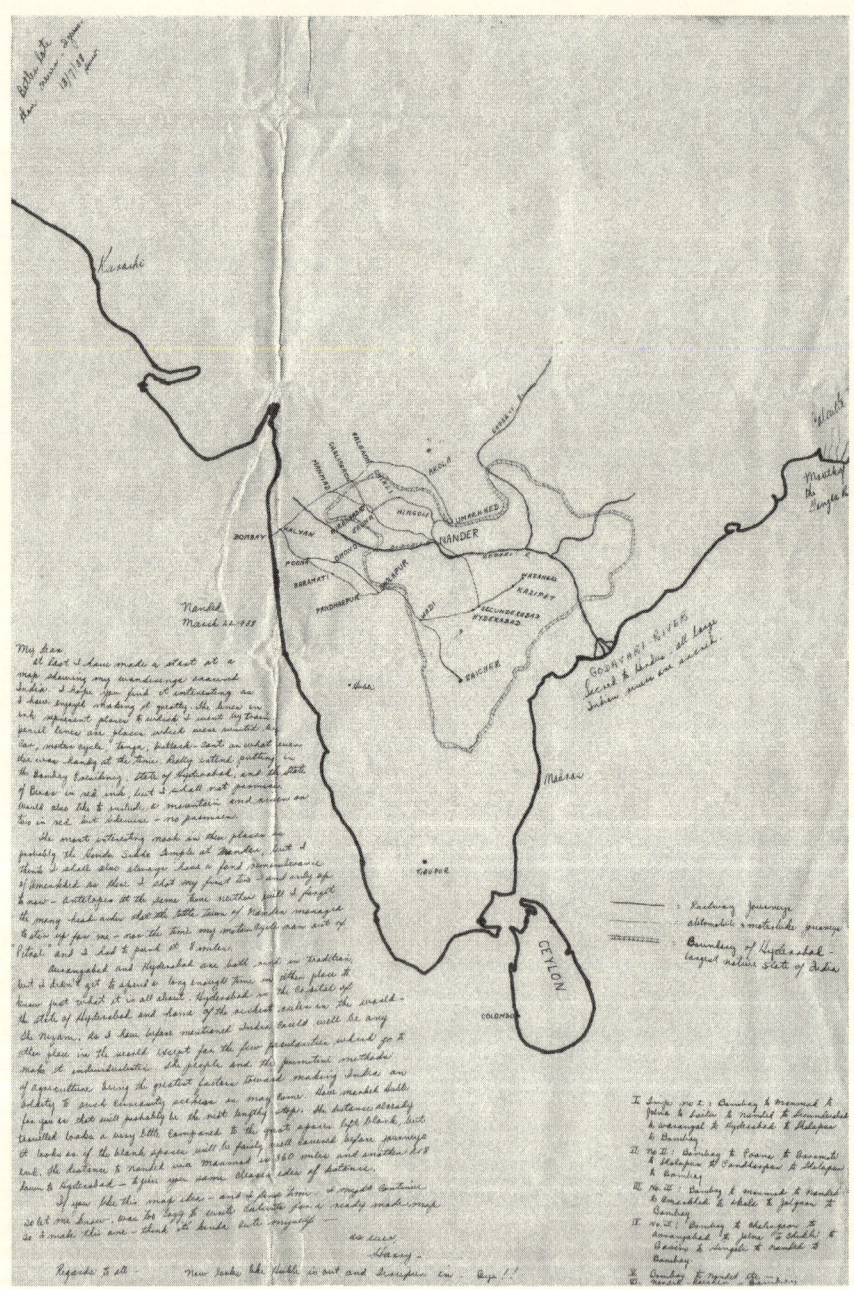

Harry's Hand-Drawn Map

24 | Harriet Claiborne

THREE

TRAINS AND MOTORCYCLES

January 1938 — Nanded

Early in 1938, I boarded a train to Nanded, the first of several small villages I would visit in the interior of India. Raised as a country boy in Texas, I was not put off by the lack of civilized amenities, such as electricity, telephones, and flush toilets. Neither was I bitten by a snake or sick from eating village food. I learned to cope with whatever came my way. Writing to Idie kept me as happy as I could be without her.

> January 4, 1938 — Nanded
>
> My darling Idie: I received your letter of Xmas Day this afternoon. If ever I feel weak before hearing from you, I feel big and strong afterwards.
>
> Here we are, away in the wilderness. The mails are very uncertain. I arrived at 1:00 this afternoon, after an almost sleepless night. Left Bombay at 11:00 p.m. and changed trains at 3:30 in the morning. Still do not know what I am to do here. My instructions were that something underhanded seems to be going on and for me to discover

what it is. Check all accounts, stock, etc. Also, personally attend to all reports which must go daily to Bombay.

What I like about this job is that I know so little about it. Some of the forms I have never seen before, but here, I am the boss. If something important comes up with any responsibility attached, I have to say yes or no, and the monkey is on my back. In Bombay, Ed comes and says, "Harry, do this" or "Harry, do that." He did say he felt sorry for me.

This district is commonly known as the Mogloi (Mog-lie) section of cotton production and is the hardest market in India to manage. I heard at the office everyone is a born crook, and all have a bag of tricks to spring on you. I haven't seen a white face yet. There is one other European here, or there was, when Ed and I came through a few weeks ago. I am supposed to stay a month to six weeks. I don't have much trouble during the day, but I have lots at night.

I meant to tell you about the human scarecrows. There are many grain fields and about a thousand big crows fly over them daily. The farmer builds a small platform in the field and stations a woman or child on it. They have long slingshots, with which they are very accurate, and do a good job of preserving the crop.

If this is going to go on for a month, my sweet, I'll have to charter a boat to send you my letters.

Love you, Harry

* * *

One night, I pondered how long I had been away from Idie. It felt like an eternity, and I was discouraged. I couldn't seem to understand things that I should have easily grasped.

I felt like kissing Chand, as his was the only friendly face I could count on. Chand's duties were to open my tins of food and serve them, run errands, take care of the luggage, and do all the tipping. He probably made a tidy commission for himself.

Every night, I made a practice of reading a few chapters in the Bible Idie had given me, the one she called "Our Bible." I always felt better afterwards and began thinking of deeper things than the annoying everyday problems I was facing.

> January 6, 1938 — Nanded
>
> Tonight, Sweetheart, I feel strangely happy. I read the Book of Job in our Bible and thought how insignificant that little book makes one feel and how thankful we should be for so many blessings. I like chapter eight, verse nine: "For we are but of yesterday, and know nothing, because our days upon earth are a shadow."
>
> I think the fog surrounding my work lifted a trifle today. The fellow who is the agent here is old and hard to deal with. He resents me telling him what to do, and so I say as little as possible, but I have a job to do too. I think it will be done right before I leave.
>
> I will have to travel about eighty miles to Latur tomorrow. Bombay telegraphed me to go and check those statements too. They don't know what a daze Nanded has me in.
>
> Love you, Harry

* * *

The trip to Latur was bumpy and dusty, but the countryside was nicely rolling with the usual oxen, water buffalo and black goats. Saw my first camels; they were enormous! Their knees reached the tops of the doors of the car.

That confounded Ed Waddell sent me out here, but every day he telegraphs someone new that "Mr. Harry Witt would be instructing him how to do this or that." All he told me was to use my own judgment! A fine kettle of oil to boil a rookie in, says I.

Another telegram from Bombay arrived a day or two later with the directive that I was to take a train to Basmathnagar, which is even smaller than Nanded. Our agent and broker wanted to meet me. I had not been there before and did not know what to expect.

Two passenger trains ran daily, one going east, the other west. Several small towns hugged the line, about twenty-five miles apart. They were cotton markets I needed to visit by rail because they were not connected by a drivable road.

At 11:45 p.m. I began pacing the station platform. The westbound train, due at midnight, arrived at 2:30 a.m. Chand was there to see me off. Since this would be a one-day trip, I left him there, saying, "Who will look after Sahib?"

I boarded the train at 2:30 a.m. and got off at Purna. Thirty minutes later, a grumpy old stationmaster told me the feeder line to Basmathnagar would not leave at seven a.m. as scheduled; never does. I squeezed into a wicker chair too small for a full-grown Texan, dog-tired. I hoped to sleep.

At 3:30 a.m. "Salaam, Sahib" rocketed around the small, dimly lit waiting room. I wiggled up, mad enough to fight. The voice couldn't be calling me; nobody knew I was there. Before I could utter one mean word, a little guy declared, "Witt, Sahib, I am your agent, Ram Chand."

It was my first meeting with Ram Chand. He came, he said, to pay his respects. I wanted to say I was fine without them but I didn't. I sent him away happy because I promised to visit his office on my way back. I squeezed back into my wicker.

At 4:30 a.m. "Salaam, Sahib" again rattled my groggy brain. I struggled to my feet, grumbling, gawky, blinking. Our company's cotton broker draped a flower garland around my neck and announced, "Sahib will take tea."

Not a question, a statement of fact. In the dim light from one naked, low-watt lightbulb, the teacups looked dirty and the tea, thick and unappetizing. I hesitated. I thought I could hear Guy Schilling's voice in my ear: "Don't eat or drink anything at native places in the interior."

The broker seemed puzzled. Was the young sahib refusing to take tea with him? I downed the tea in one gulp. Crisis averted. The broker downed his portion with lip-smacking gusto. I told myself I must learn to do that. His duty done and his respects paid, the broker departed.

How did these people know I was here? Chand later told me. Our Nanded agent had put his coolie on the train with me to alert the Purna people I would be passing through. Why? "It was his duty, Sahib."

At seven a.m. I began pacing the Purna station platform. There was no activity around the train for Basmathnagar. When would it leave? "When it gets ready."

The train finally "got ready," and I arrived in Basmathnagar at eleven a.m. The agent and broker were on the station platform, two half-pints carrying flower garlands as if they were crown jewels. They couldn't reach high enough to hang them over my head. I took off my topee and bent almost double. I tried not to laugh, but onlookers did!

"I am three hours late. What happened when the market opened this morning?"

"Market will not open until Sahib arrives. It is customary to delay opening, if necessary, when important person visits."

Important person? Me? Little did they know how far down I was on the company totem pole. This "important person" had much to learn about up-country India.

The cotton market was one room in a small, mud-walled, thatched-roof house. When I arrived, a gaggle of barefoot men was sitting on cushions on the floor. We went through Salaam again, without flowers. A chair was found for me, and as I sat, the room became quiet; all eyes were on me. Visitors from headquarters must say a few words. I did, very few. Our agent translated my words into Hindi, using more than a bushel of words.

Bargaining in Hindi began immediately—a noisy, hand-waving affair. When finished about an hour later, our broker informed me we had purchased the entire one hundred bales for sale that day.

"Is Sahib not overjoyed at our good fortune?"

"Of course, I am, but why did we have to pay the highest price of the year?"

"To show everybody," said the broker, beaming, "that my sahib is a raja sahib!"

It was two p.m. when I arrived back in Purna. The train to Nanded was due at four p.m. Ram Chand was waiting for me, collecting on my promise to visit his office, one room in his small house. I sat on a wide verandah on an overstuffed chair, upgraded to a throne by throwing a purple cloth over it. Two bullock carts, almost in touching distance, spread barnyard aroma. A dozen town bigwigs gathered to take refreshments with the young Bombay sahib.

Two barefooted, bare-chested male servants brought large circular brass trays, heaped with mounds of fruit, nuts, and parched grain. Orange segments tempted me, but buzzing flies brought Guy to mind. I munched instead on peanuts, joining others in littering the floor with shells. I tested the tea and was surprised. I enjoyed this aromatic tea—from Darjeeling, I was told. I had several cups while talking cotton with Ram and English-speaking guests.

As train time approached, I lifted my teacup, saluted Ram, and managed a small, embarrassed burp. Ram snapped his fingers. The two servants reappeared, one carrying a heavy flower garland, the other, a small silver bowl on a wooden tray. Dipping his fingers in sweet oil from the bowl, Ram gently touched both of my cheeks and said, "May mercy always smile on you." Then he draped the flowers around my neck.

WOW! What would small-town Texans say about that?

No more platform pacing; my train was on time, I arrived back in Nanded at 4:30 p.m. My business could have been finished in one hour; it had taken eighteen, navigating the vagaries of up-country train travel. I decided to get a motorcycle.

* * *

I knew letters from Idie would take time to go to Bombay first, then be forwarded to Nanded. Trying not to be discouraged as I looked through the daily mail sack, I yelled, "Yes!" whenever I found one. Sometimes there were more than one.

January 1, 1938 — Houston

Happy New Year, Beloved Boy! Thanks for the Christmas cable. I just got back from Fort Worth and, to my delight, found four letters from you! I had no idea you would be so sweet to write as much and as interestingly as you have. Words are inadequate to tell you how thrilled I was! I am going to read them again and thoroughly digest those sweet words.

I have driven over one thousand miles in the last week, and hardly know whether I am coming or going. Will you really be gone three years? Oh my! You will succeed with the language and the buying. Let it go the upward route, and you can't go wrong. Each night I pray for wisdom and protection for you.

Am really tired tonight. I think I will go to bed after I tell your picture how very much I love you and how precious you are to me, even if you are halfway around the world. Idie

January 16, 1938 — Houston

My beloved Harry: Your interesting letters always receive an enthusiastic welcome! I am, by your letters, like I used to be about your phone calls. I get cross when they don't come. I look forward to every letter because they are now our only connecting link.

I am swamped with requests for stamps from your letters. Even the postman wants an airmail. Said airmails from India are very rare, about one in every ten thousand. I have divided them up fairly, so no one person will receive them all. I don't have one stamp left. I trust this letter will travel more quickly than the others have done.

My darling, it is late, and I must say good night. May your work become easier, and may you enjoy it more each day.

Love you, Idie

* * *

I carried Idie's letters with me on my trips to the up-country, giving me a sense of purpose. Poona's Napier Hotel reminded me of the Bird Cage Theatre in Tombstone, Arizona—a rambling stone building with rickety stairs leading to the two upper floors. My room was just large enough for me to turn around. There was no running water, and bathwater was carried up the unsound stairs by a servant. Tubs were galvanized tin. With my big feet in it, there was hardly room for the rest of me. An old-fashioned wardrobe and a chair too weak for me to risk sitting in, plus a much too short bed completed the furnishings. The walls were paper thin with enough cracks to eliminate any possibility of privacy. That seemed unknown in India anyway. I slept well.

Surprised by local customs, I frowned when I saw a young, laughing girl rush into a dirt village street and scoop up cow dung the moment it hit the ground. I watched as she ran back to a house, made it into a pancake shape, and plastered it on the wall.

"Repulsive!" I said to Chand, who gently chided me.

"Not dirty, Sahib. A useful gift. Poor people have no other fuel for cooking."

Over time, I became accustomed to the blue smoke from cooked dung hanging over villages at cooking times, daybreak, and just before sundown. It was not unpleasant; nor was it a perfume but it did help override the "bad smells of India."

The road to Baramati was dusty as I passed herds of goats, sheep, and cows. Primitive forms of irrigation and mud huts dotted the rough countryside.

There was no official *dak-bungalow* (guest house), but Gangappa, our Hindu agent in Baramati, had built one near his home in honor of Ed Waddell and Guy Schilling. He named it Wadshling Hall. It was comfortable, except for the bed. Pictures covered the walls, his wife's idea. She was studying English, a rare activity among the Indian women I had met. At the end of the room, in a prominent place, was a large picture of the king and queen of England with pictures of Ed and Guy on either side. Ed's was a little higher than their majesties.

Each day began at five a.m. with tea and a bath. I read the Bombay paper from the day before while the Hindu household said prayers. I worked on reports and took tea again during the morning work break, had a bite to eat around noon. After resting until three, I worked on more reports until six. I drank *chotta*, also called *chotapeg* (a small whisky and soda), with the family and talked until dinner was served at 8:30. The household went to bed around 9:30. I was still hungry after the Hindu dinner, so I secretly opened a couple of the tins that always traveled with me and had a little more to eat.

* * *

A surprise was waiting for me when I returned to Nanded: a letter from Idie!

> January 20, 1938 — Houston
>
> My darling boy: The movies you took have arrived! Wait until I tell you how I worked to get them. I was out all afternoon getting ads for our school paper. It was 5:15 p.m. when I came home and found a notice from the post office saying I had a package from India, but an affidavit was required.
>
> I called Bill to see if he could drive. We found a parking place and rushed in. The man at the registry said I had to fill out two papers and have them signed by a notary. My heart beat faster when I got a glimpse of the size of the package.
>
> We asked the postmaster if any notary would do—yes. I knew Aunt Nettie had several. It was getting close to 6:00. We jumped in the car and rushed to her office. We filled out the blanks, swore they were not movies of prize

Postmarked Bombay | 33

fights, etc., no vulgarity or lasciviousness, not for public exhibition. It was so funny!

It was ten minutes to 6:00 when we rushed back to the post office. The man at the window read it slowly, finally said it was okay, had me sign another slip, and then handed me the package.

I took Bill back to work (he didn't have time to see the pictures) and drove home. I showed them once, then had to go to church for a conference. When I got back, I lay flat on my stomach and showed them again. I was in heaven. I thoroughly enjoyed the movies of the sea and the arrival in India. If only I could talk; writing is inadequate for me.

Mother laughed, but oh, my darling boy, I felt I was right with you. When you said, "Hello," so distinctly, I felt your presence and could look into those brown eyes and marvel at being with you. Think how often I can "go to India" and see my love!

Since you have been away, all the lovely traits of your character have magnified until I can't find a single fault. How well I remember the many happy hours we spent together.

When I write to you, I put your sweet picture in front of me, and then I talk to you. I feel hindered when I must put my thoughts in black and white. I anxiously wait for your interesting letters.

Bless you, my sweet. Love you, Idie

In February, Ed sent me to a remote village in the up-country. I arrived late in the afternoon, feeling a bit anxious, as a British friend had warned me it would be "primitive, man, primitive."

FOUR

UMARKHED

February 2, 1938

I stood in the center of a small cluster of mud-and-wattle houses, looking back at the road over which I had just come. It was really a narrow dirt track, ending where I stood, becoming the village's only street. I watched naked children playing in the dust and thin stray dogs slinking around them. Bullock carts came and went, bringing newly picked cotton to the gins and then taking it away in bales from the press. There was no running water or electricity, except at the gins and press. The nearest telephone connection was ten miles away in a larger village. Cotton was grown here, and ACCO bought some of it.

Bullock Carts Coming and Going with Cotton

"Eureka!" I said, when I realized my temporary home would be the dak-bungalow, a short walk away from the village hubbub. I saw it was a sturdily built, western-style country cottage with a thatched roof and wide covered verandah across both front and back. An ancient banyan tree seemed to grow upside down in the bungalow's backyard, and a little Hindu temple capped a nearby hill. I relaxed; anxiety fell away. *Smartly new, exciting things pop up wherever I go in this country. I can be comfortable here.*

A Dak Bungalow

Morning brought second thoughts. Comfort would wait until I could get a handle on the place called "bathroom." Nothing in it but an oval tin tub with a tin-cup dipper and an apple-crate-sized wooden box with a hole in the top, dubbed "Thunder Box." No towels, no soap, no paper, no running water; the *bhisti* (water boy) lugged water in from a well outside. I grimaced, thinking out loud, "This is no place for a full-grown Texan!"

Chand stood behind me and did not seem surprised. "Sahib should just stand up in it, while I pour water over you, and scrub."

The look I threw at him said what I thought about that.

Just then, ACCO's local agent, Kuligood, and the manager of the cotton press, Shaik Rahim, a gray-bearded old Muslim, walked into the bungalow. I thought they would talk cotton, but I was surprised.

Striding into the room as if he owned it, old Shaik stuck out his hand and said, "Welcome, Sahib."

I stood there for a second, looking at his outstretched hand. No other Indian had offered to shake hands with me. Hindus do their salaams, folding their hands, never touching the flesh. I recovered enough to shake and say, "Howdy."

Then that old geezer, while still holding my hand, proudly announced, "I am the greatest hunter in Berar Province. Have I not killed fourteen panthers and too many black bucks to remember?"

My friend in Bombay warned I was being sent to oblivion, and the first man I met talked like a Texan!

Chand, not overjoyed to be there, brought tea, and rattled the cups when Shaik said, "I killed a panther right over there, just outside the front door."

I raised my eyebrows at Kuligood. He nodded.

I said I thought wild animals were afraid of people and wouldn't come near the bungalow. Shaik pouted. Kuligood said, "Panthers will go anywhere when they are hungry, even into the village, where they kill dogs and goats."

"Killing that panther," Shaik went on, "was no big thing; hardly worth mentioning except that it happened here, at the bungalow. A donkey wandered over here, away from the village. The panther killed it in the yard and pulled the carcass onto the verandah. Didn't eat much, so I knew he would come back. I came late the next afternoon to wait for him and sat on the floor just inside the door. When he appeared and started to eat, I shot him. That's all there was to it. No big thing."

No big thing? A panther kills and is killed at what is now my front door and it is no big thing? Guy Schilling warned repeatedly about snakebites, a major cause of death in India. I wondered why he had not mentioned panther bite.

Chand brought a flickering kerosene lamp as the room darkened. Shaik went to a window and said, while looking out, "I killed another panther near the banyan tree. Sat on the top step and waited for him. Killing him was a big thing: he was a monster."

Kuligood moaned. Shaik didn't miss a beat. "It happened about this time last year when a young woman went to the temple on the hill to pray for a son, her sister told me later. What can a dirty old stone do about sons? She didn't come down until nightfall. The trail runs past the banyan, and

Postmarked Bombay

when she got that far, the panther grabbed her." He paused, then said, "She died quickly."

"But horribly," Kuligood stammered. "She screamed once, heard by everyone in the village. We knew what it meant because it has happened before: one of us had died." Sweat glistened on his forehead. "Weeping broke out. We Hindus were afraid, as we always are, when jungle killers come near. We are forbidden to kill, but we can be killed."

Shaik, a Muslim, can and does kill. "I, too, heard the scream," he said. "And knew what had to be done. Grabbed my shotgun and flashlight and hurried over here, knowing that I would be too late to help the woman, but hoping I might surprise the killer. He heard me coming and crashed into the bush. What was left of the body lay near the banyan. Not a pretty sight, but I could do nothing about it; nor could I follow the panther at night. I went back to the village and got some men with lamps to follow me. They took the remains away for cremation the next day.

"Paw prints told me the panther was lame on the right front paw, an injury that turned him into a monster. No longer able to kill other wild animals, he had to find something easier. People are easier. I knew he would come back for another meal, so I came a little before sundown, took off all my clothes and piled them inside the door. I wanted to be as black as possible. Panthers don't smell well, but they see better than most animals. I sat on that stoop for four hours. What I don't like is waiting, sitting like a dumb rock, letting bugs bite you, trying not to move, not even bat an eyelid.

"The panther knew his business. I had surprised him the night before, so he took his time, came very slowly on his belly, inch by inch, working his way around the banyan. I didn't see him or hear him, just sat there with my finger on the trigger. The first thing I saw was a front paw sliding out from in back of the banyan. One paw, nothing else. Wanted to shoot but knew I had to wait for a clear shot. Finally, charging out of cover, he pounced on the place where he had left the woman and put his head down to smell. I fired, and the panther fell on the spot where the woman died.

"I inched myself back into the bungalow, my finger still on the trigger. Didn't go near him until daylight, as I might have only wounded him. That's when panthers are the most dangerous. Tomorrow I will show you his skin."

Had I come from anywhere but Texas, I might not have slept at all that night. But I did, soundly.

My first full day there began with a blow to my belly. Chand told me my in-the–boondocks pantry, a tin trunk stacked with canned edibles, was empty. It was always with me because Guy Schilling insisted that I would surely die of dysentery or another exotic disease if I ate anything that didn't come out of a can. Well, I had seen a bunch of healthy-looking men working here. Should I challenge Guy's advice? I reckoned not, so I jotted down a telegram to him — HUNGRY SEND FOOD — and handed it to Chand.

That's when I learned the post/telegraph office was ten miles away through the jungle. "You can't get there from here," Kuligood said, "except on foot, by bullock cart, or by bicycle. Don't expect a quick reply."

He warned it could take at least a full day to get there and another to come back.

Three days passed with no word from Schilling. I was not starving; tangerines were in season—plump, tasty, and cheap—but I had begun to hate the sight of them. Kuligood, Shaik, and Chand worried about me, Shaik most vocally. "Look at me," he said. "I eat village food, and am I not healthy? Tomorrow we will go hunting and shoot something for you to eat."

I told him the only thing I had ever shot was a tin can on a fence post.

"Did you hit it?"

When I said yes, he said he would pick me up at six in the morning. I was not a hunter, but I decided to go with him even if Guy's food arrived.

At daybreak, Shaik again shocked me to the core. He was standing tall, shouting, waving a long stick, and driving a bullock cart drawn by an immense Brahma bull. He wore two bandoliers forming an X where they crossed on his khaki shirt, shotgun shells in one, rifle cartridges in the other. And with him, his servant, the blackest man I have ever seen, brawny arms folded over bare chest, shotgun in one hand and rifle in the other. *Banditos* crossed my mind, as in a Western movie, and I was to go with them!

I have now ridden in a bullock cart. Didn't enjoy any part of it, especially breathing its strong, barnyard odor. How that bull could run! Encouraged by Shaik's shouts and pricks from the pointed stick, the bull rocketed across dormant fields. Shaik and Ishmael were in high spirits while I desperately hung on. We stopped about a mile from the village at a farmer's grass hut.

The farmer, pointing all over the map, said he had seen antelope and black bucks "out there." I saw nothing but waving, knee-high grass. Shaik took the shotgun, Ishmael gave me an old single-shot rifle, and we began to walk.

I was dressed to go to the office, not on a trek, and it was no walk in the park. Being "out there" isn't a place for a tenderfoot, especially without boots. While Shaik glided over and around obstacles, I stumbled repeatedly and found it hard to keep up. Burrs clung to my socks, and insects gnawed at me. *If this is the joy of hunting, I want nothing of it.*

I don't know what I expected—certainly not that a sixty-year-old man could walk me to a standstill, but old Shaik nearly did.

By ten o'clock, tired and sweating profusely, I stopped and shouted, "We are wasting our time …" when two antelope exploded almost from under my feet. Racing away with long leaps, they were a thrilling sight. I managed to raise the rifle.

"Don't shoot!" Shaik yelled. "Just babies resting. Now we will find the herd."

Following the fawns, we found eight to ten antelope cropping the tall grass about a hundred yards away. We stopped walking. The antelope raised their heads, looked at us, and then went on eating. Excited enough to pop the buttons off my shirt, I wanted to shoot, but Shaik shushed me, whispering, "No shooting yet, and no more talking."

Ishmael, knowing the routine, hunkered down in the grass. Shaik, taking hold of my shirt sleeve, began to walk a narrowing circle around the herd, tugging me with him. They continued to eat, and we continued to walk. Having walked halfway across India to find antelope, I thought Shaik was risking spooking them without firing a shot. But they didn't spook. The gap between us narrowed to less than fifty yards, and Shaik whispered, "Can you fire now?"

We stopped, and at that moment, every head snapped up, eyeing us. My nerves jangling, I fired, only to add another shocking surprise to this day. Off went the entire herd in great leaps and bounds, including the big buck I had aimed at. A standing broadside shot at less than fifty yards, and I had missed!

Shaik whooped, fired off one barrel of his shotgun, took a step or two, fired off the other barrel, and began to run. Ishmael kept up with him.

"Why hurry now?" I yelled.

Then I saw my buck fall, and I, too, began to run. When I caught up, they were standing over my first black buck, giving praise to Allah.

Forget what I said about riding in a bullock cart; the ride back was pure joy. Words gnawed at me all afternoon, Shaik's words: "We will go hunting and shoot something for you to eat." And Schilling's dire warning: "Eat nothing that doesn't come out of a tin." Then Shaik's boisterous enthusiasm when he came to the bungalow at sundown. How that man could talk!

"What a day! We hunted together, and you shot your first black buck, a very big thing. We must celebrate to seal our friendship. I am happy; you are starving; let us eat."

I had grown up among men for whom hunting and shooting were as natural as breathing. To shoot my first antelope, a black buck, was a rite of passage. It was a thrill for me to become a man in my father's and brothers' minds. Given the opportunity in my later years, I would not shoot that black buck with anything but a camera.

* * *

The tangerine *walla* (merchant) lost his best customer. No red-blooded Texan could resist the tantalizing aroma of antelope curry served by the barefoot, partially dressed, widely grinning bungalow cook.

The food I requested had been purchased upon receipt of my telegram some weeks earlier, then found by Schilling in an office closet. Thinking he had left me in the wilderness to starve, he "blew a gasket" and ordered my immediate return to Bombay. If I had told him I had thrown away the tin trunk, he would have blown another one.

Unsettled by the terse tone in the telegram, I thought I was in trouble with Schilling, but I wasn't. I had been called back to Bombay to pitch the North/South ball game. Anticipation had filled the American community with great excitement and having me pitch seemed more important to Ed than anything I was doing in the interior.

"Keep the ball high to Mac," Ed cautioned. "He plays cricket, and if you give him a low ball, he will lose it."

I didn't listen well, as youthful arrogance surfaced, and I served Mac a low ball. He squashed it.

All was not lost, however, for that was the only run the North got. The South won the game and, most importantly, bragging rights. All day Sunday, I was a hero. Then, early Monday morning, Ed sent me back to Nanded.

* * *

After I had worked steadily for three weeks in Nanded, trying to find the fifteen hundred more bales of cotton Ed had hoped for, I was anxious to finish and get back to Bombay. The days slipped into matter-of-fact workdays. When I felt discouraged, I wrote to Idie, hoping what I said would make her feel as if she were with me.

February 24, 1938 — Nanded

Dearly Beloved: it is almost March 3rd. Think of me on that day, and I'll return the thought! I remember, so well, our meaningful conversation after the Rice dance, the day we first met. It became a magical memory that we still cherish and celebrate. It gave us a mutual understanding, probably the first, threading a needle which eventually knit our souls together. I like that—think I'll write a book.

Be sweet. All my love, Harry

* * *

Idie never stopped making me smile when I read the sweet things she said.

March 2, 1938 — Houston

Harry, my dearest: tomorrow will be the most important day of the year for me. Yes, my darling boy, March 3rd is here again. It has been four years since that memorable evening. I can vividly see the first one, and all the following ones. It reminds me of a baby learning to walk, our friendship, you know, first steps rather uncertain and shaky, then as time passes, stronger and stronger until it becomes a part of you.

No one can look back to a more precious beginning. You are my inspiration, my life and my all. The Good, Gracious Lord saw fit to have us meet one March 3rd and knew all we needed was one night. Then a future filled with joy, sorrow and love that could be shared by hearts as though they were one. I loved you then, now, and forever. Your Idie

March 6, 1938 — Houston

Darling boy: your sweet letter with good wishes for March 3rd arrived on March 3rd. How's that for good timing? I celebrated by showing the movies you sent, inviting Bill Hanks to join Ruby and me. We, of course, talked a lot about you, so I had a splendid March 3rd.

I am hoping Ruby and I can visit my brother and his wife in Arizona sometime this summer. Please enjoy every minute of your stay in India and be as sweet as you have already been by giving me the privilege of seeing it through your eyes.

I send you all my love from the bottom of my heart, Idie

March 23, 1938 — Nanded

Ah, my dear, my dear, it came today, your letter of March 2nd and so many memories with it. I have not forgotten— how could I forget? The one night when we both began to live, and yet it was never so real or so vital to me as while I read your letter. I could see you sitting there—you might have had on a white dress, I might have tilted your head back against the Chrysler cushion, then bestowed my heart, soul, and body into your safekeeping with that first, so well-remembered kiss on that so well-remembered night.

I am returning to Bombay tonight. I hope not to come back until December. I feel lesson one has been a good one. A lesson that I shall not soon forget. Don't believe I have done so well. Don't get me wrong. I'm sure that everything was as good as could be expected, but it won't do. When Nanded is behind me and the work finally closes on chapter one, I shall be relieved.

May our love continue to grow. Harry

* * *

People in the Bombay office asked what it was like to live for a time in the up-country. I told them my most enjoyable moments in Nanded were just after dark when Mickey Junior came to call. Sometimes he was late, but if I were patient, he always turned up.

On first becoming acquainted with Mickey Junior, I tried to get rid of him, but as the days grew into weeks, I looked forward to his visits with genuine pleasure. Had there been a choice, I would have preferred someone else for a companion, but in Nanded, one takes what one can get.

Mickey Junior was a rat, and about as friendly as one can expect a rat to be. He measured about a foot in length, not including a long, skinny tail. He twisted his tail when wiggling his ears and whiskers in an arrogant way. It seemed as if he was trying to say, "I am a handsome fellow and clever, too, since you can neither frighten me nor hit me with your poorly aimed old shoes."

My quarters, although none too spacious, were roomy enough for Mickey, coming through his own little doorway, under the backdoor sill, which he probably gnawed himself. Always gentlemanly, Mickey never hurried, even when shoes were falling around him. With his head poking through the doorway, he paused to survey the room. I imagined if Mickey had been a smoker, he would have lit a cigarette before strolling in.

I would gather my shoes and old books and settle down across the room just before I expected Mickey's grand entrance. When he stopped to look the room over, I heaved a shoe in his direction. He would duck out of sight but then return for another try. When this game first started, Mickey was silent, dodging in and out as quickly as possible. Later, he seemed to understand it was a game and would give me fair warning. He hung around the outside of his hole for a moment or two, squeaking all the time, as if to say, "Get ready, here I come."

When shoes and books crashed near his head, he scampered away with loud and seemingly gleeful squeaks.

Since I had no wife to talk to, Mickey provided a pleasant half hour of relaxation for me every evening and seemed almost tame by the time I left Nanded. It got to the point where he would stay in his hole, washing his face.

My job was a new one. Part of the time, I was doing things I did not know how to do. Mickey Junior helped me not to worry all the time, and so I owe him a lot.

I also experienced some amusing moments with Chand. He worried when he saw the littered floor every morning, probably thinking a devil had taken possession of me. As the days went by, he became accustomed to the mess. Then, one night, I did not play with Mickey Junior. Chand came in the next morning, stepping high over the mess he expected to be there but wasn't. He looked at me, waiting for an explanation, but I got busy with my tea, and he left.

When the day came for us to leave Nanded, I told Chand to pack for Bombay. He said that was good; Sahib had been out a long time and needed a change.

FIVE

CLASSING COTTON

March 1938 — Bombay

I arrived back in Bombay after four days of traveling. Radiating a big smile, I checked the mail bag at the office and found letters from Idie. She told me about seeing Walt Disney's new color film, *Snow White and the Seven Dwarfs*, calling it a work of art and encouraging me to go.

She also sent a note she wrote in the midst of her science class, sensing I had experienced an unusual success that morning. I couldn't wait to tell her my news.

> March 29, 1938 — Bombay
>
> Dearest heart: I am back in Bombay. This time to spend several days. Looks like I'll get my ten days this month. Nanded is about finished, thank goodness. Now, there is another job I am learning here. Really is enjoyable, being able to go to a show every now and then.
>
> I am learning to class what ACCO calls California Cotton. It is the long staple variety, very high quality and makes into luxurious sheets and blankets, and even clothing. I

am making lots of mistakes, but they say a cotton classer never gets it letter perfect. It is a really good experience.

Went to see *Snow White* and thought it a wonderful piece of work but would only enjoy it as a novelty. Once a year would be ample.

Be a sweet girl – miss you—Harry

* * *

Ed told me I would stay in Bombay until I had classed ten thousand bales. I knew it would be a hard job but a responsible one. The difference of 1/32 of an inch in staple length meant about two dollars per bale. I was flattered I would be allowed to do it.

I learned to concentrate, taking my thoughts away from Idie, except at breaks. A great miracle needed to happen before we could be together in less than three years. I felt as if I had already learned a lot, yet the road seemed endless.

I sent Ed a report from Nanded, which he particularly wanted, but it was somewhat short of what he was looking for and I knew it. After we had gone over it together, he grinned and said, "You know, Harry, we're a good pair. Both of us do things alike, sort of haphazardly. Guy could teach both of us a thing or two. When you have time, look at his notes—maybe you'll get some ideas. If you do, let me know." I relaxed, thankful to be working with a man like that.

Guy was just as considerate. I made lots of mistakes, but I never heard an unkind thing. I once bought four hundred bales of inferior cotton. Later (before Bombay saw the samples), I saw my mistake and wrote Guy. His reply was "Congratulations on having learned the most important lesson in buying cotton at such a cheap price." I did get some royal razzing from both Ed and Guy—Guy said I couldn't be more than eighteen!

Gene began talking about moving out of the hotel and getting a flat. I decided to go with him when we ascertained it would be more economical. I was still going to be out of Bombay most of the time but thought it would be nice to unpack my trunk and know where things were for once.

Moving Day

April 10, 1938 — Bombay

Beloved Idie: here I am in our new home! Gene and I took a temporary flat until May first and then we will move to the second floor. Even though I enjoyed the hotel, I believe I shall like this better. We have a Chinese cook named Ming. We are renting the furniture until we move and know what we need. Was great fun picking things out but could have used your advice while buying towels, bed sheets, and other little odds and ends like dishes! Empress Court is part of a large, new apartment complex called Churchgate Reclamation. There are many already built and more under construction. All are quite modern and comfortable.

Saw an American newsreel today. I recognized the speaking voice which you and I have heard innumerable times. Today makes almost one and half a year since I left. Does it seem long? Wonder if the remaining two and a half years will go more quickly.

Don't know when I will be going back to the interior. It will be a long time if they keep me here looking at ten thousand bales of cotton.

I love you and miss you, Harry

* * *

I talked to Ed during a tea break one afternoon and listened to his plans for the toughest cotton market in the world: Hyderabad and Nanded. The state of Hyderabad was producing about four hundred thousand bales of cotton, the same as South Brazil. ACCO was thinking of setting up a permanent office there.

I also used tea breaks to read or reread Idie's letters and to converse with Gene. Knowing Guy would soon be taking a home leave, we agreed that we would miss his good company. It was Guy who said he thought either Idie or I would change before our three years of waiting were over. One day Guy said, "I think it is expecting too much to ask Idie to wait while you are enjoying India. If I meet her, would I be talking to the future Mrs. Witt?"

"Yes," I managed to stammer back.

May 8, 1938 — Bombay

Dearest Idie: another day, another week and school will be over when you get this. Six months ago, we were thousands of miles together and now we are those same thousands of miles apart. I have missed you. Once in a while, it seems the time will never come when I shall hold you again, but I know that is a foolish thought.

Yesterday there was a great sporting event in Bombay. The American Association's softball team played in the semifinals of the Bombay Y.M.C.A. league and won. It is an annual affair and last year the Americans played for the first time and won. The finals are today. Everyone plays, chiefly because they want to keep physically fit. There is one fellow who makes twelve hundred dollars a month, another who makes a thousand and most of the others make around five hundred. Your big bruiser is the pitcher, and he has lost only one game since coming to Bombay. Consequently, he is considered somewhat of a ball player. Aren't you proud!

I am still happy with the work and India. Still miss you and want you—and that about covers it all for this time.

Your Harry

* * *

Idie once asked me, in a letter, if India had many Christian churches. I thought there wasn't any country in the world that had more missions or missionaries than India. The difficulty, as I saw it, was that it encouraged people to live a lie because they had been told by becoming a Christian they would be helped. Practically everyone in India needed help.

Living conditions were primitive, and the things in which they had unbounded faith were insignificant, in my opinion. I believed the Indian people would be better off with their own religion until they were educated enough to grasp the teachings of Christianity. Many went to Mass, for example, then returned home to their pagan customs and prayed to them as they had for generations.

Neither did Indian men seem ambitious. "The work which my father did is the work I should do. Why should I try to improve upon so great a man as my father?" That was their way of looking at things, but education was gradually gaining a hold.

A Catholic church had patron-saint statues lining the walls. I noticed that the saint having the brightest robe received the most attention. Many worshipped the saints and the Virgin Mary without a thought about her Son as Savior.

I thought the real function of missionary work should be limited to teaching Bible stories until education could pave the way to understanding.

* * *

In the midst of my musings of what to write back to Idie, I heard the Bombay cotton market was on the decline. The year before, July/August figures were two hundred fifty rupees, and the same month this year, the figures reported one hundred forty-two rupees. The natives were heavy losers because they continually speculated. ACCO did not, so we made a lot of money before the bottom fell out.

Meanwhile, Chand's attitude became worse and worse, asking for a large loan (compared to his salary), so I had to get a new boy. Ed gave me fatherly advice and told me it was an old game which is played in order to ensure their job. So, I hired a Catholic Christian who seemed to be a good worker. Chand was Hindu.

* * *

Dark clouds began to hang low the first few days in June, and showers were frequent. The real monsoon, which is a season of rain and wind, was expected to start around the tenth. People in the office told Gene and me it would burst with fury and malice. The seaside drive would no longer be safe with water lashing over the seawall. Special tops would need to be put on automobiles, and the hood should be amply protected, or the motor would drown out every five minutes. What gossip we heard that first year!

SIX

MONSOON

June 12, 1938 — Bombay

Beloved Idie: I couldn't wait to tell you that last night the great dam in the sky broke. A powerful wind blew through a quiet night and a terrible load of water fell out of the sky, enough to make me wonder why I had not asked for directions to Noah's Ark!

Today, people are jubilant. The rains have come. The earth, some say, will be reborn. One of the clerks in our office said the monsoon is a fight between good and evil. He may be right—a battle between clouds, wind, and water. Whenever I can, I go to a window and watch with conflicting emotions; glad the great heat is gone for now, unhappy at the thought of having to slosh through ankle-deep water.

Week by week and in between, I find myself almost face-to-face with you, writing my heart and soul, in the hope that your days will be gladdened. I'm learning to think about several things at once, although I'm not certain I like having my thoughts rudely disturbed when thinking of you.

My social life consists of going to the cinema and playing ball on Sundays, plus an occasional midweek poker game (seems different here, as I usually win!). I have acquired a liking for cigar and pipe (not to excess), and as for the drinking, I indulge mostly in tomato juice unless I am at a party. I can usually mange to carry a half-empty glass all evening, until the dice game starts. What kind of a boy am I being, my darling?

Love you, Harry

* * *

One thing I appreciated about Idie was that as much as I knew she loved me; she had her own mind and would push back at things I said. Then, sometimes ...

June 18, 1938 — Houston

Dearest boy: I have a surprise for you--I agree about missionaries and teaching foreign people about our Lord. I believe schools and a simple gospel message will gradually help their state of living.

I can see more plainly every day our separation was in a great plan and decidedly for our good. When you analyze it, you can see the benefits. Had this not occurred, we would not know the full extent of our love. I don't think we realized how necessary we are to one another.

I looked at your movies last night, the ones we took at Rice. It is grand to see you move and talk. I sat, telling you over and over how very much I love you and how precious you are in my eyes, and how sweet! Idie

* * *

I took a step backwards as I read Idie's letter, realizing I had only tasted contentment, peace, and happiness when she and I were together. Baseball season was over, and learning how to properly class long-fibered cotton seemed an unending chore, but I could still dream about the future. ACCO Bombay was selling more cotton than ACCO Houston. I wondered, if business continued to grow, would an office open in Persia? Guy might move to Teheran, and Gene or I, with Idie, might go to Karachi.

My attention was interrupted by a problem in the sample room. I had been given the messy task of rearranging everything in it, and often things did not go smoothly. Ed came to me at one point and told me some of the workers were complaining I was working them too hard. They felt it wasn't healthy to stand and pull cotton all day. I got a big laugh out of that!

* * *

I learned a lot about monsoon as I watched it descend into the city. The wind blew with the rain at a terrific rate, making its patter sound like machine-gun bullets, squashing against windowpanes. Heavy purplish-black clouds rolled in from the sea carried by gale-force winds. They lopped inland, dropping their load of water as they went. Tall palms were whipped into a frenzied dance, giving the whole scene strong overtones of unreality.

Lacing sheets of water spewed from boiling clouds, reminiscent of a giant waterfall covering everything one could see. So great was the concentrated fall, it seemed the clouds would empty in an instant, but they continued dropping their load over a wide area. Bridges went, roads went, houses caved in, and communication halted. Walls sweated, mold collected on leather goods, rubber goods simply fell apart, wheels rusted, and destruction generally had a roaring good time.

Monsoon placed the "indispensable" label on one's "boy." No matter that he needed to be repeatedly reminded to perform his chores; his services remained a prime necessity. Sahib's clothes had to be dried out every day over the ingenious cane framework under which the *segari* sat. A segari was a metal or pottery brazier with glowing coals. It sat in a room set aside during the monsoon to serve solely as a drying-out place. Clothes and segari had to be attended to by my boy, or Sahib's clothes would stay damp, whiskers would grow on leather, and bed sheets would stay damp.

Despite its destruction and the frustrations that go with it, such as whiskers on one's best shoes and getting soaked on every venture outside, the monsoon is a thrilling experience. For all is not destruction. Who among the native Indians would wish for no monsoon? Not one among them would vote against it. It is the replenisher of cracked, thirsty, hungry soil and heaven-sent succor for agricultural peasantry and merchants, soothing the human brow after months of stifling heat. Monsoon is king here; no emperor ever had a more adoring populace.

SEVEN

RUGGER

June 1938 — Bombay

British friends told the captain of the rugger (rugby) team, the Bombay Gymkhana, I had played American football and was a fast runner. I was invited to a practice and observed the players standing in a circle, passing the ball around, then locking arms and heads in what they called a scrum formation. It looked like real work.

I kicked the ball high and long for them, longer than sixty yards. Practice broke up while I demonstrated it was not an accident. The men were eager to see if I really was fast before putting me with the backs. We lined up on the goal line, and I took a little edge on the start, stopped running when the others caught up. They gave up trying to get me to finish a race. I explained I had not yet learned to breathe correctly in the humid climate and so avoided the scrum. I got my chance in the backfield and wrote to Idie later.

> July 1, 1938 — Bombay
>
> Dearest Idie: I went to a couple of rugger (sometimes called rugby) workouts and find it pleasant fun and good exercise, somewhat different than our football because

most of it is kicking, with no forward passes. Tomorrow, I will play my first game.

For some reason you are mighty close to me. You seem to walk by my side more than ever before. I can't explain it, but it might be your letters saying the same things mine do. Can it really be that we will soon be together again, sweet girl of my heart? How much I hope, no one will ever know.

Be sweet – Adore you, Harry.

* * *

    I stirred up some controversy with the British as an American who wanted to play rugger. It seemed unbelievable to them that an American could make the first team in his first year of play, but I thought I could do it. I told Gene the fellows who play are fine people. As far as the game went, it could be explained as a glorified form of American basketball, played outdoors on a hundred-yard field. A try counted for three points and the goal after the try is an additional two. I made a try in my first game but thought I should have made two more.

* * *

July 6, 1938 — Bombay

Dearest Idie: The American Association had a big fourth of July party at the Taj Mahal Hotel. I dreaded having to go, but in such a small community one must keep in touch with one's fellow countrymen. I seem to be their representative American youth since I'm younger than any of the others and manage to win all their baseball games.

The big, air-cooled Taj Mahal ballroom was reserved for the American Association and guests. The festivities began with cocktails, in the American manner. The English use few mixed drinks; the common, almost universal, drink is the "Chota peg" or "small measure," which is a whiskey soda and a sane drink, if there are any sane alcoholic drinks.

Two Negroes supplied piano and drum music, playing American songs, such as "Streets of New York" and "California, Here I Come." Some of the braver guests, or more hopped-up ones, began to sing, and others joined in. I enjoyed that part of the night.

Then came dinner, consisting of a small steak, baked potato, etc. After dinner, the president of the Association asked us to toast the President of the United States. It was the first time I had done that, and I felt quite a thrill. A band (the Negroes had gone) played "The Star-Spangled Banner" while everyone raised their glasses and said, "To the President of the United States."

Afterward, we were asked to remain standing and drink a toast to His Majesty, the King-Emperor. This time the band played the British national anthem and then offered the toast, "To the King-Emperor." The American foreign policy, as enumerated by Secretary Hull, was read. I was proud to be an American.

There was dancing and a horse-racing game. Ed, Gene, and I sold tickets and became quite hoarse. There was also a night club floor show. At the end, the band played "America" and then the American and British national anthems. The Chinese envoy was present with his wife and seemed to enjoy the party. Gene and I left at this point, but we heard later that the party had continued.

There were probably two hundred and fifty people: several English, some Indian couples and at least one Swiss. A cosmopolitan crowd, predominately American. Everyone likes American parties because anything can happen! This one was surprisingly calm. There were groups of balloons strung around and the usual fun of bursting them lasted but a few moments.

I was interested in your ideas of missionary work here. I am afraid the great masses of people will never have faith in our deities because of their traditions. Hindus cannot touch us, eat from a dish we have touched, or allow us to enter their homes because we immediately make them unclean. Inroads might be made with the untouchables, such as coolies, sweepers, and cleaners, but education must come first to the masses.

The more intelligent people read the Bible as a great philosophy but do not believe it. One of our employees has read it all (so he says), but he cannot believe a deity can be within oneself because he cannot be materially detected. My friend would rather live this life somewhat sinfully and take his chances in the next reincarnation.

I set out to remind you that you are still the light of my life. There is nothing I would not do for you if I thought it beneficial to you, or nothing I would do if I thought it harmful.

Thanks for being a guiding hand; for making something of my life, for sending me to India. Thanks for your faith, your devotion, your love, Harry

* * *

I played rugger on weekends and scored six points in a game we won. Three additional points were not counted because I forgot to stop running at a certain point. Still with the B team, I felt we hadn't seen any real competition yet, but I would be ready when it came.

Conversations with Ed were not only about business but my hope to bring Idie to India. Ed guessed we would get married someday if we had made up our minds to do so. I smiled at that and told him neither of us were worrying about it. Ed's only objection seemed to be the kind of life two people could live on with three hundred dollars a month. I knew Ed spent more than his five hundred, and Guy more than his four hundred, plus receiving a slice of the profits. I hoped Idie and I could do well on what I was making, but I didn't think the time was right to ask.

Things continued to be difficult in the ACCO sorting room. I had to fire one of the workers for laziness and constant grumbling, bringing down the morale of everyone else. I hated to do it, but those whom I fired never seemed to mind being out of a job.

I did have some fun on the rugger field when I showed the team a "good old American forward pass." It wasn't legal in rugger but thought the boys would enjoy seeing how it was done. I often sent Idie newspaper clippings about our rugger games and waited impatiently for her reply.

July 31, 1938 — Houston

> Harry dearest: my hero is again making headlines, as you did at Rice! I am delighted you are enjoying the company of nice Englishmen, especially while playing rugger. Wish I could watch, cheer, and pray for your success as I did when you played football. You have my best wishes to make the first team and my utter disappointment if you don't. So there, get busy!
>
> By the time this arrives you will have had a birthday. So, my dearest one, a very Happy Birthday to you! I am sending you a magazine, The King's Business. Yes, it is a religious magazine but the best I have seen. No, it is not a Baptist book, it is for all beliefs and has articles by beloved Christians. I know you will enjoy it.
>
> I shall be with you in spirit on August 15th and am sending you blessings for your 25th birthday. They are coming

a long way so they will be sweeter when they arrive! I know the Lord will bless you and give you peace and contentment.

Your love satisfies my every desire. I do not want to go places with other men. I constantly refuse and am perfectly happy to stay home. I know you feel the same way. The Lord will unite us when the time is right. You will rise above others if you hold steadfast to your faith. I am thankful for all the blessings you have received.

Thinking of you constantly, Idie

* * *

Ed, Faye, Gene, and I went to the exchange together on the night the U.S. Bureau of Agriculture issued the "Annual Crop Report Estimate of B/C (Bales of Cotton)" to be produced in the U.S.A. for 1938. Without knowing the people involved, it would be difficult to understand the importance of this report. It affected the whole world, but nowhere as much as in India. This exchange did more transactions than New York, as many of the Indian brokers and merchants are millionaires several times over.

The report was half a million bales more than anticipated. Such activity! The brokers and members of the exchange gathered on the floor and in the balconies, jammed together, very colorful in their bright turbans and painted faces.

The market broke at five rupees here and about twenty points in New York. Immediately hands began to wave, hundreds of them. They were waving away from themselves, meaning "I am a seller." The market declined, and as it went down, the hands gradually turned until many were waving toward themselves, signifying they were buyers. To me, it looked like chaos.

They kept no books but had the most wonderful memories. Some old brokers would sell a hundred thousand bales from August 1st to July 31st and never make a book entry, or a mistake!

* * *

August 15, 1938 — Bombay

My dearest: today I am a man! Your sweet letter came this morning, right on the dot. You're getting awfully good, as your greetings are exactly on time. And many thanks for the magazine. I haven't seen it yet, but I know I shall love it.

And so, my darling, I am a success. Saturday, I will play with the Gymkhana "A" team, which is evidently no mean achievement. Have been making a score every now and then and they have decided to give me a try. If I do well, I'll try to send you the news.

You were given to me so I would learn the importance of faith, and how to live the kind of life that will help me make you happy. Life is interesting in a way that it has never been before. I have incentive to go forward, hoping our hunches will work out.

Love you, Harry

* * *

The city was quiet as the monsoon continued with daily storms. Even the office did not have much for me to do. The Waddells hosted a party given by the ladies of the American Association, called a "hard times" party. The object was to replenish their treasury which had been sorely taxed by paying passage home for a doctor and his wife who couldn't adjust to life in India. The Waddells hoped to make three hundred rupees but took in fifteen hundred rupees.

Games were set up all over the house, with small prizes for the winners. Gene did well, winning four theater tickets, plus crackers and toothpicks. I managed to get an alarm clock and a couple of tins of meat. Quite a few English guests were present and a few Indians. It was a successful party, but not being a party man, I went home early.

The next day, Gene and I went to the bungalow of our head salesman for *tiffin* (brunch). Vallabdas (Val-ab-das) lived about fifteen miles from Bombay. We took off our shoes and sat on the floor. The Indians sat on small tables about two inches from the floor while a long pillow on the floor was reserved for Gene and me. Each person was served a large brass plate about twelve inches in diameter with sides two inches high. No meat was served as Hindus were present, but vegetable curry, peas, beans, okra, potatoes, and other vegetables were piled high on the plate.

I told Idie later, everything was highly seasoned with chilies. We also were served a native bread, resembling Mexican tortillas. Gene and I were given spoons; the Indians used their fingers. Such noises! I discovered the more noise one made, the more highly he was regarded.

* * *

About this time, Gene and I heard Guy was in a hospital in Houston, but no one seemed to know why. Then I received a letter from Idie.

August 25, 1938 — Houston

Harry dearest: Surprise! A letter not written on Sunday! I simply could not wait. Your last letter was too cute. I, too, am pessimistic about ever being in India, but it is fun to build our castles. It has kept me in the clouds all summer. I am lonely without my constant companion.

As you probably know, Mr. Schilling is in Houston and is quite ill. His case has not yet been diagnosed. I called the Methodist Hospital and told the nurse who I was and asked her to ask Mrs. Schilling if I might come by and talk with her for a few minutes. Mrs. Schilling asked me to come at one p.m.

I bought some lovely flowers and went to the hospital. Three nurses went with me to his door. Mrs. Schilling suggested we go on the porch and talk. I told her I came to offer my services and car because Guy had been so kind to you. I invited her to lunch when he was better, and she said she would love it.

At least three times she said how much he liked you, and how anxious he was to meet me (what did you tell him?). She said she would call as soon as she had any news about when he could have company.

They are afraid he has something infectious. She seemed grateful, telling me the hospital was getting on her nerves. Before I met her, I wondered if I could be successful in India. I didn't think I was competent, but if the other wives and American women are like her, then I know I could be a success.

My darling, I will keep you posted on Guy. Only the Lord knows what next month will bring. My prayer is that we may be together again to share love, happiness, sorrow, and whatever life gives us. Love you – Idie

EIGHT

THEORETICALLY, IT OUGHT TO WORK

August 29, 1938 — Bombay

My dearest Idie: I am a little discouraged about taking pictures these days. I may just bring them home when I go, or let you come here to see them. As far as the movie, I am afraid it has become the forgotten man. I have little ambition to do such things without you. I haven't seen the places tourists visit. I've been in the jungle and in towns where only a narrow-gauge railroad goes. No Europeans, never a hotel, sanitation terrible, mosquitoes horrible. These things don't photograph well. All the towns do have small temples though.

Today is another Hindu holiday—they have plenty. When you come, we will visit all things and see how they tick. Next weekend is the Parsee New Year. Gene and I are planning a short excursion.

Be sweet. I love you – Harry. Regards to Ruby

* * *

Gene and I left Bombay on a Friday afternoon, dreaming of a great weekend vacation. Monsoon rain, usually finished by then, was beating down furiously. The road was barely visible, so we drove at a creeping pace. Our first stop was to be Kalyan, forty miles away, to meet Ollie Olsen, from the office.

It was still pouring when we reached Ollie's cutoff. We missed it and drove ten miles further before becoming suspicious enough to turn back. The rain, having delayed us sufficiently, stopped. The sun glistened on wet grass and trees. What a wonderful world! One mile from the cutoff, the motor belched and stopped.

Gene opened the hood, wiggled wires backward and forward, then declared, "Theoretically, it ought to work." The motor was more practical and refused.

Theoretically, It Ought to Work

While I ate Vienna sausages from a tin, Gene puzzled with contacts and theories. Finally, he gave up and joined me on the running board. We sent Sukla, Ed's boy borrowed for the occasion, into Thana, just ten miles away, to ask Ollie to come for us. We did not see him again until we returned to Bombay the following Monday.

Hours passed. Gene mulled over the possibility of the motor theory being wrong. We tried making new parts out of the Vienna tins, but they didn't work. The moon came up; we continued to sit.

We had been waiting several hours when an Englishman came along nursing a flat tire. We lent him a jack and his driver found the wire that put Gene's theory back in line. Gene's smile told me he was relieved to find that the motor was orthodox after all. We drove on.

Ollie, meanwhile, had roused the countryside. He had servants watching all the roads. If Kalyan had possessed a fire department, it would have been out too.

Dirty and hungry, we arrived at Kalyan about nine o'clock. Forty miles in six hours! Not a grand beginning, if one believes in omens.

Sukla was still missing the next morning, so we went on without him. Neither of us spoke any of the Indian languages, but we hoped sign language would get us through.

As we climbed the Western Ghats, monsoon rain and heavy clouds were again with us. Miniature waterfalls rolled down the mountains on all sides. Even under melancholy clouds, green trees and grass sparkled. The road wound upwards, sometimes too close to the rim.

We passed a long-forgotten vine-covered bridge that seemed to walk right into the side of the mountain, as distant peaks gave an impression of endlessness.

Near noon, we climbed onto the great plains. The air was crisp and clean, not full of water. We had a flat tire but also found a small dak-bungalow, where we spent the night.

Sunday morning was bright, with no misty rain, black clouds, or musty monsoon smell. We drove to the Ellora Caves, fourteen miles from Aurangabad, in the state of Hyderabad. No one seemed to know how old they were, but we were told that Buddhists, Brahmins, and Jains had built them in the third or fourth century for worship and meditation.

Having practically no archeological knowledge, Gene and I had to depend upon a native guide, who knew little more than we. The sculptures were massive and magnificent. We enjoyed looking at them, even as we were bewildered by the many Hindu deities and their reincarnations. I cannot do them justice; one must see them to appreciate the wealth of art and history they represent. We left determined to learn more about our Indian brothers and their beliefs.

We ate baked beans and canned fruit salad at Aurangabad in the first-class dining room on his Exalted Highness, the *Nizam's* (ruler) private railroad.

After a short drive through the old Moghul stronghold, we visited the mausoleum of Rabi Daurani, wife of the Emperor Aurangzeb. A small replica of the great Taj Mahal at Agra, its white dome with corner minarets, is a landmark for miles around. Natives proudly refer to it as the "Chota (Little) Taj."

We climbed to the top of one of the minarets, and the countryside spread out below in a crisscross of fields and pastures. We saw a solitary goat herder and a lonely-looking bullock cart winding its way to market, a tiny village in the distance. We were reluctant to climb down.

Sunday night found us situated in the roomy Jalna dak-bungalow. The last thirty-odd miles were the most pleasant of the trip. The road was a grassy track used mainly by bullock carts, but without ruts or dust. Not even a wild-eyed bullock to menace us. Green trees, grass, and fields brought back memories of our Texas countryside. We thought that road the best of all the Nizam's dominions.

After ordering dinner in the station dining room, we sent a note to our Parsee agent, Rustomjee. As this was a pleasure trip, we only meant to say we were passing through and would call again at another time.

Rustomjee would have none of it. He arrived with his best friend, the police chief, just before dinner. A celebration was in order. Scotch came out, and drinks began to flow.

We learned a great deal. Did you know that the Nizam has the power of life and death over his subjects? Or that there can be only two motives for crime? Money or women, or both. We also learned that the average village criminal was more difficult to deal with than the city dweller. Uneducated and simple, animal instinct dominated his existence.

Our dinner sizzled in the hot box while the waiter dozed. Finally, near midnight, the scotch began to see the bottom, and the police chief remembered it was his wedding anniversary. He guessed he better go home as his wife was having a party. We saw nothing of Jalna, except the smelly bazaar, which we drove through coming and going.

Early Monday morning saw us homeward bound. The road, though lined with bullock carts and gaily dressed pedestrian traffic, was good. We drove at a fast clip for India, making one hundred fifteen miles in the first three hours. Then the ax fell again. It took six hours to do the next forty-five miles.

It was very difficult in India not to accumulate a crowd of inquisitive natives wherever you stopped, be it desert, plain, or river. The most difficult of difficulties was to find an English-speaking native in the up-country.

We came to a small village; we needed petrol. Was there petrol? Yes, someone nodded. We drove from one end of the village to the other at least ten times. We ended up, after checking every hut, without petrol, near the breaking point.

Natives enjoyed our dilemma. It was a good game in which the whole village participated. There was still enough of the precious juice to take us to the next village. We decided to risk it, praying for petrol all the way.

"Does anyone here speak English?" Silence descended upon the jabbering mob that had gathered around us. Gene and I looked at each other. This then, was the end of the line. It might be weeks before we could get back.

We heard a small voice say, "Yes, Sahib. I English well speaking."

Have you ever been lost? Ever thought you were going to be stranded in a dirty little hole for weeks with no food or place to sleep, except under the stars with wild dogs and cobras? Then you know how we felt.

"Where can we get petrol?" We could almost see the wheels turn as our interpreter wrinkled his forehead in a masterful effort. "Ahmednagar, Sahib. Forty-five miles."

Back into gloom we plunged. Lady Luck was on holiday!

We had left the main road to see a more picturesque India. Buses never traveled this road during the monsoon because water crossings were particularly bad. What prize tourists we had turned out to be!

Suddenly, we saw a bus that had also taken the wrong road. The driver gave us just enough petrol to reach Ahmednagar. Life was good again.

I was driving. There were water crossings every few miles. To make sure we did not get stuck, Gene waded at each one. We safely negotiated many crossings. Confidence returned. Then, rather recklessly, we drove into an innocent looking hole, without Gene wading. We started sinking and water poured into the car. The engine conked out. I expected the hood to submerge at any moment. We finally stopped with an axle and running board resting on the riverbed.

As if enough trouble had not already dogged us for one day, the seemingly impossible happened. Not a coolie was in sight. No jabbering mob disturbed the peaceful murmur of the water as it trickled through the car. Gene took off the fan belt and dried the plugs. Still no coolies. We dug the soft gravel away from the wheels and built a short runway of big stones.

Gene made a quick check on the motor and again said, "Theoretically, it ought to work." Surprisingly, it did. We rocked her backward and forward. Inch by inch she came through. On the other side, we measured the petrol with a stick. The tank was practically empty.

Off again I felt lighthearted, despite knowing we would soon run out of petrol. Five miles from Ahmednagar the engine died. We knew, by then, what the last sputtering cough of an engine sounded like.

We discovered four miles an hour makes for pretty good walking. Ahmednagar looked better than good when we got our red, perspiring faces into the first available telephone booth.

The dak bungalow was comfortable, the air crisp and cool. The curry and rice were as hot as anything we had ever eaten. We slept the sleep of the just and arrived back in Bombay Monday afternoon without further mishap.

* * *

Happy to be where we could once again take in a movie, Gene and I decided to go to a film we heard was bringing controversy into the streets. A hundred police officers were at the entrance to the theater where *Drum* was showing, trying to keep rioters away. Some people seemed to think the film was anti-Indian, but neither Gene nor I saw anything against India in it.

There was often trouble on the northwest frontier and in Burma, but little of it in Bombay. If anything, there were tussles between Hindus and Muslims, but mostly, it was peaceful.

* * *

The situation in Europe, however, did not look good. ACCO had practically suspended all operations in Germany, as there seemed to be no immediate settlement in view. Japan had been on a pay-in-advance list for a while, so their business losses were no great disappointment, except for those merchants who were willing to speculate.

In contrast, I heard ACCO Bombay was enjoying a nice profit for the first time in three years. I was not sure Gene, or I had become great assets to the company, but rumor had it we would receive a bonus of a half month's salary.

September 20, 1938 — Bombay

My dearest Idie, a very good morning to you. Rugger goes on. Right now, I am considered an "A" team member, for which I am thankful. The Bombay Gymkhana Cup Tournament is in progress and four or five teams are entered. The All-India tournament is in Madras in early October. There is a keen competition I am unable to feel without the cheering thousands and the brass band; however, we won our first game and play again tomorrow in the semifinals. We should get to the finals, but the fun will begin to fly as the "Duke of Wellington" regiment will probably win the other bracket. They are "tops" in India.

The war clouds are still dark. The market is jittery and so are the merchants. The Indian market will jump straight up if war does come and then ACCO will probably make a good profit. I think you will enjoy the attitude of the newspapers here as compared to the American ones. I would like to have some of those nice long talks we had not so very long ago.

Love you, Harry

* * *

Gene knew of a little fishing village about fifteen miles from Bombay. I heard there was a golf course there, but Gene's intent was to introduce me to a meal called *sukaika*.

We went there at sundown one Sunday. While a Japanese cook with a big cleaver chased a squawking chicken, we toured the grounds. Small tables were scattered on the grass, and tall trees made an effective screen from the dusty road. A small arched bridge graced an artificial lake, decorated with beautiful flowers and swimming ducks.

I also noticed a cookhouse, in which food was partially prepared, with living quarters for the proprietor and family. The only other building was a small pavilion with open sides for rainy-season customers.

Japanese lanterns, liberally placed, gave off a party spirit during the day. They could not be seen at night as there was no electricity. Petrol lamps were brought to the table as darkness fell. It all seemed quite primitive.

After what seemed like hours of waiting, food began to appear—chicken, tomatoes, carrots, onions, potatoes, cabbage, string beans, and a sauce. I sat silently, surveying the raw food, my brows raised in concern.

Each separate ingredient was artistically arranged on a dish of its own, but I was in no mood for raw food. Gene seemed content, and he had been there before, so I waited to see what would come next. A charcoal stove with live coals arrived, and then I began to see light. Sukaika would be cooked on the table in front of us.

Using chopsticks with amazing dexterity, the cook began putting the chicken and various vegetables into a small pot now simmering over the coals. He made his job a work of art. Before the cook was finished, he had accumulated enough food to fill a pot many times the size of the one he had.

Fascinated by the ease with which the cook, the chopsticks and the food all came together, Gene and I bent closer to the pot, watching intensely. It seemed no trick at all to pick up a carrot, a slice of onion, even a pinch of salt. As the cooking progressed, sweet aromas became deliciously penetrating. We fingered our chopsticks and asked, "How much longer?" every few minutes. We always received the same answer, "Pletty soon."

Finally, small bowls of steamed rice arrived, and despite the cook's protests that he was not finished, we started to eat. I smiled between mouthfuls, declaring it, "Delicious!"

We ate several bowls each. The cook kept stirring the pot, adding more from time to time until we finally gave up eating.

* * *

September 27, 1938 — Bombay

Dearest Idie: The Bombay Gymkhana won the Bombay Cup! We leave Saturday afternoon for Madras, there to try for the All-India Championship. Our victory was overshadowed by the dirty play of one of the fellows on the other team, but we were happy anyway.

People here take their sport a little more seriously than we; some get excited enough to do a small amount of cheering. After the game, a lady something or other presented us the cup.

Saturday night there was a banquet. It began with a toast to the King-Emperor and then their national anthem. Next, we had some of that raw English beef they eat and the usual potatoes, peas, and ice cream. Afterward, the speeches began, and a great din ensued until the would-be speaker mounted the top of the table. After each speech, there was a toast and then the song, "For They Are Jolly Good Fellows." At the end of the speeches, toasting, and jolly good fellowing, most chose serious drinking and harmonizing around the piano. I quietly slipped out at midnight.

The next day I heard the whole troop had gone to the Taj Mahal Hotel, closed the place with them inside and proceeded to take the furniture apart. These Englishmen are utterly amazing. They are stiffly conventional in public until they are all by themselves, and then they have a fun time. I feel reasonably safe in saying I felt better on Sunday than any of them. I was informed I was most fortunate and honored to play with the Englishmen, especially on the first team my first year. I feel lucky but not at all surprised because as I have often said, there are guardian angels.

I will write from Madras, if possible. Love you, Harry. How's school? Regards to Ruby

* * *

My trip to South India for the rugger tournament coincided with ACCO business. I enjoyed playing in the All-India Championship, even though we lost. In driving back to Bombay, I stopped at one cotton mill after another and was so tired I could not write even one word to Idie.

Back in Bombay, I discovered Gene had moved both of us into a bungalow with plenty of room and space for a darkroom. Faye Waddell helped us with getting curtains and bedspreads made. She reminded me so much of Idie and how much I wanted to send for her.

I wrote a twenty-five-page report for Ed about my trip. After finishing, I leaned back in my chair and told Gene I was seriously thinking of asking Ed to give me a special Christmas present, especially after receiving another letter from Idie.

> October 16, 1938 — Houston
>
> Dearest Harry: your letter of September 27th made me so happy. I was delighted about your team's success but was confident you would come out on top.
>
> I have an awful bunch of children this year in school. There! It is out! I thought I could keep it to myself, but I didn't. My heart isn't there sometimes. I wonder if it ever will be again.
>
> Saw Bernice Barker in town yesterday. Do you remember her? She asked about you and seemed shocked when I replied I still heard from you. I said you liked India and were happy. It would be at least two years before you came home. People seem disappointed when I don't cry and say I miss you and it is all horrible.
>
> I went to see *Drums* last night. I thoroughly enjoyed it. Do you remember how it started with the map? I had a strange feeling when they stopped at India that I was there too, with you. I thought the scenery was very lovely!
>
> I love you—you and only you. Idie

* * *

November 7, 1938 — Bombay

Dearest Idie: how time has slipped away! You must be wondering what happened since my first letters were long and often. They were interesting and now are shorter, say less, and are farther between. I'm sure you know I love you, think of you just the same, and wish for you even more.

I've been fifteen hundred miles through Central India, Khandesh, Berar, Mogloi, and Baramati since then, and written another long report. Ed said he intends to send the first report to Mr. Whittington. I hope he does. If I do say so myself, it was good!

I missed your letter this week, and Monday was a dreadful day. I hope you were just too busy to write. I try not to be selfish, as I know the things you put up with. Our separation is harder on you than on me. I can never say I am happy away from you; I work, keep busy all the time, and so time passes.

I send loving thoughts—hoping your children have reformed. Harry

NINE
CHRISTMAS AND THE TIGER

November 12, 1938 — Houston

My dearest boy: at last, I have heard from you. It has been four weeks since I had a line from you. Ruby threatened to cable if my disposition didn't improve. Can I help it if I am cross when worried about you? I did not complain aloud to anyone, but Ruby surmised my early retiring in the evenings was due to something.

One year ago, you were starting on your life journey to India. One year down, perhaps two to go. It has been a great blessing in many ways. If nothing more, it has indelibly stamped my heart that I can neither love nor enjoy any other person. To know what love means in one's life is its own accomplishment. We will never regret this separation but realize it was for the best. May your second year be more successful than your first. I am for you!

I am glad you have a new place to live. I hope you enjoy it—a darkroom did you say? How about proof?

After one full year of not being with you, I still have only love in my heart and one name on my lips. Always yours, Idie

* * *

November 12, 1938 — Bombay

My beloved Idie: one year ago, you went to school. I went by train, a ship, a faraway country. Today, I wonder what changes have occurred, what magic has worked on you and me. I know fundamentally we are the same two people. We may look a bit older—you may have a gray hair and I, a more pronounced wrinkle in the forehead, but we still have the same heart, the same thoughts. I wonder—have we grown older?

I must say yes. I have found my thoughts don't dwell so much on the pleasures of the day, as on "What progress have I made today?"

I also wonder what has happened to our love. I say it has mellowed and become no less a part of both of us. It is bound inextricably into an everlasting light by a tiny flame which burns, and sometimes even hurts, inside. Then comes the most important wondering of all, the future.

I would not say what I am about to say, except that I want your answer, from your heart as well as your head. Please weigh one against the other and then let me know.

I am certain I can bring you here anytime I ask Ed. My heart cries for you, but my head cautions me to go slowly. Three hundred dollars is not much money in Bombay. I doubt the company would pay your way since we are not already married. It is essential we have a car. I have only two or three hundred dollars put away, so we would start in debt. The company would advance any necessary funds for a while, but these are not the main considerations.

I want to do everything well in whatever I undertake, feeling my stubbornness has certain value. Progress I have made, but I am not satisfied. I am sure Ed is not disappointed in this past year's accomplishments, but at the same time, I am still an indefinite quantity in the business world. Should I ask anything of Ed?

You might like Bombay or the people, but I think you would love India. I am equally sure you would be a tremendous help to me, becoming an asset to the company. There would be three objections, I think. Can we live on my present salary? Can you accept the lifestyle of Bombay people? Will I be able to travel for six weeks at a time and not worry about you?

Think it through and let me know your reactions. I may not have painted a clear picture. I hope you puzzle it out. Let us pray that this will be the beginning of the end of our separation.

I send all my love and hopeful anticipation. Harry

* * *

A discussion in the Bombay office opened a new adventure for me. ACCO had made sales of about five thousand bales of cotton, but two hundred thousand bales of good quality were usually available at that time of year. Due to untimely rains, the cotton was stained and needed to be cleaned enough to pass the sample they sold against. It could make an enormous saving in money and prestige for ACCO if we could do it.

Ed said, "If you want to try this, you will need to spend a month or two in the Central Provinces." *I am anxious to go because everyone says it can't be done. We shall see!*

Before I left, Gene and I went to a movie with a short film, *Peace, and Remembrance,* about the Armistice and the war scare. I settled into my seat and looked at the empty seat next to me, feeling Idie's presence. I felt as if we were together again, thinking as one. At that moment, I decided not to ask Ed for permission to bring Idie to Bombay yet.

The decision was not an easy one. I spent much time pacing back and forth, wanting to believe this was the time for Idie to come, but I couldn't. I loved Idie more than anything and knew she loved me. Yet, I winced as I imagined Ed saying, "No, not yet."

* * *

December 10, 1938 — Ulun

Sweetheart: tonight, my heart and soul are filled with things I should like to say, and when I lay the pencil aside, I will not have said a fraction of what I wanted to say.

I am writing from Ulun, in the Central Provinces. It is very small, and I have been staying at a cotton gin. I feel fortunate because there are electric lights, which make writing and reading somewhat easier than the usual oil lamps. The climate is one you so often read about, as I wear a jacket every morning until about nine and sleep under a blanket at night.

As to the business side of my being here, I can't lay claim to any great success. My job is to make good cotton out of muddy cotton. It can be done, and I think I'm the fella who could do it, but I feel terribly restless. This is one job I want to do well. Yes, my darling, our Bible is with me.

It has been a long time since I wrote you an interesting letter, hasn't it? The truth is the rare and new has become commonplace. It was a shock when I woke up one day to find that dhotied men and saried women were no longer a novelty, that the bullock cart, beggar, and street vendor were to be passed over as trivial everyday sights. I am afraid, my darling, that on that day, India opened her arms and yet another young sahib took her as his own.

When my leave comes, I know I shall sail with a song in my heart for you, but I shall miss the lazy old bullock cart, the jingling bells of the gherry (horse-drawn Victoria carriages), the shrill high-pitched Indian voices, the painted faces, and the bargaining, cheating, lying, yet likable Indians. I imagine I shall gladly sail back when the last leave is up. When I dream, I see you by my side.

I've rambled along, supposing you love every word, just as I do. Never will you know how I cherish each word you write. I can only say thank you for your loving hope, faith, and guidance.

I know you understand my heart and soul as I cry out with this little note that I am forever and eternally yours, Harry

Best to Ruby–Merry Christmas!

Harry at a Cotton Gin

* * *

I was content as Christmas edged closer, telling Ed I was "getting along all right." He had visited me in Ulun, to see how the work with the muddy cotton was progressing. We discussed many things, including Ed's belief that Indian cotton milled in the U.S. would become too expensive to be competitive in big European markets. Therefore, the up-country mills in India would consume an ever-increasing quantity of Indian grown cotton. Ed was working on developing a larger organization in which ACCO would get a percentage of about a million bales per year in India. ACCO's reputation was becoming the *pukka* (the best) of all cotton merchants.

I said I thought the Indian merchant felt smart when he could make a shady deal, especially with a European. Nothing seemed crooked in business to Indian businessmen, but ACCO, called "Anderson," seemed to be different, respected by Indian merchants. That trust could be worth untold future business.

Ed also told me he had asked Houston to send someone to study up-country India, inferring that he was looking for a future partner in the firm. I bent forward and thought, *I am beginning to love this job; it is very young, and we can grow together.*

* * *

Gene and I were happy to accept an invitation to spend Christmas with Ed and Faye and a few others at a hill station in Mableshwar.

December 28, 1938 — Mableshwar

Dearest Idie: Christmas at Mableshwar was joyful. There was a Christmas tree and children, making for a perfect Christmas, except for the snow and you. Mableshwar hosts many shady drives and gorgeous mountain views, bridal paths and old forts, jungles, and waterfalls. I stayed four days, but everyone was so nice it seemed like only so many hours.

Besides Ed, Faye, Gene, and me, Mr. and Mrs. Bob Noble were there with their son and daughter, plus two older men and Faye's mother. We were up early in the morning and retired early in the evening. There was very little drinking, singing of hymns and carols, golf, tennis, bridge, and shooting.

Merrymaking was at its highest at mealtime, especially on turkey day. Bob Noble is the manager of "Kodak House" (Eastman) in Bombay, and he gave me a comprehensive criticism of my pictures. They are coming along slowly; some are nice but others, only so-so. I have begun an album for you, as we should have a record of events here.

The Christmas tree was a real fir, decorated with tinsel. Packages made several heaps, and there was much discussion about when to open them. Bob's children were thirteen and ten, anxious to begin untying things. The girl is sweet, with personality plus; we got along well. My best present was your letter and magazine. Thank you, my sweet! There was also a box of stationery, five monogram handkerchiefs, a couple of good books, cigars, a big bath towel and mat, and several other little things. A real Xmas!

Sitting by the fireplace was wonderful, I felt your presence more than once. I got one big shock when they gave me a small package. It so looked like you had wrapped it, as it was blue, with silver ribbons and stars, a real Idie package. My heart missed a beat. It was from Faye.

Your Christmas Day letter answered the questions I asked in November. I am so glad your answers were what I thought they would be. Ed asked me if I had received a good letter from you, and when I answered yes, he said when he went to Houston, he wanted to meet you and tell you all the things about India which I might not have told you.

I was stunned when Ed said he thought meeting you was important before you came out. It means he approves! I still feel I cannot ask until the end of the first three years. Ed knows I want you and that you want me. I'm sure he would have suggested you come long ago if he were sure we would be the same here as back there. Hopefully, we shall celebrate next Christmas together!

Love you, Harry

* * *

I learned something new about the boss at Mableshwar: he had a strong itch to get a tiger. I don't know why I was surprised; almost everyone I knew in India wanted to shoot one or more of the big cats. The first thing Ed did was to hire a local hunter, a *shikari*, to scout the nearby jungle for signs of the cats.

Excitement ran through our hotel like wildfire when we heard the shikari had found fresh pugmarks of a big tiger on a game trail. Energy was flowing out of Ed like a wayward typhoon. He went into the jungle to see for himself. Then he bought a water buffalo calf and hired villagers to stake it out near a tall tree.

I had heard a lot of stories about "tiger shoots," but I never thought I would be on one. I was up early that morning and rushed to breakfast. Ed was already there, all smiles. The tiger had killed the calf! Ed and the shikari returned to the kill site. I tried to tag along but was told, "The tiger may be lying up near the kill; we don't want to spook him."

Ed was busy all day, hiring villagers to build a hide, or *machan*, in a tree near the kill. He said "his" tiger had eaten only a small part of the calf and would probably return that night for a second helping. Ed would be sitting in the tree all night, if necessary. It gave me shivers, but I sure wanted to climb into the machan with Ed.

Bad news! Gene was chosen to be in the machan with Ed, to shine the light from a powerful flashlight on the tiger when it began to eat. That's what happens to low men on totem poles: hold the fort while others go off to war. Ed said it was only fair because most of my time was spent in the interior where I would have other chances. Gene stayed in Bombay; this might be his only chance. It made sense, but that didn't keep me from disappointment. Envy, too.

An hour before sundown, Ed and Gene shimmied up the tree but not before Ed sternly lectured: "Stay awake and alert; remain absolutely still, all night if necessary; don't move a muscle, not even an eyelash. The tiger will come silently and slowly, inch by inch, belly to the ground, watching and listening. The slightest movement will spook him."

Maybe I was the lucky one. Could I pretend to be a dumb bum on a log, up a tree in the dead of night? I went to bed, head whirling.

Ed and Gene came in at sunrise, looking like they had been on a binge. Pugmarks, read by the shikari, told the story. The tiger had come down the trail and stopped, crouched on his belly, then moved on into heavy jungle cover. Something had frightened him.

Gene said he couldn't sit still, probably spooked him. Ed was still hopeful, said no one was at fault. Hustling off to bed, he said he would try again, and I could go with him.

I was having second thoughts, but the die was cast. I had become custodian of the flashlight. Ed, the shikari, and I approached the tree near the kill. Ed and I silently climbed the tree, and the shikari left. Ed seemed calm and expectant. I was a bundle of nerves. Up a tree in the jungle, I was trembling with excitement, not fear; sitting on wood planks laid across tree limbs, looking down on what was left of the calf.

Birds chirped in nearby trees, and a breeze rustled the leaves. There were no other sounds, nor anything moving that I could see.

The sun went down behind a mountain and extinguished the light. For the first time, I realized what complete darkness was like. I was uneasy, imagining dangerous things, other than Ed's tiger. I couldn't see anything at all, hoping the tiger would make a noise so I could shine the light, giving Ed a target.

A full moon came slowly, the way Ed said the tiger would come. Its glow gently tinted treetops, leaving shadows on the ground and bringing the kill back into view. Swarms of biting insects came with the moon. I wanted to swat at them but didn't.

Very slowly, I repeatedly brushed my hand across my face. A breeze refreshed us and carried the bugs away. Nothing else happened, hour after hour, and excitement dribbled away; it was hard to stay awake.

I fell asleep clutching the flashlight. I dreamed the tiger was slipping up on me. I awoke in a cold sweat, terrified.

A long-tailed rat was on a tree limb only a foot or so over my head. I froze as I watched him crawl down to my feet. I was not afraid of Ed's tiger, but I was afraid of that rat. Its nose touched the toe of my shoe, whiskers sensing the air. I had a blanket over my legs and the rat crawled on it. I wanted to shake it off, but that could spook the tiger, and put me in the boss's doghouse. What to do?

Boss or no boss, I decided, tiger or no tiger, if that rat got as far as my belly, I was going to raise some Texas noise and get out of there.

Suddenly, the rat jumped onto Ed's blanket, and he raised as much noise as I might have. He threw off the blanket and shouted the only words spoken in the machan that night: "Let's get out of here!"

SHABASH SHR KHAN!
Hooray, Mr. Tiger, you won that one!

TEN

DREAMBOAT IN

January 1939 — Bombay

1939 began quietly enough, but pivotal changes were happening in the world at large. Talk of war heated up in Europe and in the Bombay ACCO office. If war broke out, I wondered if I could bring Idie to India, or if we would have to wait even longer to be reunited. There was nothing to do but wait and trust in providence, as Idie always said.

> January 1, 1939 — Houston
>
> Happy New Year, my precious boy! Your letters are always timely. The last one surprised me with the wonderful smiling picture of you! I immediately rose to the clouds—how in the world did you manage to take such a grand picture? India has given you freedom, prestige, work, and opportunity. I am confident I could feel it if you were not. I am thrilled with the picture, but how my heart longs to see and be with you!
>
> I am sorry you haven't heard for two weeks—I literally breathe, eat, sleep, and work Harry. Constantly, the back of my mind is saying, When can we be joined again? I know

all things work together for good for those who love the Lord; perhaps this new year will give us our hearts' desire.

Your lovely gifts arrived Wednesday morning. I could hardly pay the man the duty for wondering what was in the box. Ruby was looking over my shoulder when I opened it. It has done more than anything to satisfy her with India, as she remarked. "Why, they have things just as we do."

Each thing you do gives me so much joy, May the new year bring you strength and happiness; may you grow spiritually and mentally and be successful in all undertakings.

Once again, I give you my life, my love, my trust—Idie

* * *

January 8, 1939 — Yeotmal

My dearest Idie: another year is here. Where it will lead is a mystery. Last year was a great one for surprises and advancement. This year must also bring its share of good things along with the bad.

I'm about to become a bachelor, as Gene is moving to Karachi; Ed is going on leave in April or May, and Hal will go to Bombay with Guy. Gene and I will give up our bungalow, and I'll move back to the hotel. I have always liked staying in hotels, and there will be music with my meals.

I made a resolution not to let a week pass unless I write to you, but already I have broken my resolve. It seems strange I don't write to you every day because I am never happier than when thinking of you and sharing my experiences.

I came here intending to stay only a day but had to stay three. Must brag a little by saying I had the foresight to bring a blanket and towel, because I had a slight accident in front of my travelers' bungalow. The brakes locked on the rear wheel of my motorbike, and I bit the dust like any other good Indian. Although I was unhurt, my pride and my clothes have taken a definite turn for the worse.

I do love you. Nothing else matters in this old world. Your Harry

* * *

Yeotmal was a little bit of nothing stuck away in that great space called up-country. I had to go there occasionally, to look at things and rant and rave because the progress was so slow. Sometimes I went further into the wilderness to a couple of smaller places called Dharwad and Degras. Part of the trip was through jungle, drab to most people, but I came to see the animals that inhabit them rather than the vegetation. Contrary to my original opinion, jungles are not always filled with enormous trees, trailing Tarzan-like vines, or crocodile infested swamps. They are dense, filled with millions of small scrubby trees, tallish grass, and thick bamboos.

The other kind of jungle, with the enormous banyan tree, trailing vines, etc., was there too, but not to such an extent. I saw a great many monkeys; they always amused me, scampering around the road and up the trees.

There were times I had nothing new to say to Idie but sometimes I just wanted to share my emotions of loneliness and longing with her.

January 20, 1939 — Yeotmal

My beloved Idie: I have a bad case of nerves this evening. Something rare for me, as I can usually keep steady. You mean more to me than you will ever know, if for no other reason, to keep me from becoming a drunkard.

Things have not been moving as swiftly as I should like. I am all alone out here, not having seen a white man for three weeks. I'm sure I need a little association with a fellowman, and you are supplying that.

I went into the interior of Nizam's state (Hyderabad) yesterday. It's only about seventy miles, but ten of them are awful, just a cart track, over fields, around mountains, through jungle and rivers. Driving two hours yesterday and again today was the most physical effort I have made, not forgetting I once dug ditches on a pipeline. I am exhausted, and tired enough to bore you with pages of nonsensical nothings. Are you ready to spend hours listening?

I also read an upsetting novel. The book was *Spears against Us* by Cecil Roberts. It was a story of an Austrian Tirol family and their friends, some of them English, before and after the war (World War I). There was no villain, some of the characters were weak, perhaps morally bad, but I loved every one of them. They were happy until they began to suffer with injured pride.

The signs of those times are like the signs of our times. Once again, the race of fiery blooded German/Austrians/Prussians are rushing headlong into a maelstrom of misery. I believe Europe will be at war before too long.

We have spoken about both of us changing, learning the ways of the world on different sides of it, possibly drifting apart far enough to need adjustment. However, don't you think fundamentally we have not changed? Incidental changes will be balanced by our letters. I think we are closer today that we were two years ago. I also feel we are more willing to sacrifice self to make common happiness and a joyful home. This brief "excommunication" has given us a reverence for the joy of companionship. I am sure that come what may, ours is love which has no weak link. Through patience and faith in one another we shall soon be as one once more.

All my love, Harry

* * *

January 22, 1939 — Houston

Harry dear: I did enjoy the letter describing your Christmas. I am delighted it was so nice. I was quite flattered you thought the blue package was from me. Had it been, you would not have received it well tied. The reason I am sending only magazines is the post office here said packages are subject to being opened by each country handling the mail and they truly tear up the ones we get.

I wonder about the tiger hunt! Bill vows you couldn't stay still long enough, especially if a rat were nearby. I am sincerely devoted to that man!

Last night, as I was walking up the steps, Ruby was listening to the radio playing Bolero. I don't remember how I ever got to the top of the stairs because the minute I heard it, I thought of you. Little things like that upset my equilibrium!

I love you, my dearest—now and forever—Idie

* * *

I was somewhat off my beat as I drove to Nagpur, a larger place than the usual ones. It was close by and offered an American cinema, a real hotel, and a good meal. I couldn't resist! As luck would have it, the car broke down, so I spent a lazy day, hardly leaving the hotel.

I saw many churches and good work being done in them. It was fertile countryside, densely populated. Missionary organizations had been working in that area for years, and I saw their efforts bearing fruit.

One point, if resolved, could solve most missionary problems, that of Christian brotherhood. Though some pretend not, I believed most Indians were still class conscious. Sweepers and menials were "untouchable," and even though some orthodox and the untouchable were being converted, the strictly orthodox would not sit beside the untouchable in church. I heard the church set aside different parts of the sanctuary for people of the same class to sit together. Were they really Christians, or do they see in Christianity a means to an end under the Europeans?

Such segregation seems opposed to very basic Christianity. Many beliefs in India were based on superstition. I argued with people and sometimes muddled their brains by showing how every Indian manipulated his religion to fit his daily needs. One of the salesmen in the office went so far as to say lying and cheating were separate from religion. He didn't know what heading they came under, but certainly not religion.

When I first arrived, most of my writing was about India because when I looked at something, I automatically thought Idie would be interested, and I still do. Later, a new thought appeared; I felt I was building a philosophy of life, stone by stone. Then I wondered how anyone so young and who knew so little had a right to speak of a philosophy of life.

My strong body was a good gift, and I was trying, with Idie's sweet guidance, to make it a worthy one. Of all the wonderful gifts, Idie was the most treasured.

* * *

Ed called me back to Bombay in February, telling me he had been watching events unfold in Europe. He then asked me, "Are you still sweet on that little girl in Houston?"

"Yes!"

"War is coming, and we don't know when it will be over. Perhaps you should marry her sooner rather than later."

On February 18, I sent a Western Union cable to Idie:
> DREAMBOAT IN. SUGGEST ENGRAVE CHANTILLY

When I didn't hear back right away, I sent a second cable:
> WILL YOU MARRY ME

March 1, 1939 — Bombay

My darling Idie: this is the letter I have wanted to write for so long! It is hard to believe that at last you have really said "Yes" and soon we will be together again. I think more than anything, I want to say thank you for loving me, for being so faithful, and for making me so happy.

Another March 3rd is nearly here, our last one apart. There will be no gift for you this time except my love and myself. March must be our month of destiny.

Tell anyone you like but I think it best to hear from the office before you tell too many. I'll try to get an airmail letter to the family on the same plane as this one. I will also try to write to Ruby, but things are moving fast now.

As to the wedding, I can't add to Faye's brief suggestions except to say she would be happy to be of any assistance to us. She and Ed seem to have adopted me. Ed might have great plans for us, as you are a part of the cotton business now. Your job is to see I carry my ideas to the end. There are great opportunities here, my darling, and we must not let them pass unnoticed.

Faye suggested we have a quiet ceremony at her place (which is lovely), but if you prefer a church, you may have it. Afterward, she thought it would be nice for you to meet around fifty people at a reception. This is only her suggestion, and we will make no plans until you arrive.

Our life will be somewhat muddled, as we may live out of suitcases for a while. We do have an upcoming home leave in about a year or so.

There are so many things I want to say. I love you so much, and I am so happy you are coming! I am going around in a daze most of the time—please forgive me. Always yours, Harry

PLEASE HURRY!

PART II
GETTING TO KNOW HER

Getting to Know Her

ELEVEN

BOMBAY AT LAST!

March 1939 — Houston

Idie and Ruby had prepared for Idie's departure long before my cables arrived, as they had no doubt their collective prayers would be answered, or I would send for Idie as soon as I could. Linens and Chantilly silver had been monogrammed, summer dresses sewn, gifts from friends packed, her passport and visas secured. I heard that gossip in the office and talk between family and friends had changed from wondering if our romance could survive to an awed excitement, reverberating around Houston society.

It was hard for me to wait for Idie to arrive after finally seeing "Yes!" in a cable, but I knew it would take another month before I could hold her again.

The MV *Saturnia*, like my ship, the *Rex,* a year, and a half earlier, was beautiful. Idie kept pamphlets with pictures of the interiors and filled her time with watching movies, bathing in the pools, "horse racing" games, and musical concerts. Mandatory lifeboat drills for passengers and crew occurred intermittently, sometimes at odd hours.

Idie told me her birthday on April 18th was celebrated with a special dinner of broiled baby lobster and roast turkey, topped off with "Ice Cream Bomb Ida" and birthday cake.

The ship's itinerary included stops in Boston, the Azores islands, Lisbon, Gibraltar, Algiers, Palermo, Italy, and Naples. Idie made a scrapbook of her trip and included postcards in lieu of photographs. She wrote Ruby and friends postcards and sent them from the ship. One draft read:

> Greetings from the Red Sea—only it is blue. Suez Canal was interesting. Weather warm, trip pleasant – thinking of you – Love, Idie

* * *

I smiled when I read the cable telling me Idie had left the SS *Saturnia* on April 28th and boarded the MN *Victoria*, the same ship on which Gene and I had sailed. Idie confessed she could not sleep the night before they docked in Bombay, as every male voice in the hallway woke her, thinking it might be me. She finally got up at six a.m. and impatiently waited for her first glimpse of Bombay.

MN *Victoria*

* * *

May 8, 1939 — Bombay

Idie seemed so close and yet so far. I nervously paced the dock as I watched two tugboats push and pull the big ship into Ballard pier. When at last we could see each other, I waved awkwardly. Idie's white handkerchief fluttered briefly. I had not gone for her on a galloping white horse, so she came to me on a big white ship.

A toot-toot goodbye from the tugs signaled their job was done, and a mob of chanting coolies took over manhandling the gangway: bare-chested and bare-legged, with red turbans on heads, they were naked except for brief loincloths.

Nothing could have prepared Idie for the sights and sounds on that wharf. A horde of jostling people greeted the ship, some looking like they were at a costume party, others hardly dressed at all. Idie peered around the mass of upturned faces—white, black, tan, olive, brown—all adding to the noisy frenzy with greetings in a dozen or more languages. I wondered if Idie thought it would have been better to wait for the galloping white horse.

A group of Indian officials, in starched white uniforms, marched importantly onto the ship. I could not board until they said so. The crowd became restless as minutes ticked away. Then, as if a dam had burst, a thick slab of Colonial India surged across *Victoria*'s decks.

Welcome to India, Idie! Indian men, wearing white cotton Gandhi caps or turbans in various sizes and colors, and white business suits; English ladies in printed cotton frocks, other Indian men in form-fitting tunics with Jodhpur boots; Hindu men in billowy white dhotis and petite Indian ladies dressed in colorful saris, looking like tiny Madonnas with a jewel set into one side of the nose, plus rings on fingers and bracelets on brown arms; British and American men in tan topees, resembling big game hunters in business suits.

Hindus, Muslims, Parsees of many castes, sects, sizes, and colors surged up the gangway, carrying me with them. I found Idie waiting demurely, a radiant "Hello!" in her smile. Our reunion was short and subdued. Shyness set in, only a quick sizing up after a year and a half apart.

Lordy, she is prettier than I remembered. How has school teaching changed her without me to heckle her? Who was that guy standing so close to her at the rail?

Ed and Faye Waddell; Hal and his wife, Stella Connor; and Guy Schilling were there to welcome her. Faye invited her to stay with them, where she would sleep on futons on Ed's dressing room floor. We slipped away as soon as politeness permitted.

R.S. Mani, the number one Indian in the office, greeted us as we stepped ashore. He gave Idie her first gracious salaam and placed a flower garland around her neck. Her eyes sparkled; her face lit up in a wide smile.

I drove to the American Club for lunch, on the wrong side of the street, the right side in India, scaring the daylights out of Idie. I watched her trying not to stare at men wearing western-style shirts, long tails hanging down to their knees over white dhotis, socks held up by supporters on bare legs. She seemed fascinated by the sacred cows and unwieldy bullock carts in the narrow streets and the tall, bearded Sikh policemen directing traffic.

I enjoyed watching Idie's obvious enchantment with the jumble of sights and sounds, and from that day forward, her joy set the tone for our lives together. I was not surprised by her enthusiasm because I knew her so well, but really getting to know her wasn't always easy. Even getting married wasn't easy.

TWELVE

THE WEDDING

May 9, 1939 — Bombay

Why is it so hard to get married?
I just wanted to say the words, take Idie by the hand and head for the hills, to Kashmir and a lush valley nestling amidst the Himalayas.

Faye and Stella said that was outrageous, a proper wedding it must be. "Settle down, Buster." Meet the minister, finalize plans, buy a ring, get topee and bedroll for Idie, arrange for a U.S. consul to certify the wedding and issue new passports, and Idie must have her hair done!

What is wrong with her hair?

Learning to cope in British India began on Idie's first night in Bombay when the Waddells invited friends to dinner to welcome her. Sleeping on the floor would not deprive her of sleep, but a growling stomach did threaten to keep her awake.

When the guests departed, the Waddells retired. We were alone. I said I thought Kahn, Waddell's Chinese cook, had put on a lavish feast. Didn't Idie agree?

"Yes, indeed," she said, "the table was beautiful, the food looked luscious, but I am starving!" *"All the delicious food,"* soup to nuts, *and she is starving?*

I knew at home in Texas, dinner would be served at six p.m. In Bombay, not before eight p.m. It had been a long day and Idie seemed weary and hungry. She said it had been wonderful to hear Number One Boy announce, "Dinner is served, Sahib."

All at the table, except for me, were strangers to Idie, and I was too far away for a whispered conference. All the well-wishers had questions for her. There was the difficulty! Before Idie answered a question, she politely placed her knife and fork on her plate. Every time she did, the server snatched her plate, full or empty.

"He was barefoot," Idie moaned, "and kept silently slipping up on my blind side. I didn't know how to stop him without embarrassment, so I barely took a nibble from each course."

I roared with laughter.

"It's not nice to laugh at starvation," she remonstrated.

While the "boy" might have been overzealous, he was doing his job. In British India, one must cross your knife and fork on the plate if you are not ready for it to be taken away.

The solution was easy: we raided the Waddells' icebox.

Faye, with assistance from other ladies at that table, planned and executed the proper wedding they knew would not happen if left to me. It became the only game in town for a while.

Idie and I heard later what some people were thinking: we were both twenty-six, a mismatch that wouldn't last. I was too young, Idie too old. A man shouldn't marry before thirty, after he had "established" himself and could "provide" for a wife. Twenty-one was the best age for a woman to marry, so she would not become an "Old Maid."

Faye and Stella took Idie under their protective wings, banishing me when necessary. Ed checked me out. I don't know if the ladies talked about birds and bees; Ed never mentioned them. He did ask what I would be wearing at the wedding. I said I hadn't thought much about it. I don't know what I would have worn if he had not sternly taken me to task, and to his tailor, where he ordered the poor man to suit me up in white sharkskin in record time.

It occurred to him to ask about my dressing robe. I had to admit it was getting thin. Looking like a father about to spank a bad boy, he snapped, "Do you want to scare that little girl to death?" And he took me next door to buy a new robe, a big-sleeved Japanese yukata, draping all the way down to my toes.

Before Idie arrived, Faye and Stella had pestered me about buying her a ring. Since Idie would have to live with it the rest of her life, I said I wanted her to choose it.

"A groom gives the bride a ring. He doesn't ask his bride to shop for it."

But I did. Jamnadas, an office friend, took us to a jewelry bazaar, located on a dusty street clogged with loudly bargaining people. Idie seemed thrilled to be in an oriental bazaar for the first time, making bodily contact with India's masses. She walked elbow to elbow with dhoti-clad men and stood at jewelry stalls hip-to-hip with women in saris, light scarves draped over their heads. She looked at dozens of silver and gold rings; was fascinated by where they were worn on fingers, toes, ears and in the nose, with tiny tinkling silver bells on them, A vast assortment, but the right ring was not there.

Bombay Bazaar

Jamnadas suggested we visit his friends in the diamond market, but that meant looking at stones only, having the ring made to order. That would take two weeks. We needed a ring for the wedding the next day. Reluctantly, we went along and met his friends in a somewhat dark room in a not-too-sturdy house. It was empty of furniture except for an iron safe the size of a small closet and a low rectangular table, around which four turbaned, dhoti-clad men sat on the floor.

The men rose when we came in, murmured salaams, and offered dirt-stained pillows to us. Idie hesitated. She had never been in such a shop: the pillows looked unsanitary, and the turbaned men didn't look like merchants she was used to. Following my lead, however, she sat.

Cups of steaming tea, brewed together with milk and liberally laced with raw sugar, appeared as if by magic. I took a quick sip. Idie looked at me in disbelief, genuinely concerned for my well-being.

During our short time together in India, I had expanded upon the "dos and don'ts" of eating and drinking; and there I sat, blatantly breaking my own rules. Looking more than a little nervous, she cautiously lifted her cup and took a tiny sip.

With that bit of hospitality behind us, a *chockra* (assistant) swung open the doors on the safe, exposing stacks of wooden trays, side by side, top to bottom. One tray, filled with soft leather pouches, came to the table and one pouch was opened. A stream of sparkling diamonds ran out in front of Idie. She gasped and became vibrantly alive.

"Oh, how beautiful!"

The dealers liked that, and her radiant smile. They urged her, in perfect English, to pick up the stones, examine them and see they were honest men, dealing in top-quality gems.

More trays came to the table; more pouches were opened. By the time we had to leave, Idie had handled enough diamonds for a queen's ransom, but there were no rings in that shop.

Outside, Jamnadas reluctantly said, "Foreigners buy rings at an English style shop." It was our last resort, held back to the bitter end, I suspect, because Jamnadas would receive a smaller commission (or none) at a foreign style shop. With time running out, we went there: carpets on the floor of a bright, airy room, display cases glittering with gold and gems of many sizes and colors. Idie seemed right at home.

Tea was not served. An immaculately western style dressed Hindu, without turban, speaking English, asked how he could be of service. Idie, knowing exactly what she wanted, told him. He brought it, without hesitation. Idie put it on her finger, and it fit perfectly. The search was over. Idie had chosen her wedding ring.

* * *

The day after Idie's arrival, Faye took us and another older couple to lunch at the Wellington Club—to talk, we thought, about wedding plans. But when lunch was over and coffee served, the man introduced Idie to a major pastime: telling big game hunting stories, some even gory, ending with spellbinding graphics.

Who was that man? The preacher, gentle Reverend Warner, who had been a missionary in India for twenty years. We would be the first American couple he would marry. By the time Faye emphatically said, "Enough!" I thought he was more interested in scaring Idie than in marrying us.

* * *

On May 10th, the day of our wedding, time stood still for me, a day of jitters. I packed early, to be ready to leave for Kashmir shortly after the ceremony. Telephoned Idie. Was not permitted to speak to her. I went to the office, where the office manager ran me off: "A moon-eyed calf is no use around here." I was not due to Waddell's until six p.m.

Time did not stand still for Idie. It wouldn't dare stand still around that woman! Many things filled her day, hours with an Italian hairdresser for one. He "knew" how to make a bride beautiful. Idie knew how a bride should look: Texan, not Italian. Verbal swords clashed. Waving expressive hands, the Italian talked loudly, asking other customers to help persuade her. Idie remained calm but firm, not budging an inch. The Italian did her hair the Texan way.

Midafternoon at Waddell's, Emily Meeken skillfully gave Idie a facial and then fashioned a headband of tiny, delicate flowers for her hair. The "girls" searched for and found "something old, something new, something borrowed, something blue." Idie's full-length wedding gown of French lace, sewn by Ruby, was new. A handkerchief, carried in her hand, a gift from Ellen Clark, was old. The sash on her dress, blue. A handkerchief Faye had carried at her wedding was borrowed. Deeply touched, Idie wore it inside, next to her heart.

I arrived on the dot at 6 p.m. Hal Connor, the best man, took me in hand, saying, "To get you off cloud nine long enough to say, 'I do.'"

Someone should have been assigned to keep Hal cool. More fidgety than I, he experimented on where to carry the ring for easy access; he practiced like a western gunslinger at getting it out smoothly, settling on a vest pocket. He checked his watch every few minutes.

"Want a drink?" he asked.

"No, thank you."

He paced while I stood looking out a window. "Are you sure you don't want a drink?"

"Sure. Real sure."

"Well, I do!" He dashed out into the kitchen for a quick swig.

Stella Connor, at the piano, began the wedding march. Idie, radiantly beautiful on Ed's arm, appeared at the end of the large room. For the first time in my life, I wanted to be a poet, to express the jolt of pure bliss running through me. Bliss is what poets call it, but what hit me must have been something else because when the preacher said, "Repeat after me: I, Harry, take thee Ida Dell" I, hardly able to muster a whisper, said, "I, Ida Dell, take thee Harry!"

What happened next was a pregnant silence. Fortunately, the preacher calmly started over, and I got it right the second time, loud and clear. We were married! Could we now head for the hills?

Harry and Idie at Their Wedding

Certainly not! Sign documents and receive new passports from an American consul, invited to the wedding for that purpose. Idie was introduced to all the guests. That took considerable time, but Ed's toast was short, sweet, and prophetic: "Here's to Harry and Ida Dell, from now on, Ida Dell and Harry."

A highly agitated little man kept following Ed around, repeating, "Sir, may we start? Please, sir, may we start?"

Ed was moving among the guests and ignored him. Who was that little man? The photographer, with no flash equipment and fading light. We finally posed for time exposures with the little man constantly chanting, "Hold. Hold it."

"May you live happily a thousand years," was written in bold, red Chinese characters on the top of the wedding cake, made by Kahn. He honored us by bringing it in himself. Red is the color of happiness and good fortune where Kahn is from, and a thousand years doesn't seem like any time at all. Idie gave me the first slice as she nibbled at a tiny piece. While others were being served, I edged her toward the door. *Thoughtful old Ed!* He came alongside and whispered conspiratorially, "Wouldn't you like to slip out this way?"

With heartfelt thanks, I opened the door and was met by what felt like a ton of rice thrown by three male guests waiting in ambush. We were on the second floor, and I sighed with relief as the lift door closed—and then thought about coming out swinging when it opened on the ground floor. The agile rice throwers outraced the lift to continue pelting us all the way to my car.

Pressing hard on the accelerator, I shot us away, Idie laughing. I, too, was highly exhilarated. We were finally on our way to Kashmir! Then a rattling noise erupted. Worried, but naively unsuspecting, I pulled up, untied, and threw away a large pile of empty tin cans.

That, I thought, was the end of horseplay. But I was wrong again. It really is hard to get married! The time for rejoicing was still hours away.

THIRTEEN

HONEYMOON BLISS?

May 10, 1939 — Bombay

We arrived at Bombay Central with time to spare, confident we had outsmarted the merrymakers. I had told no one we would leave on the Frontier Mail, the only train out of Bombay with an air-conditioned coach. The station was another eye-opener for Idie, her first venture onto an Indian train platform: a crowd of noisy, jostling people; a mélange of dress, hats, turbans, topees, saris, and dhotis; kiosks selling newspapers, books, and magazines in many different languages; trainmen in stiffly starched white uniforms, and hustling coolies shouting for the right-of-way, bulky baggage on their heads.

Take a good look, Idie. This is the sort of neighborhood you will soon move into.

She got the briefest of looks. A gang of raucous guests from the wedding took over the platform as if they owned it, littering our compartment with rice and announcing to the world we were just married.

Daya, my "boy," tried to sweep out the rice, only to see twice as much thrown back in. Large "Just Married" letters were scribbled over the outside of our compartment. A trainman, almost in tears, tried unsuccessfully to stop the madness. I was close to exploding by the time the train left. Idie seemed to enjoy every minute.

When the train finally pulled out of the station, joy did not immediately return. Since the first stop at Dakar was only twenty minutes away, Daya stayed with us to tidy-up as best he could. Business done, he stood at the door, ready to scamper out the moment the train stopped.

Consternation! Throttle open, whistle screaming, the train thundered past Dakar and on into the night, leaving us stranded with Daya, not knowing how long it would be to the next stop, if indeed there would be another one during the night. Indian trains have no corridors. There was no way could Daya leave. We were stuck with him, and he with us. Our honeymoon began with a chaperone!

Three embarrassed people in a closet-sized train compartment, two trying not to lose their cool, the other crouched on the floor, face to the wall, struggling to mute giggles. We began to shiver because the thermostat had been set as low as it would go and jammed beyond adjustment. What to do?

I opened my suitcase.

More consternation! Not only was it loaded with rice, but my pajamas had been tied into hundreds of tight knots. Idie burst out laughing. It is best not to repeat what I said. Idie chided me for not having the foresight to lock my bags as she had done.

Discarding rice and untying knots kept us busy for a while. Then, with a flourish, Idie opened one of her bags. Consternation in spades! Every nook and cranny was heavily laden with rice. Thoughtful Faye had finished off Idie's last-minute packing. We howled with delight at how easily the two of us had been duped.

The train roared on for two hours, at the end of which, Daya shot out of the car before the train came to a full stop, racing to his quarters as if Hindu demons were in hot pursuit.

I had traveled uncounted miles on Indian trains, but this was the only time in an air-conditioned coach. Not because I enjoyed the heat, dust, and insects that came with the others, but because there were so few air-conditioned ones. We lost that one too, about eighteen hours out of Bombay. We changed trains to a feeder line for Agra, trading the tightly built steel car for an aged, wooden one, the temperature pushing 120 degrees.

We were barely settled into our "new" compartment when the door was suddenly flung open. Four grinning, babbling coolies stood outside, wearing bulky red turbans and sporting large brass badges on their chests, indicating they were in the service of the railroad. They shoved in a large tin tub, all four coolies coming in with it, followed by Daya, turning the narrow compartment into a mob scene. Idie quickly pulled her feet up onto a bunk. Daya directed placement of the tub. The coolies then trotted off, Idie demanded an explanation. I didn't have one, and Daya had gone with the coolies. They returned immediately, each with a large block of ice on his head to be dumped into the tub.

Coolies, their humanitarian job done, lined up outside the door, stepping forward one by one, saluting, and saying, "Salaam Sahib. Salaam Memsahib," while receiving baksheesh. Daya closed the door and windows, turned on two small fans in the ceiling, aimed them at the ice, and "Presto!" the compartment was delightfully cool.

* * *

At Agra, even before the train jolted to a full stop, Daya scrambled into the compartment with two coolies. Each one hoisted a bedroll on his head, took a suitcase in each hand, and trotted away, Daya followed at a leisurely pace, carrying nothing. Carrying is coolie work, beneath the dignity of Number One Boys.

Idie, seemingly indignant, thought something should be done. The door had been flung open; no one asked permission to enter. Half-naked men came in, snatched everything we owned and made off with it. Her troubled eyes tried to follow the coolies, but quickly lost them in the melee on the station platform.

I knew the train would stand still for exactly ten minutes. A whistle would blow, the engine would give a little toot, and the train would chug on. People with masses of baggage would get off, other people would get on, talking and shouting in the language of Babel. Idie stayed close beside me, a vise-like grip on my arm, watching the tumult surge toward the exit gate, heavily laden coolies leading the way.

When the crowd began to thin, a small man in a business suit, eye to eye with Idie, threaded his way to where we stood. He gave us a smart military salute, and said, "Witt Sahib, I am your guide."

How, in that throng, could he know with such certainty?

"No problem, Sahib. I was told to look for young American newlyweds. You are the only lost-looking Americans here." His name was Ramchand.

Agra, during the month of May, is terribly hot. Everyone who can, including "mad dogs and Englishmen," avoids it. Off-season turned out to be perfect for us because, when checking into Laurie's Hotel, the manager gave us a wedding present: the luxurious bridal suite. Idie's face lit up, especially when she saw it. It had, she exclaimed, everything a bride could wish for: a large sitting room, bedroom, separate dressing and bathrooms, brocade-covered furniture, rich drapery, thick pile carpets, lace frills on the pillowcases, and silk sheets on the bed.

Escorting us around the suite, the clerk said our baths had been drawn at four p.m. It was then eight p.m. *A thoughtful but strange gesture.* They knew we would arrive at eight, but neither of us asked why so early. After a twenty-three-hour train ride, the thought of a cooling immersion in a deep tub was marvelous. I hustled into mine. Idie took her time, she later told me, and then happily approached her brimful tub and tested the water. It was too hot. She pulled the plug. The precious water flowed out. In came a fresh tubful. Without testing it again and humming to herself, she stepped in and let out a rattling yell. The water was hot enough to scald.

I suppose the proper thing to do in such situations is to scream. That's what she did, lustily, scaring the daylights out of me! Erupting out of my tub, I staggered into her room, shedding water like a shaggy dog over much of the regal finery around us.

She was standing almost waist deep in the tub, eyes closed, arms folded demurely across her chest, trembling violently. Relieved to know that neither snake nor human viper had caused her distress, I lifted her out.

I have a vague memory of a celebrated painting, called *Dawn*, I think, of a young damsel standing in a pool of water. Had I remembered at the time, I surely would have exclaimed, "How beautiful you are!" but even that would not have pacified her.

We knew then why the water had been drawn so early: the hotel supply is stored in cast iron tanks on the roof, in 120-plus degrees of temperature. Idie was all right, no bruises or blisters, but the bridal suite had other surprises for her.

In India, in 1939, modern bathrooms had the latest thing in toilets: a cast iron box high on a wall behind the stool, with a chain hanging down from it. Give the chain a smart tug, and water rushed down to flush the bowl. They were unfriendly, almost demonic to Idie. She tugged, then tugged again and again, but water refused to come down. A sensitive matter, almost a crisis to Idie, so she approached the subject gingerly:

"Don't you think the bathroom facilities are quaint?"

Quaint? Who would describe a toilet as being quaint?

I laughed. "You find them only in the best places, and they work."

"Work, you say! Show me."

I pulled the chain in my bathroom. Much to Idie's surprise, water splashed down. Idie pulled, and nothing happened. We went into her bathroom. I pulled. It worked. Idie pulled. It didn't work. I told her it was an art. Idie never mastered the art of chain pulling.

I realized I was present at the creation of a psychological block which became Idie's companion all her days in India. When confronted with one of those monsters, a special intonation crept into her shouted "Harry!" and I hastened to her aid.

While strolling in the garden after dinner, we were surprised to find zealous guide Ramchand. I was not pleased. It was almost eleven p.m., and instinct told me he was up to no good. On the way to the hotel, he had persuaded Idie to rise at five a.m. so we could see a deserted old city, Fatehpur Sikri, at six. Uncivilized hours at best, but I ask you, on one's honeymoon?

Nevertheless, that's what she had agreed to. Travel guides have a genius for sniffing out who really runs the show; Ramchand, with barely a nod to me, aimed a question at Idie:

"Does Lady Sahib know the most romantic time to see the Taj is by moonlight?"

Gotcha! I had him there. The sky was perfectly clear, no moon. "It will rise later, Lady Sahib, only a quarter moon, but still the most romantic way to see the Taj for the first time."

Idie clapped her hands, "What marvelous luck! What time will it rise?"

"At four a.m. Lady Sahib. We should leave at three thirty. It is a sight you will never forget."

Rise from my nuptial bed at three in the morning, to look at an old building, no matter how beautiful? *That's carrying things too far!*

That was one man's opinion. At 3:30 a.m. we mounted an ancient touring car disguised as a taxi. I chided Ramchand for telling us there would be a moon. "Patience, Sahib," he said. "It will greet us at the Taj."

Agra had gone to bed. We passed through dark, empty streets, boarded-up houses and shops, no bullock carts, no half-naked children, not even a slinking pie dog. Most unsettling was the lack of a noisy mob of people. Idie and I sat close together holding hands, not talking. Even Ramchand, Mr. Loquacious, didn't talk.

Entering a narrow, tall-tree-lined lane, the taxi driver killed the motor, and we coasted up to a massive red sandstone building towering over our heads: the gateway to the Taj Mahal. We sat, huddled in darkness, feeling an oppressive silence, rarely experienced anywhere in India.

Ramchand quickly ended the silence. Striding up to a huge wooden door, he began to pound and shout, every stroke of his fist creating a hollow boom inside the great building. *A shocking performance at a mausoleum.* Ramchand continued pounding and shouting, not a sound emerging from inside. Embarrassed and nervous, I wanted to leave.

"Not to worry," he said, "Once awake, the guard inside will welcome us."

Finally, shouts from within joined those outside. I didn't know the language, but the meaning was clear: belligerent anger.

High up on the door, a peephole opened, through which Ramchand and the guard seemed to heap insults upon each other. An iron bolt clanged open from a small door, low down inside the big one. A tall, broad man emerged wearing a gray-white garment, arms waving, shouting lustily.

Idie and I had gotten out of the car and were walking slowly toward the gate. I was agitated with Ramchand's behavior and wanted to get out of there and come back in broad daylight. Idie and I turned around to go back to the car when I stopped dead in my tracks upon hearing, in perfect English, "Enough! Enough! By Allah, have you no respect for the dead or for the living who sleep here? What heathens are you to mock this holy place with unholy pounding?"

I motioned to Ramchand that we should go.

"Ah no, Sahib," he said. "One of the great mysteries of the Taj is that silver drives away ill humor."

Knowing who carried the purse, I had again temporarily become his leader. A silver rupee changed hands.

"May Allah bless you, noble Lord! Enter, Master; enter, Lady Sahib."

Inside, after nervously entering what looked like a hole in the wall—a high step up for Idie, squirming through a keyhole for me—our feet came down on squirming, grunting bodies. The floor was carpeted with stretched out, sleeping men. Hearts throbbing, adrenaline racing, we froze against each other, unwilling to press feet to flesh. I was ready to crawl back out and be done with it.

Ramchand appeared out of the gloom as if by magic, raised an arm and pointed toward a dim light coming through a very tall arch about fifty feet away. Heads down, watching our steps, we threaded our way to it where we could look up.

Idie gasped. There it was, the Taj Mahal. I will always think of it as the most beautiful building built by man: its great white dome, spires, and minarets, framed in the curved archway, bathed in the soft glow of Ramchand's quarter moon. We feasted our eyes in awed silence on what someone called (I don't know who) "a priceless jewel set in an indigo sky." The guard called it a holy place. Ramchand had said Lady Sahib would never forget that first view. No greater truth has ever been spoken.

Ramchand stood apart for a short time; then, touching my arm but speaking to Idie, he said in a hushed, gentle voice, "Let us go there."

"Going there" meant walking through the Taj garden beside the "Stream of Life," a shallow, stone-lined canal filled with water, past a square pool in which the great dome shimmered in reflected glory; then up narrow stone steps leading to the platform on which the Taj was built.

"Lady Sahib, and Sahib too, will have to enter on bare feet," Ramchand said, "unless the guard can be persuaded to lend canvas covers for your shoes."

Our silver persuader glinted briefly in the dim moonlight as we sat on a stone bench in a shadowy alcove while the guard, taking our feet in his cold hands, slipped covers over our shoes.

Another man, wearing a turban and loose-fitting robe flowing down to bare feet, met us at the top of the stairs. He looked old enough to be Aladdin's genie, holding the fabled lamp as he escorted us across the marble terrace in front of the Taj, swinging the lamp from side to side. Waving black lines set into the white marble seemed to move gently up and down as the lamplight moved across them.

"These lines represent flowing water," Ramchand explained. "You and Lady Sahib are walking on water." He was wrong. Idie looked as if she were floating on air.

Strolling amid oriental splendor in dim light from an ancient, shaped brass lantern, held by a bearded and turbaned old man, etched a place in our souls we would always carry with us. Shadows danced, every quiet step bringing new discovery and strange sounds, like hearing our muted voices ring hollowly back to us in the crypt below, where Mumtaz and Shah Jahan rested side by side.

The Taj Mahal

Shah Jahan had planned to build a replica of the Taj in black marble on the other side of the river but could not do it when he was deposed by his son, Aurangzeb. He was often seen sitting on a wall at Fort Agra, where he was imprisoned for eight years, silently staring at the Taj.

Moghul emperors were great builders of forts, palaces, and gardens, especially in Agra and Delhi, both capital cities at one time. Being a schoolteacher before I rescued her, Idie wanted to tramp through all of them, which we did, dawn to dusk, for two whole days in each place.

* * *

Tradition says one should choose a romantic place for a honeymoon. I found one, far away: hard-to-get-to Kashmir, which poets call "the Vale of Happiness." It is a lush valley, eighty-five miles long and twenty-five miles wide, hemmed in by snowcapped Himalayan mountains, the Jhelum River flowing through it.

Though often subjected to copious bloodletting by invasions from without and strife within, it speaks to the receptive visitor in gentler tones, regaling the eye with superb vistas, enfolding one's whole being in an aura of serenity and peace. Paradise gardens of the great Moghul emperors were built there, their very names expressive of love and romance. Lazy living on spacious houseboats allows time on Dal Lake to observe master craftsmen working at ancient arts, plus trails to walk, fish to catch, game to pursue, and flowers to pluck.

Getting there was adventurous, even in 1939. I guess everyone is interested in finding "Paradise on Earth." I had to go to Kashmir to find it, feeling Idie would be entranced.

I almost gave up on Kashmir because of the long train ride. Indian trains rattled, were sweating hot, and belched coal smoke, which seeped into your compartment, as did the insect world. Having suffered the heat, dust, and boredom myself, I wondered how Idie would react to a primitive style of traveling.

Moghul emperors, on horseback or elephant back, took several months to get from Delhi to Srinagar, the capital of Kashmir. Train and motorcar would get us there in about three days. Does that mean we traveled more comfortably than they? I am not sure we did. The first Moghul emperor, Babur, wrote three things that greatly annoyed him in Hindustan: its heat, its high winds, and its dust. They were with us too, until we reached the foothills of the Himalayas.

Surprises never ceased when I was with Idie. I watched her bubble with the excitement of new discovery, almost a biblical pageant.

Out of Delhi, our compartment was built to sleep four, with upper and lower bunks on two walls, but we were alone on that trip. Bedding was not included; bring your own bedroll. Two cane-bottomed chairs, a small room with a shower, commode, and wash basin. No soap, no towels, no paper; bring your own. Daya dusted off two lower bunks, rolled out our bedrolls, gave a quick flick to the chairs and departed, doing nothing to the bathroom, for that was work for lower-caste people.

We pulled out of Delhi at 8:05 p.m.

"A shower on a train? How quaint!"

There's that word again. "Who would use it or anything in that room? Everything is thick with dust."

Out came antiseptic and wads of cotton wool. Idie scrubbed, finally declaring, "Well, that's done for this trip." Words spoken on the wind.

She got the bad news early next morning.

Yawning, only half awake, she slipped into her sandals and glanced at my bunk, with me still in it. I was covered in a film of dust and soot. Indian trains burn soft coal. Old wooden coaches leak. She shook me, not too gently.

Even less awake than she, I pointed toward the bunk she had so recently vacated. Idie gasped and stared in astonishment. The place where her head had been on the pillow was the only clean white spot to be seen, a perfect profile etched in soot.

A panorama of village life in the raw unfolded in fleeting glimpses as we rolled toward Rawalpindi, where we would trade steel rails for a country road. Idie, glued to the window, was entranced by "quaint" thatched-roof houses; small naked black boys atop water buffaloes belly deep in water; enormous white Brahma bulls hitched to high-wheeled carts; waving children tending goats; women carrying piles of firewood on their heads; other women standing in a stream, washing clothes by flailing them against large stones; straight-backed women carrying large brass jugs filled with water on their heads with queenly grace.

Mile after mile of biblical scenes flickered past us, like a slideshow. Such scenes became real when the train stopped for lunch at a small town. While it continued to roll slowly toward a full stop, urchins appeared, running beside our compartment door, offering orange soda pop in glass bottles, sealed at the top with a glass marble inside. Suddenly, we were eye-to-eye with a chubby fellow carrying a large brass tray on his head, filled with parched grains and nuts, which he sold for a pittance, wrapped in squares of old newspaper.

Getting down, we strolled past a covered wooden hutch holding large, segregated earthen jugs of drinking water; Hindus drank from one side and Muslims on the other. In the first-class restaurant we found a curry spicy enough to scald Satan's tail, served with a fried potato patty.

We watched people cross from one platform to another on an open-air foot bridge spanning the tracks; saw both child and adult, male and female, answer nature's call beside the track. We looked at books, magazines, and newspapers in several languages in kiosks, but few in

English. We saw women in saris, rivaling the rainbow, men in Hindu dress and Muslim dress, Hindu men looking uncomfortable in western suits. It was a throbbing but orderly scene that paralleled, I thought, Idie's heart, throbbing with it.

At long last, we arrived at Rawalpindi, on India's northwest frontier, where I had planned to overnight and head for the hills early next morning. "Pindi" in the afternoon was extremely hot. I asked Daya if he could find a taxi to drive us at least as far as Murree. I had heard it was a delightfully cool hill station only forty miles away, 7,500 feet up in the Himalayan foothills.

Smiling at such a naïve question, Daya shouted one magical word, "*Taxi!*" Half-a-dozen jabbery taxi drivers closed in on us, eager to pick up a fare. They all sported tan wraparound turbans and loosely fitting khaki shirts and pantaloons.

Idie stepped back as Daya, and I haggled with the drivers.

I don't know why we chose Abdul; several others said that was their name too. I suppose it was because he offered to take us all the way to Srinagar. We hit the road with the heavily mustached young Muslim driver oozing machismo.

Abdul's "Beautiful Car," an aged touring model ready for a car museum, gave us a wonderfully cool wind in our faces for twenty-five miles on a gravel road. Happy Valley, on the other side of that mountain, was so close. But when gravel changed to a narrow pavement, we began to climb steeply, and the road became an obstacle course of sharp curves and switchbacks.

With the throttle wide open, Abdul stormed the mountain, slithering around sharp curves, mountain on one side, sheer drop-off on the other. Daya was in the front seat, looking pale, while Idie and I were bumping against each other in the back. I asked Abdul to slow down, but he pretended not to hear and pushed harder on the gas pedal. Idie began to turn green.

Discarding friendly persuasion, I pummeled Abdul on the back, bellowing at him to stop. He did. He was so startled at the sahib's behavior; he almost took us over the edge.

A short roadside walk did wonders for Idie, and a severe heart-to-heart with Abdul turned machismo almost to servility. He was only trying to please, he said. He knew Americans were fast drivers. How did he know? Why, all Americans drive fast in American movies!

We entered Murree just before dark, at a serene pace.

At the hotel, still a bit wobbly and needing a stomach replacement, Idie preferred not to face food, so I dined in the room while reminding her that India was noted for "bad" diseases, no laughing matter. I was genuinely concerned. She said she would be fine in the morning. I said okay, but if not, the honeymoon was over, and we would return to Bombay.

There she was at daybreak, dressed, raising a ruckus, heckling me into rushing off to a hearty breakfast. And her stomach? How had she replaced it? "Ah," she flippantly answered, "last night you ordered me to get well."

What can a man do with a woman like that?

* * *

Leaving Murree, we snaked down the mountain on a narrow road through a great forest of deodar and pines—old, thick-trunked fellows, standing tall—into a small valley cut by the Jhelum River. We heard its angry roar long before we could see it slashing at enormous boulders and huge fallen trees. We pushed on, and the valley narrowed into hemmed-in gorges; the air, trapped between two stone cliffs, didn't move. The temperature shot up. We sweated, while adrenaline rose again on the ribbon-like road, clinging to the cliffside, with the roaring torrent below.

Beyond the valley, big trees thinned out. By the time we reached Pir Pongal Pass at eleven thousand feet above sea level, all vegetation disappeared. An icy, bone-rattling wind welcomed us to a desolate place surrounded by sublime wild beauty. Snow-capped peaks glistened like pristine gems in an immaculate blue sky.

An old hermit lived at the pass, in a cave near the roadside. When we arrived, he was standing beside the road, waving his arms, shouting at the few people trudging on foot across the pass. His long, unkempt hair and white smock were cruelly whipped by the stinging wind. That didn't seem to bother him, but people did. Wild-eyed, called holy by some, he had set out small pottery jugs full of water for weary travelers.

"Drink quickly and get off my mountain," he shouted again and again.

That was what Idie seemed eager to do. Cold enough to imagine she was freezing, standing on a mountaintop in a strange country, eye-to-eye with a Hindu religious fanatic, was not high on her list of things to do on her honeymoon.

Abdul seemed even more eager than Idie to get off the mountain. Not that he was afraid or superstitious, no sir! He just didn't like being around wild-acting people. Nevertheless, he gave the hermit a small coin and suggested I give him a rupee. Why? We had taken none of his water. To make sure, Abdul said, as he got back under the wheel, we would go safely down the mountain.

I gave the rupee but not because I was superstitious. We drove safely down the mountain. The valley of Kashmir, walled in by an unbroken ring of majestic snowcaps, opened before us. The gravel road was lined on both sides with plane trees, dressed in brilliant green, reflecting jabs of sunlight pointing the way to Srinagar.

* * *

Abdul took us into Srinagar at a leisurely pace while Idie and I gawked at unpainted wooden houses resembling Alpine chalets. Some were several stories high, decorated with hand-carved window frames and doors. Blossoming flowers in window boxes; busy people, mostly men and boys, in narrow streets; picturesque wooden bridges spanning canals; fleeting glimpses of exotic wares in shops; all were a fitting end to our long trek.

We stood on the bank of one of the many Srinagar canals, surrounded by a gang of houseboat owners, vocally advertising houseboats for rent. "First class houseboat, Sahib?" "See my houseboat, Lady Sahib."

A happy but disappointed mob, for I had booked a houseboat and a water taxi in advance. Our three paddlers skimmed quickly across the canal, where Idie and I scrambled onto the deck of Houseboat *Mandalay*, our home for the next ten days.

"Oh! How beautiful!" Idie exclaimed as we stepped into the sitting room. Not the boat, for we had not yet explored it. It was the sight of spring busting out all over in pottery jugs on every bit of flat surfaces, filled with cut flowers.

The houseboat owner beamed. I smiled. We were off to a great start.

Mandalay, moored among small willow trees, was a top-heavy wooden box floating on water, unimpressive on the outside, but close to luxury inside, with plenty of elbow room, plus a cook boat, tied to the stern, housing five servants: cook, houseboy, cook's helper, *bhisti* (water boy), and sweeper. Could any bride ask for anything more?

Interior of the Houseboat

All the above, plus food for two and a water taxi, cost the princely sum of nine rupees per day, about three dollars and sixty cents at the time.

The houseboat owner proudly took us on a tour. The sitting/dining room, paneled with natural plane wood, spread over the front half of the boat, above which was an open top deck with a movable blue and white canvas awning. Padded deck chairs, small tables, and large pottery urns filled with blossoming flowers invited us to sit and enjoy the spectacular view of the mountain and broad lake.

The sitting and dining areas were separated by two steps down into the dining room with a round walnut table and graceful high-backed chairs. A small hutch on one wall held tableware, and another, on the opposite wall, sported gleaming brass ornaments on its highly polished shelves.

Overstuffed chairs with end tables sat in one part of the combined rooms, with a small writing desk and chair gracing another corner. A coarsely woven matting, strewn with beautiful Persian throw rugs, covered the floor. They were soft, almost caressing one's bare feet.

The rest of the main deck was taken up with bed, dressing, and bathrooms. Seemingly enchanted with everything she saw, Idie entered her bathroom. But there, words failed her. She gave me a startled look and said, "This is a bathroom? You've got to be joking!" But I wasn't.

Idie was speechless for a moment, as she surveyed a typical houseboat bathroom. Though the bare wooden floor, and everything else in it, was spotlessly clean, that little room was something that a bride would not wish for: two wood pegs set into a wall to hold a robe and towel. "How rustic!" A porcelain water jug and bowl sat on a crudely built wooden stand, with tiny flowers embossed on them. A small oval tin tub sat on the floor with a tin dipping cup in it. A square wooden box, also on the floor, nicknamed "thunder box," masqueraded as a commode, no chain, no paper. "Primitive!" said Idie.

Questions came later, over tea, when we were alone. Hot tea with scones and native Kashmiri strawberry preserves helped set the scene:

"There are no water taps. How does one get bathwater?"

"The bhisti brings it from the cook boat and dumps it into the tub."

"How can one properly bathe in such a small tub?"

"One doesn't properly bathe. Stand in the tub and ladle or sit in it and ladle."

I had another idea, but maidenly modesty saw it coming and stifled it unborn.

Other questions remained unanswered for the moment because the houseboy glided in on bare feet, announcing baths awaited the pleasure of Sahib and Memsahib.

Pleasure? More like a moment of truth for Idie.

She had eagerly looked forward to this moment, but with visions of a tin tub and dipping cup fresh in mind, enthusiasm vanished. Rising reluctantly, "Off to the slaughter," her body motion said, she marched off to her first encounter with tin tub bathing.

Going in meek as a lamb, she came out exuberantly happy, ready to roar like a lion. Idie knew how to cope. She told me later how she had ladled, hummed, and splashed. "It was a delight!" she said, "Really a pleasure." She said that!

I had been introduced to tin-tub bathing in many out-of-the way places in interior India, and the most expressive thing I can say about it is "Bah, humbug." No way can a bulky mass of blubber get a bath in a tin tub. I always tried to be hopeful going in but usually came out cursing and growling. When I stood in the tub, my feet took up more than half of the bottom. Sitting, my rump used almost all of it, with water splashing out, while the rest of me hung half in and half out. Whenever I could, I played hooky from my job and went to an interior hotel where I could have a shower.

After bathing, awaiting the call to dinner, we went up to the top deck as the sun began to sink below the mountain peaks. The air was cool and invigorating. Across the canal, Takht-i-Sulaimon rose one thousand feet about the valley floor. It was crowned by a Hindu temple, which could not be seen from below, said to have been built in 200 BC.

The placid canal had become a one-lane highway, with swift water taxis carrying tourists and peddlers' boats filled with Kashmiri handicrafts, returning to bazaar or workshop.

Darkness came gradually, and canal activity slowed. When we were called to dinner and went inside, night had enshrouded the valley, leaving only flickering lights on land.

We asked the cook to join us after dinner, British style, soup to nuts, with savory at the end. Idie thanked him for a job well done. He beamed at her pleasure.

"Would all evening meals be like that?"

"Oh yes, Memsahib." Proudly, it seemed.

"We would prefer not to have quite so much at every meal."

"As Sahib," seeking authority, "and Memsahib pleases."

"Sahib also pleases."

"Soup?"

"Yes, but not at every meal."

"Fish?"

"Likewise."

"Rare meat?"

"Yes, but not every night."

"Pudding?"

"Yes."

"Savory?"

"No."

Disbelief. "No savory, Sahib?"

"No savory."

"Mutton chops for breakfast, Sahib?"

"Yes, every day." A big grin.

"Fresh strawberries for lunch every day, Memsahib?" Incredulous.

"Yes, every day, please."

The puzzled cook returned to his domain.

* * *

While at breakfast the next day, a male voice floated a question in to Idie: "Flowers, Memsahib?" She scurried to the wide-open door facing the canal.

There, in a small boat, sat a chunky, grinning little man surrounded by gorgeous cut flowers. *Beauty and the Beast;* a bare head crowned with dense black hair, a smock-like robe stained with mud and dirty water and a face full of untended bristles. He held a large bouquet of spring colors aloft in each hand. His cheerful grin was wide, his manner gentle while handling the flowers, his voice soft: but he had no other words in English except "Flowers, Memsahib" and "Four annas, please."

It was Idie's first meeting with a traveling salesman, Kashmiri style. The man handed in bouquet after bouquet, Idie happily exclaiming over the beauty of each, while I stood by, shelling out four-anna pieces. Our boat would have been overloaded had not another arrival distracted her. He offered fresh fruit.

"What gorgeous colors!"

"Look at that pile of luscious strawberries!"

"What tantalizing aroma!"

"Oh, I must change. I'll hurry. Don't let them go away."

Let them leave? As newcomers, we were fair game. Later, it became necessary to rope off our landing to signal that we were not home to boat peddlers.

Even as Idie left to change, her arms loaded with "four annas, please" flowers, another boat paddled up. "Good morning, Sahib, I am Cheap John. May I show you my goods?"

What stunning contrasts: suave Kashmiri merchant replaces humble toiler of the soil. He, too, was soft-spoken with twinkling eyes, neither short nor tall but somewhat rotund. He wore clean leather shoes and a business suit with a turban.

I said we would be leaving shortly.

"A short visit only, Sahib, just to look. To become friends. Sahib can visit shop later."

I invited him to come aboard. Sitting on the floor inside the houseboat, his assistant handed him box after large box filled with Kashmiri handcrafts: embroideries, copper bowls, ornamental brass objects, wood carvings, silver work, a dazzling array of jewelry and gemstones.

Hearing Cheap John talk about each piece, Idie, still in her to-the-floor white satin housecoat, came to stand in the doorway. One look galvanized Cheap John. Rising quickly, he salaamed respectfully, bowed, and breathed gently, "Ah, a true lady. Enter please, Lady Sahib, and see my treasures."

Captivated by the man's grace, she joined us, sat down, began to handle, and extol the beauty and workmanship of each piece. Cheap John's prices shot up.

Fortunately for my thin bankroll, our water taxi appeared before she became totally immersed in the "treasures" surrounding her.

Idie changed quickly, and then we skimmed over the lake. Having to get something off my chest, I got right to the point. "I hope you won't do that again."

Idie sounded surprised. "Do what?"

"Appear before Kashmiri merchants wearing that rich-looking housecoat. Makes you look too prosperous, too regal." As she did indeed, standing in the doorway.

She laughed. I suppose all women want to look and feel regal sometimes.

"Kashmiris are famous for bargaining skill. To buy well, one must bargain."

"Haggle? I will not do that."

"If you look and act prosperous, prices go up. If you praise something, prices go up."

"Well, it's no fun if you can't be honest about beautiful things. I'm afraid, dear Harry, you will just have to pay a little too much for the few things we will be able to buy."

And dear Harry did.

* * *

The water taxi, or *shikara*, was a gaily decorated little boat: long and thin, tapering to a point at both ends but wide enough in the middle to sit two side by side on spring cushions. Spotlessly clean, a canopy of straw mats provided shade and separation from paddlers in the rear. Cushions and side curtains were decorated with flowers embroidered on white cotton cloth. All had fanciful names: Shangri-La, Flying Dutchman, Mickey Mouse, and Mae West among them. Ours was Big Air Ship.

Three men, wielding heart-shaped paddles painted red, supplied the power. But if you were a speed demon, two extra paddlers could be added. Three were more than enough for us. Occasionally, the muscular brown arms raised the tempo a notch or two and sent us racing across placid water at speed enough to fantasize that we were riding a Kashmiri flying carpet.

Idie trailed her fingers in water so clear the bottom of the lake seemed within touching distance. We set out for Shalimar Garden.

Dal Lake was alive with activity: a fisherman, knee-deep in the water, repeatedly cast a large circular net; other men, naked except for a G-strip, used poles to dredge up living vegetation from the lake bottom; boats overflowed with fruits and/or vegetables. We passed boats loaded with masses of flowers and in the distance clusters of ducks and geese, some wild, some domesticated. "Hellos" echoed across the water from other tourists in their shikaras; a steady stream of peddlers' boats came close beside us, armed with friendly persuasion.

"Look at these nutcrackers, Memsahib, chenar leaf carved on walnut wood handle."

"My goods are the best in all of Kashmir, Sahib, and I sell cheap too!"

"Memsahib, buy this ring shawl, made from belly of young ibex."

"I see in face of Memsahib a very great lady. Buy this silver bowl, lady."

Idie wanted to look at and handle every piece in every boat. While I tried not to be rude, I knew I had hocked my salary for months to come just to get here. Eyes sparkling, she exclaimed at the beauty of every piece handed to her. She ran sensitive fingers over wood carvings, lovingly caressed scarf and shawl, asked for explanations of this or that, and declared each piece more exquisite than the last.

Idie quickly became the apple of every merchant's eye; sure, given time, Memsahib would choose many things, and Sahib would pay. But time ran out for them. We were approaching the garden. Our captain spoke quietly to one of the merchants, who immediately pulled away and passed the word to others, who also paddled away. One moment we were surrounded, the next quite alone.

Idie asked, "Have we done something wrong?" No indeed. Merchants and boat owners have a back-scratching pact: if you don't annoy my passengers, I will try to bring them to your shop later.

Shalimar Garden was near when our shikara nosed into a mile-long, twelve-foot-wide canal. Other boats were ahead of us, while still others, crossing the lake from several directions, converged on the entrance in fan-shaped array. They followed us in, as if through a funnel. A traffic jam quickly built up. Paddlers came alive and would have honked horns if they had had them. Collisions seemed inevitable, but skillful boatmen averted spills. The peace and tranquility of the open lake became a cacophony.

Approaching the garden gate, every boatman was eager to give his passengers a good landing spot. Most of them were too small for more than one or two shikaras. On several occasions, our boat rocked from side to side, perilously close to capsizing. Sweating over paddles, shouting, and tossing jibes, in seemingly good humor, every boatman tried to outmaneuver and out-argue the others.

Our boat did not make it to the landing. While still fifty yards away, we were surrounded by other boats. We scrambled up the canal bank onto a footpath and walked the rest of the way.

* * *

Is a garden just a bunch of flower beds? Not Shalimar Garden. Built in 1619, it was once the summer residence of Emperor Shah Jahan, builder of the Taj Mahal, and his wife Mumtaz Mahal. Shah Jahan called it "Paradise on Earth." As tradition demanded, it was divided into three parts: outer or public garden, middle or emperor's garden, and most beautiful of all, the empress's garden on the topmost terrace. The public part of the garden was no longer there.

Most of the buildings had been destroyed, except the empress's black pavilion. It was built over the Stream of Life, surrounded by waterfalls flowing into deep tanks, fountains spraying water a few feet into the air. We lingered there longer than any other place in the garden.

While we wandered from terrace to terrace, a dumpy old fellow, a *mali* (gardener), timidly approached. Making a half-bow, he held out three freshly cut, delicately shaded pink peonies. "For Lady Sahib," he softly murmured.

Idie's face lit up. I still remember her radiant smile. It was, for me, an abiding souvenir of our visit to a royal garden. After Shalimar, I needed no urging to visit Nishat Bagh and Achibal, which we did on separate days.

Though deeply impressed by the beauty of the gardens, I was not aware of their close association with the Muslim faith. Wanting to learn, I hit the books and found the Moghuls were trying to duplicate paradise on earth as described in the Koran. It says true believers will find in paradise a garden bliss, with flowing water and companions pure and holy.

The garden will have all kinds of trees, fruits of every kind, and something to please all the senses. For the eye, the color and shape of flowers and the sheets of water; for the ear, the song of birds and cascading of water; for the smell, perfumes of foliage and flowers; for the taste, exquisite fruits; for the touch, soft rose petals and the caress of cooling water.

All the gardens are magnificent but in stunning contrast to each other. Shalimar is a royal garden, Nishat, a private pleasure garden. In Shalimar, there is an aura of maturity, dignity, and reserve. In Nishat, flowers, dressed in all the boisterous colors of spring, fairly shout, "Come play with us!" while fountains on every hand exuberantly join in the playful chorus.

At Nishat, twelve graceful terraces sweep up the mountainside, while the Stream of Life frolics down. It carts the water more swiftly than at Shalimar. Cascades, waterfalls, and fountains are more numerous. Our first impressions were of lively water and a glorious profusion of flowers. Neither of us had ever seen nature's paintbrush so lavishly in action. Millions of pansies line pathways, with irises, poppies, and peonies bringing happiness everywhere.

Being a private garden, Nishat was divided into only two sections: the main garden and the *Zenara* quarters (Harem) on the upper terrace, eighteen feet above the next terrace. The Stream of Life starts here on its journey through the garden, foaming over a wide, carved stone into a large, deep pool liberally dotted with fountains.

Those who live in hot, dusty plains know the joy of high mountain vales, crisp mountain air, and sweet, pure water. Kashmir was glorious relief from the burning summer sun of Agra and Delhi. How easy it was for me to believe Emperor Shah Jahan placed greater value on Kashmir than on the rest of his Indian empire.

Achibal Garden was said to be a small but gorgeous pleasure ground, a sparkling gem, and a lure which we could not resist. It was not so when we arrived, for the Stream of Life was not flowing, the fountains not bubbling.

Seeing our dismay, the caretaker mali apologized for the drab appearance of the garden.

"Only on Sunday, Sahib."

"Surely you can turn it on?"

"Oh no, Sahib. That is forbidden, except on Sunday."

We strolled with the mali in the dead-looking garden, and Idie exclaimed how beautiful this or that would be if only the fountains were playing. The mali, agreeing, added, "Picnics used to be held here, there were many flowers. Lady Sahib would have liked it very much." It was the opening in a little game one plays in such situations.

"Yes," I replied, "Lady Sahib would be truly happy to see the fountains at work. It is a shame that you do not know how to turn them on."

"Me not know, Sahib?" Indignantly. "Am I not in charge here?"

"Perhaps so, but I will bet this whole rupee you cannot turn on the fountains."

The mali, eying the coin, hesitated for a second, then ran to the gate, looked down the road, and ran back past us, saying as he went, "I will show you, Sahib. I will turn on the water, but only for a short time."

As Ramchand had said in Agra, silver overcomes all obstacles.

Achibal returned to life. A gentle trickle of water hesitated at the top of a high wall and then, almost suddenly, spread out to become a wide silvery sheet, jumping off the wall into a deep tank below. Framed by green foliage on branching trees, it was stunningly beautiful. A fountain belched loudly. We laughed as one after another joined in, began to gurgle and then to spray.

The waterfall, about fifteen feet high and thirty feet wide, dove into a large tank in the center of which was a little summer house surrounded by gushing fountains throwing misty spray in the air. The mali said the emperor liked to sit there, watching slave girls swim in the deep pool. Achibal was one of Jehangir's favorite gardens, but it had been reduced to two terraces of well-tended lawns and great trees but few flowers.

Since neither of us had ever been confronted with lofty descriptions such as the Stream of Life, Pleasure Garden, Abode of Bliss, and Paradise Gardens, we thought we had stumbled into fantasy land.

In Moghul times, the banks of Dal Lake were lined with gardens, some royal, some private. Shalimar is sedate, Nishat rambunctious, Achibal even more serene than Shalimar. Flowers dominated our senses at Nishat, spring was bubbling out all over, while water dominated Achibal. Rollicking and misappropriated nature made us want to laugh and shout. They were out-of-the-way places, where royalty could escape pomp and ceremony, a hideaway. Three gardens, all designed by following descriptive passages in the Holy Koran. Someone had written they should be thought of as family: Shalimar, sedate grandfather; Achibal, overworked father seeking peace; and Nishat, boisterous teenage son.

* * *

Back at the houseboat, pleased by Idie's bubbly talk about the gardens, our houseboat captain started the Gulmarg thing. He described a hill station, eighty-five hundred feet above sea level, twenty-four miles from Srinagar by car, and four miles up a mountain on pony back. "Lady Sahib would have enjoyed that place," he said. "Gulmarg means Meadow of Roses. Unfortunately, it is now out of season, and all facilities are boarded up."

Idie reacted instantly, "Boarded up or not, we must go and have a picnic, just us two."

The houseboy spoke up. "I must go too, Sahib."

I looked questioningly at him. He understood it to mean a refusal.

"It is my duty to look after Sahib and Memsahib. Who will serve lunch if I am not there?"

What kind of day was it? That depends on who you ask.

We set off at daybreak in an old rattling touring car taking us to a railhead at Tananmarg. We had no warm clothes, so we huddled in the open car. Discomfort was kept within bounds by the ailments of the venerable vehicle; we had to stop every few miles to scoop water for the radiator from a fast-flowing stream beside the road. After every steep climb, the motor came to a temporary jerking halt, like a doddering old man hesitating before taking another step. Impatient as I often am in such situations, I welcomed these stops; respite for us to get down and walk a little way on the gravel road, flailing our arms.

At Tananmarg, on a wide place in the road, about twenty Muslims and pony boys waited with a dozen or so horses available for hire. As we stepped down, the entire gang closed in on us, bringing the horses with them. Houseboy began to haggle with the owners. Pony boys brought head-tossing prancing horses up to us, all sleek, spirited animals. Idie was completely at home with the brutes, rubbed the nose of one, patted the neck of another, and exclaimed over the eyes of still another. I was as uncomfortable as Idie was happy.

His business done, Houseboy turned to me, saying "Which horse will you ride, Sahib?" A moment of truth: contrary to common belief, not all Texans are cowboys. I had never ridden a horse.

Houseboy let me twist in the wind no more than a second before saying he had made choices while striking the bargain: a little brown mare for Idie, which she had chosen long before, and the tallest, most powerful-looking animal in the bunch for me.

Idie, so full of surprises, did it again: mounted smartly, looked comfortable in the saddle, petted the mare on the neck, and spoke gently to her.

What does a person say to a horse she has just met?

Wondering how I had gotten into such a fix; I gingerly approached my head-tossing steed. Fortunately, a pony boy was there to hold the stirrup, or I would not have known from which side to mount.

We set out, snaking our way leisurely through a pine forest on a yard-wide path hacked out of the mountainside; steep, rough country all around us. Idie laughed happily, while I struggled to stay on top of a pile of pent-up energy.

Like most Kashmiris, pony boys have a sense of humor, so the moment my unsteady foot touched the stirrup, they knew, praise be to Allah, that I had been sent to make their day.

Using a switch torn from a trailside birch, my pony boy tickled the horse's hind legs. The horse kicked back. I wobbled and almost fell off. The horse settled down. A few moments later, the pony boy laid a sharp thwack across the horse's rump. He snorted and plunged forward. I bounced backward, shouting, "*Whoa!*" and yanked on the reigns. The horse stopped on the dime. I pitched forward, almost onto the horse's neck. Pony boys howled in glee. Idie managed not to shout her amusement but could not mask the devilish sparkle in her eye. Houseboy sharply chided the pony boy. We went on, Idie eyeballing the scenery and telling me about it. I hardly noticed; I was too busy.

Topping a ridge, we stopped briefly for a panorama of the Meadow of Roses: a plateau closed in by mountain peaks, dotted with widely separated summer bungalows. Robust pine trees towered over them. A two-storied hotel, golf course, and polo field were in view but empty of humans or roses. Houseboy said spring would blanket the entire area with wildflowers.

It was a crystal-clear day, with a chill in the air sunlight could not subdue. No longer surrounded by tall trees, the way down was open and uncluttered. The horses seemed impatient, tossing their heads. I did not know it, but another moment of truth had come for me. Without even a mischievous smile, Idie whipped up her mare and sailed off down the slope at a rapid clip.

In less time than I can talk about it, my horse, as if jabbed by an electrical prod, jolted forward in hot pursuit of the mare, tearing the reins away and bouncing me onto his rump. I squirmed back into the saddle and recaptured the reins. Overtaking Idie, still going full steam ahead, more in the air than in the saddle, hitting all parts from mane to rump, I shouted for help. Idie was in no condition to advise. The spectacle of bulky Harry bouncing in air was more than she could bear in silence. She pulled up, tears of laughter splattering all over. Pony boys rolled in the grass in gleeful ecstasy. I had made their day.

The devil horse stopped only when I pulled his head around so that we were eye to eye. I suppose it could be said I stared him down. Thus ended the runaway on the Meadow of Roses, but if a steep mountain had not been in front of us, that horse would still be running.

Houseboy trotted over to me, not smiling but with a mirthful glint in his eye, reached down, and patted my horse's neck. It would not have surprised me if, in his fashion, he had said, "*Shabash* (hooray), Sahib, Allah rode with you."

Perhaps he did; I didn't fall off.

Needing to feel solid ground under my feet, I wanted to dismount and get on with the picnic. Idie, still enjoying the comedy I had put on for her, just sat still. I felt that she and Houseboy were pretending to be deaf. Houseboy slowly moved on, the rest of us followed. We were only halfway to Killanmarg, the place he had chosen for our picnic.

Beyond Gulmarg, the trail was little more than a ribbon, winding around trees and boulders. Gone were the graceful switchback and smoothed over bridle path. Going from eighty-five hundred feet at Gulmarg to about fourteen thousand feet at Killanmarg, the horses' impatience to speed was also gone. They toiled, often scrambling for hoof hold, and had to be rested, snorting and blowing. It was also a respite for us, as long-unused muscles had begun to ache.

The snowbank gradually became larger and deeper. The forest thinned; trees became smaller and disappeared. At twelve thousand feet above sea level, where the trail ran under a blanket of deep snow, no one wanted to venture. We arrived at Killanmarg. But we did not picnic there.

Mount Nanga Parbat, off in the distance, was stunningly magnificent, rising to 26,300 feet, a shining tower of snow and ice under a sapphire blue dome.

It was not all delight. The wind blew cold, even though a brilliant sun rode overhead. We did not linger but returned to the protection of tall trees. Lunch was spread out on a carpet of pine needles, the forest aroma hanging deliciously in the air. Idie seemed happier than many brides would be on a high, wild mountain. She was starved, she said, and could eat more than her share of whatever was in the basket.

Sad to say, that was a delusion. Nature has its own inscrutable way of returning tit for tat. Those who laugh at another's misfortune are apt to pay a forfeit. For her hearty laughter at my expense, Idie paid the piper at the picnic spot.

Full of vim and vigor, she slid off the mare, took two steps and collapsed. *Altitude sickness!* On horseback she was great, but she could not walk in the thin mountain air.

I lifted her up and staggered with her to a tree stump. She sat there for a while, bowed head in hands. But a little thing like that couldn't subdue her for long. Shortly, she was back in the saddle.

The venerable auto deposited us back at the houseboat, where, after set-tos with tin tubs, we relaxed on the top deck, rehashing the day: Idie describing how she thought each of us would feel the next morning: I would be stiff and sore. She would feel no pain.

I said, "Exercise will cure my stiffness. Let's go to Akbar's fort."

She shook her head. I never got to the fort.

"A long, relaxing ride in the shikara will be best for you."

I pointed across the canal toward Takht-i-Sulaimon, the throne of Solomon, rising one thousand feet above the valley.

"We could go there and have a look at the temple on top."

"That might be interesting. After Gulmarg, it doesn't look like a hard climb."

"Piece of cake, only a thousand feet on a smooth pathway."

So, it was agreed. We would challenge the mountain.

Next morning, Idie staggered to breakfast, stiff and sore. I breezed in, feeling no pain. "That's not fair" was all she said.

A deal is a deal, so we set off, walking side by side, stopping often to admire the view: traffic on the canal below became smaller and smaller as we gained altitude, while the lake beyond spread out, becoming much larger. The temple on top was a disappointment, but the view was worth every step. Far below, Houseboat *Mandalay* became a floating toy, Srinagar housetops a patchwork of shapes and sizes, with Akbar's fort, atop its one hill, jetting up royally.

Getting to the top, however, was not without incident.

To her considerable dismay, Idie learned one thousand feet straight up becomes many thousand steps when winding back and forth. Starting bravely, hiking briskly in bright sunshine, we found that early gradients were easy but soon became steeper. Stops were more frequent as she tried to match my long stride with two or more of her short steps. Inevitably, she lagged behind. I strode on but suddenly stopped and exclaimed, "Look at that!"—only to turn and see that Idie was not there.

I went back and found her sitting wearily on a large wayside stone.

"Are you all right?"

"Yes, I am all right," she said.

Then, in a few choice words, she summed up our honeymoon to date. No complaints, no tears, no whines, no threats. Well, maybe.

"I froze in the air-conditioned compartment, choked in dust on another train, got stiff from riding horseback, and now, you are trying to walk my legs off. If you don't want me, just tell me!"

An epiphany came to me that moment on the mountain: getting to know each other posed as many surprises for her as it would for me. From that point on, I tried to match Ida Dell's paces. Yes, indeed, I still wanted her.

FOURTEEN

HOUSEKEEPING IN BOMBAY

May 1939 — Bombay

The Pali Hill house, in a suburb of Bombay, was our first home. A place loaded with pitfalls and pleasures, where we learned to cope with each other and life in a faraway place. It had been lent to us by the British manager of Kodak, Mr. Bob Nobel, and his wife, while they were on a six-month leave in England. We had much to learn coping in a polyglot environment as we translated English English to Texas English, befuddled with English clans and Hindu caste systems. Neither one of us were accustomed to live-in servants, such as my Hindu bearer, the Chinese cook, and the "untouchable" Hindu yardman.

Then, how to sleep on a bed almost too small for two, high on one side and low on the other, or crows stealing toast from our breakfast table, or warnings about cobras in the garden?

The house turned out to be a delightful beginning. A wide covered verandah ran across one side of it, overlooking a lovely garden. Fringed with small trees and blossoming bushes, it also served as a breakfast room with one small table and two chairs.

Feathered friends patiently awaited our arrival. Large, black crows, perched atop trees in the garden, bided their time, then came with wings flapping, our toast their lure. Ming, the cook, brought the toast; they swooped in, stealing it during their fly-by, shocking us the first day. We later came to respect each other, and Ming made extra toast. We looked forward to our guests.

All I remember about the rest of the house was a small entrance hall, a bathroom, dining room and kitchen. Idie memorized every inch of it because something happened every day.

Pali Hill House

When introducing us to their home, Bob had brought out a Persian prayer rug, a prized possession. "Every husband should have one," he said. When he rolled it out and got on it, it became his haven. No matter how long he sat there, his wife was forbidden to speak to him.

Mrs. Nobel showed Idie around the kitchen. In that house, as in other British homes, coffee, tea, etc., were kept in a locked cabinet, the only key held by Mrs. Nobel. Every morning, she rationed supplies for that day: so much for the Nobels, so much for the servants. "Do that," she said, "or the servants will steal you blind."

Idie kept her thoughts to herself while learning from Mrs. Nobel but later said to me, "I don't care what another memsahib does; I won't do that. If you can't trust servants, you don't deserve to have them." Needless to say, we didn't do that and were not stolen blind.

All vegetables were washed in permanganate of potash before cooking to ward off dysentery, following memsahib's policy in the kitchen.

Everybody joked about it but also considered it a life-or-death process. I don't remember ever eating a raw vegetable while I was in India or a piece of fruit with even the slightest bruise on it.

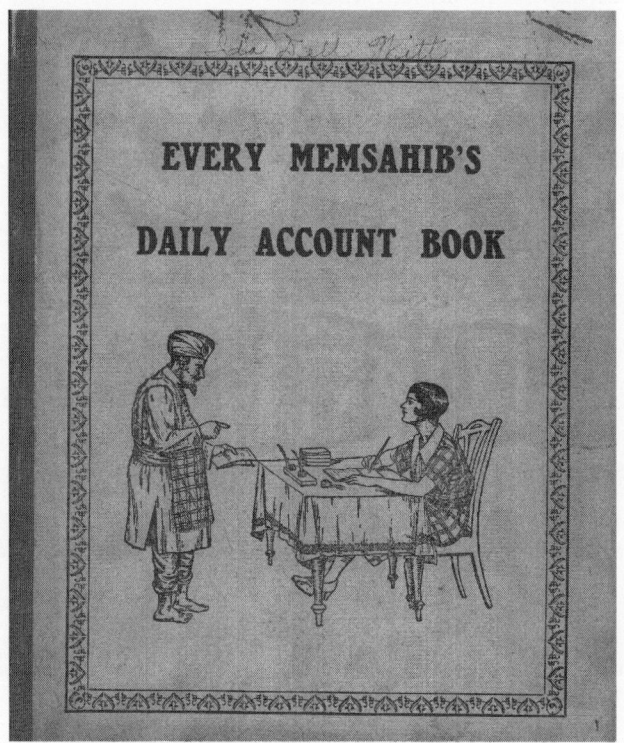

Idie's Memsahib's Book

We slept under a mosquito net because malaria was rampant, but it did not keep away crawly things. Little green lizards capered across the top of it as soon as the lights went out, and when, on occasion, one got inside, I grudgingly got outside and tore up the bedding while ridding it of the varmint. Idie asked a friend what to do about them. "Nothing," Beth said. "In India, lizards symbolize a happy home." So, the lizards kept doing what they were doing, and I kept doing what I was doing. Idie said she was glad the lizards were happy; she was not.

We were not in town long when Idie and Faye Waddell called on the Kilachand family—or more precisely, Mrs. Kilachand—to thank her for the loan of the potted greenery for our wedding. Idie, still unaware of cultural pitfalls, seemed delighted at the prospect of meeting Indian ladies.

Hindu families tend to be large, as was the Kilachands. Large, because sons, when they marry, bring their wives to live with Mama and Papa. There were several married Kilachand sons. The senior mama ruled the household. I mention this because several well-disciplined Hindu women of varying ages "took" tea with Idie and Faye. Idie told me that Mrs. Kilachand, the senior, served the tea and when passing a cup to Idie, asked almost the first words addressed to her, "Are you pregnant yet?"

A shocking bolt out of the blue and unpardonable rudeness in Idie's world. I imagined an astonished Idie, a surprised and embarrassed Faye, and a bevy of rapt Hindu ladies eagerly awaiting Idie's reply.

The room became oppressively silent. Idie said she felt hot all over, and blurted out, "But I have only just been married."

The matriarch soothingly said, "Never mind, dear, just keep trying."

The question was not rude; it was the polite question in woman-to-woman talk in a culture in which the first expectation of a wife is to have many children, preferably sons.

After that bombshell, normal tea sipping went on until one of the younger women said something that piqued Idie's interest. So doing what in Idie's culture was proper, she spoke directly to the girl, asking the question. Ghastly silence descended again.

The startled girl glanced sharply at the matriarch, who gave an almost imperceptible nod, and the girl answered Idie's question. She could not answer without permission from the older woman.

* * *

Into each life, they say, some rain must fall. Idie had a cloudburst the night of her first dinner party. She had carefully planned it, running in and out of the kitchen, coaching the butler and cook in detail on what to do. how to do it, and when to do it.

Her table was beautiful, sparkling with silver goblets and Chantilly flatware laid out on a hand-embroidered Chinese linen tablecloth. The flower centerpiece was flanked on both sides with tall candles and crystal bobeches atop the silver candlesticks.

Frank and Beth Hornell were the first guests to arrive. They had been Idie's shipmates all the way from New York to Bombay, about thirty days at sea. The party was meant as a thank-you to Beth for "mothering"

Idie during the long voyage and a thank-you to the minister who had married us, and his wife. In addition, E. Stanley Jones, the world-renowned Methodist minister, was also invited.

Beth joined Idie for a last inspection of the kitchen. It almost reduced Idie to tears. Idie told Beth the chicken was mutilated. Everything was the cook's way; nothing was her way. Ming insisted on doing it his way, not Idie's. "Kitchen belong me," he said, only to find out, with help from Beth, that the kitchen really "belong" to Idie.

Until that day, Idie had accepted Ming as he thought of himself, lord and master of the kitchen, never asking or wanting guidance from anyone. This special occasion was meant to have a Texas flavor, not Chinese, especially as to how chicken should be cut, prepared, and served. Whose kitchen was it, anyway? Idie won the skirmish but lost the war. Shortly thereafter, Ming took leave of us, to become master of the kitchen somewhere else.

Other memorable things happened at that party. After dinner, Stanley Jones went to the kitchen to visit with Ming, and spoke with him in the Chinese dialect used in the remote village where Ming had been born. Jones had, in earlier years, visited there as a young missionary. It was also Jones who enlivened the dinner conversation with a story about another Chinese cook who was told everything had to be perfect because his master's boss was coming to dinner—a "red altar" occasion, red being the Chinese color for happiness. The cook outdid himself: the turkey was served with a flashlight stuck into its cavity, gleaming with a red-light bulb.

* * *

An important part of our new married life was learning to live in community with office people who became family, plus the British and the natives. Weekends were often spent outside Bombay, exploring India, or hunting game we would eat and share with friends and villagers. We knew it was considered bad luck for a woman to accompany the men on shooting trips, but Idie did not want to stay home alone in Bombay, and I enjoyed her company.

After a long day of tramping in rough country, Idie and I spent the night in a dak bungalow near a small village on the edge of the desert. During the night, something moved in the room, jolting me out of a deep sleep. Idie's *charpoy* (portable bed) was empty. The bungalow door was wide open. Where was Idie? Had she wandered outside? Did she not know she would be fair game for snakes, wild dogs, jackals, and other vermin?

A full moon had risen while we slept, and there on the floor sat Idie, bathed in soft moonglow, oblivious of danger. Barefooted, robe pulled tightly around her, she was hunkered down in the doorway. She was gazing off into the distance.

I stumbled over to her. "What is it?" I asked.

"Listen!" she commanded, holding up a hand to silence me.

Tinkling sounds came out of the bush, growing stronger as we listened.

"Can you hear it?" she asked.

"Sure. Somewhere out there in the bush a bunch of camels is plodding along."

Moments later, a long line of camels came into view, each with a hunched rider on top, silhouetted in the moonlight—probably asleep, as I wished I were.

"Isn't it wonderful?" Idie whispered, "That's just the way Rebekah made her long trip to marry Isaac in Genesis."

* * *

"What is monsoon like?" I heard again and again.

"It's like a big hurricane back in Houston."

"Oh, you old stuck-in-the-mud, tell me more." When showers preceded the big show, she would shake me awake with "Is this it?"

"No, you will know when it finally breaks."

And she did! Near midnight one night, a great wind came first, rattling the house. Thunder boomed like a succession of cannon blasts, and lightning burst across the ebony black sky. Such powerful rain hammered the house, I thought it might wash down the hill.

The onslaught continued most of the night. Sleeping no more, Idie ran from pillar to post to see what havoc was occurring outside. Then, about an hour into the deluge, she went into the bathroom, where she was confronted with her nemesis: the pull chain toilet. Her yell was not long in coming: "*Harry!*"

There she was, as far from that object as she could get, a touch of fear in her eyes, aiming the little flashlight she was never without, at a large rat frantically paddling in the toilet bowl, a dragon in Idie's eyes, far more dangerous than the monsoon storm.

I thought it was funny and said so while flushing the beast away. Idie didn't and said so.

To me, the coming of monsoon brought a deep sense of relief. This intangible monsoon phenomenon muddled heads, as if something in the air caused people to do foolish things. It always began a few weeks before monsoon broke, usually in June, when the temperature was in the high nineties and the humidity so high that every cell in one's body would weep for relief. Sweating profusely, without air conditioning, soggy clothes stuck to my body like odorous flypaper. I changed from the skin out, three times daily while trying to ward off frustration.

Everyone in the office, from Number One to untouchable, snapped at one another, made mistakes, and blamed them on others, arguing over trifles. Servants would forget to do their work, the cook would forget to put pepper in the saltshaker, or the bearer, on a short errand, would disappear for hours.

* * *

Idie's first monsoon brought important changes to her lifestyle and put her in the driver's seat of my old car—reluctantly, because one drives on the "wrong" side of the road in India. It took what she termed an emergency to get her to try.

I was playing on the Gymkhana team in intermittent rain because rugger was played only during monsoon, the ground being hardened cement otherwise.

We played, and we won. I had made a "try" (equivalent to a touchdown in football), and mud was splattered all over me when I presented myself to Idie. I was astonished to hear her say that grown men should know better than to wallow in the mud. "No worry," I said. "There are no showers at this field; I will drive home and shower there."

"Not so fast, Buster! You will not cover the front seat with that filth. And I certainly will not ride next to you." She ordered me into the back seat, on the floor.

Chatting all the way home, with me on the floor behind her, Idie thought it was hilarious. I didn't and said so.

FIFTEEN

KARACHI STORIES

May 1940 — Home Leave

Hitler invaded Poland in September 1939, and the war in Europe began in earnest while America watched. Business interests in India kept a careful eye on worldwide developments.

Idie and I were allowed a home leave earlier than expected. We were still newlyweds, on our first sea voyage together—a three-month long second honeymoon, on a freight/passenger ship with few frills. Our route meant sailing around Africa to bypass the war, south on the Indian Ocean to Cape Town, then north on the Atlantic Ocean to New York. It was uneventful but added a week or two to the usual travel time.

One memorable event happened while at sea. On May 10th, our first wedding anniversary, we were standing on the upper deck, sailing down the African coast. We watched the fiery sun sink beyond the western horizon while, at the same time, the golden full moon rose out of the sea to the east, both seeming close enough for us to touch, nothing but water evident between them.

Idie's mother, Ruby, was waiting for us on the New York pier. She grimaced when she saw my Indian-sewn British-style attire and urged an immediate shopping spree to buy proper clothes. It was priority number *one*.

We also bought our first car, a used Chevrolet, for two hundred dollars. We drove it south to Texarkana with Ruby and spent a day visiting a flock of Idie's relatives. It was my first opportunity to meet them and for them to size me up. Idie was welcomed like a conquering heroine, the girl who had risked life and reputation to travel to that faraway place, now returning to congratulations with the young man they knew little about.

We drove to Houston to see more of Idie's relatives, and warm friendships blossomed. I reported to ACCO headquarters, where I heard the bad news: my home leave was over. There was trouble in the markets overseas, and I was needed back in India: "You should hurry back to Bombay," Mr. Whittington said.

* * *

We first went to Tucson with Ruby, to see Idie's brother, Ernie, and his wife, Doris. Ruby stayed with them while Idie and I drove to Los Angeles and San Francisco. I sold the car to a dealer for two hundred dollars. Then we scouted out the wharf where our ship was docked, our temporary home for thirty days. It was a time of high excitement, as holiday tourists traveled with us, hoping to find Paradise on the islands.

As we approached the Honolulu pier, "Aloha! Aloha!" rang out from ship to ship, ship to shore and back again. Hawaiian music on the wharf and barefoot, grass-skirted, brown damsels doing the hula greeted us. Leis of orchard flowers were draped around our necks. Happiness seemed to be everywhere, with no hint of war in the Pacific, hidden beyond the blue horizon.

We pushed off for Manila two days later. Idie received many flowers over the years, but I thought none thrilled her more than her first lei.

There was, however, little joy for Idie and me on the way to Manila, as an American intelligence officer, about our age, came aboard in Honolulu. He was a communications expert en route to Cavite, an American naval base near Manila. He was highly pessimistic, saying war in the Pacific was approaching. He was hungry for information on India and quizzed me at the base. I gave him the travel books on India that I had with me.

We spent two hot, muggy days in Manila, sleeping restlessly with unceasing noise from the loading and unloading of cargo. The equipment made maddening wheezing noises, laced with frequent shouting of workers. The ship's captain advised us not to stray from the ship, saying, "We may have to sail at very short notice."

We saw little of Manila. I had thought war in the Pacific was unlikely to be so close but changed my mind in Manila and Shanghai.

Many passengers boarding in Manila were businessmen, returning to Shanghai from home leave. Shanghai was the crown jewel among ACCO foreign agencies.

We dropped anchor late in the afternoon. The captain announced, "The city, except for the international settlement, has been occupied by Japanese troops, a tense and dangerous situation. Only passengers with urgent business will be permitted to disembark."

My spirit sank. We knew no one in Shanghai. While Idie and I looked on, passengers began to leave when two strangers coming aboard surprised us: Bill Triebig and Ralph Hubbard, ACCO agents. Houston had cabled them to look for us. They laughed at the captain's worry, saying there was no tension and no worry in the settlement. We went ashore for our first Chinese dinner in China, at a Chinese restaurant.

"A nightcap is mandatory in Shanghai," Bill insisted; so, we set off in Bill's car for a night spot outside the settlement. We were stopped by a barricade on a dark street with Japanese solders lined up on both sides of the car, flashlights illuminating our faces. "Papers! Papers!" were demanded.

"Only a formality," our new friends said while laughingly handing them over, including our passports. I was not in a laughing mood, and sat speechless, more than a little concerned about the rifle less than a foot from my chest. It did turn out to be a formality, albeit an uncomfortable one. We were halted at the barricade while returning to the ship, with the "Papers! Papers!" ritual repeated.

The purser had said "We sail at one p.m. with or without you." And we did, beginning the last day on our first round-the-world trip. Shanghai to Bombay was uneventful, tipping our hats to Hong Kong and Singapore, sailing past them.

When we arrived in Bombay, we were greeted with: "Not so fast, Buster! Don't unpack; you will go to Karachi as soon as possible."

One week later we were again aboard a ship, en route to Karachi on a cargo freighter. I don't remember exactly when we arrived, perhaps in early September, thinking we would now put down roots.

* * *

Karachi was then a part of British India, a sleepy little port, its purpose being to guard the frontier of southern Afghanistan. The foreign population was largely British, with a smattering of Americans. The ACCO office was on Napier Road with a small staff: Gene Graves, a Hindu chief clerk, a Jewish cashier, a Muslim accountant, two untouchable Hindus, and me.

Idie and I found a suitable apartment we could afford, not far from the office. One day after we moved in, our bearer told me Abdul, the rug merchant, was at our door.

"Salaam, Sahib, I am Abdul!" he said. "I bring beautiful Persian carpets. Sahib and Memsahib would like to see?"

Persian carpets? Right here in our apartment? Wow! Idie's face lit up.

Abdul's servant rolled out a pair of beautiful throw rugs. Abdul called them top-of-the-line, not bazaar trash. He caressed one of them with the palm of his hand. "Are they not beautiful, Memsahib?"

Idie got down on the floor beside Abdul. She simply had to touch them; the way Abdul was doing. It was a memorable moment, her first encounter with a silver-tongued master of the art of friendly persuasion and the waiting game.

Abdul unleashed a bucketful of supplication. To hear him talk, one could easily imagine Aladdin himself riding the carpets. Eyes aglow, Idie avidly drank in every silver-smooth word. I was a mute but interested bystander until time to leave for the office, at which point I became the villain.

"How much?" I asked.

"In shop, Sahib, the price is eighteen hundred rupees."

Idie caught her breath. knowing this was well beyond our means. (She would have been a terrible poker player.)

"But here, in Sahib and Memsahib's nice home," Abdul continued, "I make a special price of only twelve hundred rupees."

I laughed. "No can do, Abdul, the price is much too high." Twelve hundred rupees were almost two months of my salary. But I knew that Abdul's first offer was tantamount to saying, "Let the haggling begin," a way of life unknown to Idie.

Abdul smiled and said to me, "The Sahib, I see, is a businessman. Abdul is also a businessman. Let us make a deal. What will the Sahib pay?"

"Four hundred rupees" (almost two hundred dollars).

Abdul gasped, "Sahib makes a joke?"

"No joke, Abdul."

Abdul gave Idie a long look. I figured she had disappointed him by remaining quiet. Abdul made a precocious bow with "Salaam," and walked away with the carpets.

Idie seemed disappointed, saying, "That's that." However, it was just a prologue to a long-running saga.

Abdul returned a few days later, unrolled his carpets, and praised them at great length before asking, "Sahib will make new offer?"

"Sorry, Abdul, no new offer." So, the carpets again left us.

A week went by, and Abdul came back, waiting outside until I left for the office. Idie recounted later that Abdul had promoted her from Memsahib to Ladyship. Abdul also said he knew she loved his carpets. So did Sahib, but Sahib did not love the price. Abdul had come to make a great sacrifice. Lady Sahib could have the carpets for only eight hundred rupees. "Think, Lady Sahib, what a nice surprise that would be for Sahib."

When Idie told Abdul only the sahib could makes such deals, Abdul did what he had intended all along: he suggested the carpets remain on our floor for two weeks.

"Live with them, Lady Sahib," he pleaded. "They will bring you and Sahib great happiness."

Idie said she wavered, but the silk tongue won. Abdul departed; the carpets remained. Day by day we became fonder of the carpets.

Bubbling cheerfully, Abdul returned as promised, telling us, not asking us, how much we had enjoyed the carpets. Idie assured him it was true; we loved them.

"Look Sahib, how happy is Lady Sahib. Sahib will buy?"

"Sorry, Abdul, price is still too high."

"Sahib will make new offer?"

"No, no new offer."

Once again, the carpets were taken away.

Abdul reappeared about a month later, rolled out his carpets, and said, "I have big trouble, Sahib. My mother is very sick, maybe dying. I need money to visit her in Punjab. I must sell carpets today."

The dying relative ploy, his trump card, found no rapport with me. I had met it on other occasions. No so for Idie.

"We are sorry about your mother, Abdul, and would like to help."

"I know," Abdul broke in, "Price, always price. Eight hundred rupees is very special price. Sahib says even special price is too high. Sahib will pay six hundred rupees?"

I shook my head.

"Sahib loves carpets. Lady Sahib loves carpets. Think of happiness carpets will bring. Think of my dying mother. Six hundred rupees, Sahib."

Abdul, while ostensibly talking to me, kept his eyes riveted on Idie, pleading with her to intercede. She remained silent. Another shake of my head.

As if in despair, Abdul knelt on one of the carpets, as Muslims do when praying, and loudly called upon Allah to help him.

Stifling a sob, Idie rushed from the room, finishing it also for Abdul. The moment she was out of sight, Abdul arose, smiling, and said, "All right, Sahib."

Salaaming happily, he departed with about two hundred dollars' worth of rupees. We were now proud owners of a pair of fine Persian carpets.

Proud? Idie indicated that she was neither proud nor happy.

"You ran roughshod over that poor man," she stormed, "browbeat him. Probably kept him from visiting his dying mother."

"Get those things out of my sight. I never want to see them again!"

In a closet they went, out of sight. Where was the great happiness Abdul said the carpets would bring? They brought the first major rift in our just-begun married life, which lasted about two weeks.

Then one evening, while strolling in the bazaar, someone shouted, "Sahib, Witt!" And Abdul came running toward us. "Happy to see you and Lady Sahib," he said. Idie shook her head.

"I have been worried about your mother, Abdul," she said, "How is she?"

Abdul scuffed the dust with a nervous toe. With a sheepish smile, and a light bow to Idie, he said, "Ah, Lady Sahib. Sahib understands these things. My mother died three years ago."

* * *

We met a group of young bachelors who worked for Standard Oil and lived together in a house they called the Chummery. Easy conversation and jokes flowed when Idie and I were with them. One day, I said to one of them, "Let us know when a place becomes available here." Soon afterwards we took an apartment there for a few months, becoming fast friends with the "boys." We shared meals and a rowdy friendship.

The house was built on desert sand about a quarter of a mile from the ocean front. We could tell if the tide were in or out simply by walking into the living room. As the tide came in, a dark stain moved up the wall. Unsightly but not monstrous; still, something Idie would not peaceably live with. She found someone to stretch thin cotton fabric over a wooden frame and then attach it to the wall, pleasantly upgrading the room's decor.

Our stove was a mound of baked clay with holes on top for pots to sit in. They were heated by burning sticks shoved under them. The oven was an ordinary aluminum pot, with fire under it and live coals on top. We did have one of the early refrigerators, a symbol of affluence; none of our neighbors had one, so ours was installed in plain view for everyone to see at the end of our large dining room.

Meal preparation and the general running of the house rotated every month. For the month you were in charge, you would endure lively hazing about the food and other matters. Tall tales resounded around the table at mealtime, but no superlatives such as "best cribbage player in the world" were allowed. I did convince the boys that only superlatives were applicable to Texas, or anything related to Texas. Sometimes this worked against me, but usually it brought more jokes and laughter.

Food was the number one gripe at the Chummery—too many green peas and no T-bone steaks being prime targets. T-bone steaks were unknown in India because butchers cut beef the British way. Green peas, often the only green vegetable available, appeared on the table almost daily. The Chummery gang referred to them as BBs: hard, tasteless little pellets.

Returning to Karachi from the up-country, after a long ride in broiling sun, one Chummery dweller said the first thing he would do on his home leave, if he survived the three years until he was eligible for one, would be to order ten servings of green peas, line them up in front of him and force them to watch while he ate an enormous T-bone steak.

That's when Idie decided to give the boys a surprise they would long remember. She had a cookbook with a diagram showing where American cuts of beef were taken from the carcass. She took it to the icehouse where beef was hung for seasoning. After long negotiations, her feminine charm and tenacity persuaded the in-house butcher to cut six large, handsome T-bone steaks.

When the gang came to dinner, Idie first served a course of thin soup, with which most dinners in Karachi began, then she teased them into remembering their favorite steakhouse back home. While they thought, talked, and brooded, she sprang her surprise—luscious T-bone steaks, served on individual platters, replicas, almost, of what all of them had been describing.

Not believing their eyes, the poor brutes were silent, staring at the steaks. Then, bedlam broke out; the house rocked with gleeful shouts, and a "jolly good time" was had by all. Idie had done the impossible!

* * *

One night, Idie and I strolled along a well-lighted Karachi street after the Saturday night movie. We saw one of my rugger teammates approaching from the opposite direction. Looking me full in the face, showing no recognition, he averted his eyes and hurried on.

"I wonder what's eating him," I said to Idie.

The next afternoon, my friend said, "That was a stunner you were with last night."

"I know," I said. "If you had stopped, I would have introduced you to my wife."

"Your wife? I am sorry, old chap, but you know I couldn't stop. She might have been Chi-Chi (Anglo-Indian), and I didn't want to embarrass you."

A no-no for British men. Do not date Indian women, and never marry one! The penalty for breaking this rule was the loss of your job and being sent home in disgrace.

Some American firms also adopted this rule. One of our Standard Oil friends fell in love and wanted to marry a beautiful Anglo-Indian girl. Give up the girl or give up your job, he was told. Refusing to give up the girl, he was fired and sent home. I don't know if the girl joined him later.

* * *

I was surprised one day when a man came to the office and said he had heard, in the bazaar, from someone who had heard from someone who told a friend that I needed a hunter. I looked at him with interest when he said, "Could I be of service?"

He could indeed! Hashim Shikari was about thirty-two, a Muslim, with bronze skin, coal black hair, penetrating black eyes and a droopy mustache. Standing a bit under six feet, with a *puggaree* (a soft cloth wrapped around and over his head to form a turban), Hashim seemed to tower over the rest of us. Bare feet were stuck into cheap, open-toed leather sandals with a loosely fitting shirt hanging down to the top of tan colored pantaloons. These were tied at the waist and at the ankles with a cotton cord to keep sand out. I never saw him dressed any other way. When on a hunt, Hashim merged perfectly with the environment. When he stood near a thorny bush or crouched beside a rock, frozen into immobility, his alert black eyes would focus on a spot where he thought something would move. Even knowing he was there, I had to squint very hard to see him.

Hashim spent weekdays during the hunting season visiting interior villages and scouting for places where partridges, sand grouse, and ducks were plentiful. On weekends he took Idie and me to a different village each time. He always arranged for coolies to beat the bushes before we got there, to scare up partridges and to gather any we brought down. A devout follower of Islam, Hashim stopped the hunt briefly at sunup, noon, and sundown while he prayed aloud, with his face toward Mecca, touching his head to the ground. After his prayers, the hunt would continue.

Whether on foot or camelback, Hashim was never lost, as I often was, when off the beaten track. But at night, inside a car, he became disoriented. One such night, Hashim, Idie, and I wandered aimlessly for what seemed like hours until Hashim got out of the car and stood for a moment, scanning the sky. He quickly found himself and then walked in front of the car, leading us unerringly to our intended destination.

Hashim was a poor man, willing and eager to work for a pittance, often for less than a dollar a day. I never saw him fire a gun. He was our guide who hunted. We shot.

* * *

Mingling with the English wasn't easy. My British friend, Orne, had a similar problem: Texas English was as foreign to him as his English was to me. When I told him I was going hunting, he laughed.

"You don't hunt partridge," he said, "you shoot them. When you hunt, you ride a horse chasing a fox."

"Okay," I told him, "you go ride a horse; I am going partridge hunting."

When you go into the field to shoot game birds, or "go birding," as they say, you don't have to hunt; you already know where the birds are. It's a gentlemen's sport, and they dress up in well pressed khaddars, carry a thing they call a shorty stick, and hire a gun-bearer or two. A coolie "bird-dogs" for them. If a coolie can't find a doomed bird, the Sahib cusses him loudly-all part of the game.

The shorty stick is a metal rod you stick in the ground. The top folds out into a little seat. If I had used one of those back home, I would have been laughed into the next county. Idie, Gene, and I tried them and laughed at the British.

We went partridge hunting one Saturday, near a small village; our first outing with Hashim. Idie augmented the drive by teasing me about "going into the field," not to go hunting but to go birding! We were dressed down instead of up, no sharp creases on our khaki trousers, no holster sticks, and only one gun apiece, which we carried.

Hashim and eight gabbing coolies met us at the village. We piled into a truck, guns in hand, ready to use them on flying partridges. But the moment Idie stepped forward, the gabbing ceased. The village headman broke the silence. "Is it not well known that women on a shoot bring bad luck?" We needed his permission to hunt near the village. Superstition is strong in India, especially in the villages. If the old man stuck to his guns, there would be no shoot. A tense moment, but Hashim had a trump card and he played it immediately. No Memsahib, no shoot, no supper for the village. The old man smiled and threw up his hands.

Hunting with Coolies

* * *

Idie was pure joy for me on shooting trips, but to Hashim she seemed an enigma. The salt caper was a perfect example of how she kept him off balance.

Walking near the dry bed of the Hab River, about twenty miles from Karachi, Hashim and three coolies beat the bushes, scaring up gray partridges for me to shoot. Idie was watching, sitting on a large stone a short distance away. I bagged two plump partridges and held them up for her to admire.

"Not bad," she said, holding up one of her own. "How do you like mine?"

I stepped back, a surprised grin on my face. Hashim's eyes widened.

The bird was still warm. Hashim examined it carefully. Finding no bird shot, he looked questioningly at her. "Where did you get it?"

"Ah, I put salt on its tail."

Hashim shook his head, as he often did when with us. We had a good laugh.

The bird had flown over my head, and I shot at it. It flew on and fell dead at Idie's feet. A single, glancing pellet must have killed it, leaving nothing to show where it had been hit. Walking up to the car, Hashim sidled up to me and whispered, "Salt, Sahib? Memsahib said salt?"

* * *

Hunting with Hashim was usually a great time, but once we endured a best forgotten but memorable day. We chased after bustards in Baluchistan and took tea with a cutthroat bandit.

It all began at the Chummery, where the discussion was lively one night, almost raucous, when a British guest asked, "Have any of you ever seen a bustard?" He was almost laughed out of the house. The gang gleefully pounced on the word, tossing it about slowly, spelling B-U-S-T-A-R-D, with emphasis on the U, acting out what they thought bustards looked like.

Our visitor told us about two kinds of game birds—big ones, much like the American wild turkey, weighing up to fifty pounds, and the smaller bustard, resembling an overgrown wild chicken. Then he asked, "Can you partridge shooters imagine the thrill of bringing down one of these great birds?"

One of us could, the memory welling up in me of my father's turkey shoots in Texas and the big birds he occasionally brought home. I was already thinking about where to find one.

"Unfortunately," the Brit continued, "bustards are extinct in India, but rumored to be found in Baluchistan."

"Where is Baluchistan?" Idie wanted to know when we were alone.

"About twenty miles from here," I said.

"Let's go and surprise the boys with roasted bustard some Sunday night. Hashim will know where to find them."

Hashim did know where to find bustards. He had a Wazir friend who shot them. "Sahib wants to go?"

"Yes, we want to go."

"No, Sahib, Memsahib no go. Baluch no good place for Memsahib."

There we go again; Hashim objecting (more than any time before) to Idie going somewhere he thought she shouldn't go. We talked a little, but not enough, ending with the little toss of Idie's head Hashim knew too well.

So, we went to Baluchistan.

India meets Baluchistan at the end of a narrow, paved road, twenty miles from Karachi, at the wide, unbridged Hab River. It was dry at the time but could become a raging torrent during monsoon. We had been there before, shooting partridge, on both sides, so we expected to be comfortable with the people over there. Wrong!

Hashim told us the village was thirty miles from the river, a number I am sure he pulled out of his turban. Four unhappy hours passed before we sighted the village.

The road was a barely discernible camel track, meandering through scrub brush wilderness, over sand hills, and around boulder-sized rocks. The sand tried to bury the wheels of my car while the rocks tried to tear them apart. With every safe turn of the wheels, I worried about the prospect of a breakdown. Hashim assured Idie, "It is near, Memsahib," while we sweated in terrific heat, ate blowing dust, and gave blood to swarming sand flies.

We saw a welcome oasis, a small village, shimmering in the near distance. But when we got there, we were not welcome. On our side of the river, happy people gathered around, salaaming men, shy women, a gaggle of children, slinking pie dogs. Where were they? Here, only three surly men stood close together, eyeing us suspiciously, keeping their distance.

"What now, Hashim?"

He seemed more surprised than I, staring silently at the men for a few seconds. Then he leapt from the car and hit the ground running, shouting, arms waving belligerently. I had never seen the angry side of Hashim. One of them broke away, running toward the nearest house, Hashim in hot pursuit. Before they got there, a stout, heavily black-bearded man charged out. Hashim turned to face "Blackbeard." He pulled up sharply and threw his arms wide, shouted praises to Allah and embraced Hashim.

Hashim had found his Wazir friend. I relaxed but only briefly. Hashim was welcome, but were we? The wide bladed knife prominently displayed at the Wazir's waist was disquieting; never before had we encountered an armed man. Broad, tall enough to look me in the eye, oozing toughness, he was unlike any village headmen we had met. Nor was there any warmth in his salaam when it came. Hard black eyes sized me up, barely a half smile on his face. Hashim's early warning came to mind, "Baluch no good place for Memsahib," to which I silently added, *nor for Sahib*.

I wanted to leave the village and look for bustards, as we often did when looking for partridges in other villages. Hashim said we must first take tea with the Wazir and get his permission to hunt on his land. To refuse would cause Hashim to lose face. We reluctantly followed the Wazir into his house, a semi-dark, windowless room. We sat around a low table on a dirty, frayed cushion on the clay floor with no other furniture or anything else in sight.

I was sure Idie would not count sitting beside a burly, knife-carrying tough in a darkened room as one of her treasured adventures. She did superbly act the role of a "trained to silence" Hindu woman.

The Wazir barked one startlingly harsh word, which brought out of the dimness a heavily wrinkled, bone-thin black man, wearing nothing but a loincloth. He kept his head down, looking at no one, smoke-blackened kettle in one hand, small, matched cups in the other. I had learned the tea taking ritual in up-country India, especially the art of slurping, lip smacking, and burping. I often felt as if I was a bad boy, but sometimes these practices came in handy.

A muddy looking mixture sloshed Into our cups: camel's milk, raw sugar and water, tea leaves floating on top. Ugly to look at, but boiling hot, so I thought a little of it would not hurt us. Idie shot me her silent "Must I?" look. I tried to look sympathetic. The Wazir, hard eyes looking straight ahead, waited for me to make the first move. I took a goodly sip, smacking my lips. Wanted to spew it out, but I didn't. All eyes shifted to Idie. She took a demure sip, barely moistening her lips. It was enough. Hashim smiled, I relaxed. The two friends noisily slurped while Hashim got permission for our hunt, the Wazir deciding to go with us.

I often said I'd walk a mile to avoid riding a camel, and I think Idie would double that, but waiting for us were three of our favorite abominations. We mounted up, Idie riding with Hashim, I with a sullen, knife-carrying camel driver. The Wazir led off, and we dutifully followed for two rump thumping hours. We chased one bird, said to be a bustard, soaring just out of gunshot range, never going to the ground. The camels stank, the heat remained oppressive, and we were very thirsty; our water bottles were in the car. Late afternoon closed in and worry came with it: Could we find our way back in the dark?

I called a halt, much to Idie's relief, I thought. Hashim appeared unhappy. He had lost face; promised bustards, produced nothing but a miserable camel ride. But our day was not over. We must, according to Hashim, take tea again with the Wazir before we could leave.

The room was almost dark. A stinking, eye-watering kerosene lamp was on the table. Wazir and Hashim settled down for what they expected would be a long talk. Isolated people yearn for news from the outside. I knew, if not interrupted, their powwow would continue long into the night.

Then I remembered the burp!

When the old man shuffled to refill our cups, I lifted mine, saluted the Wazir, downed the ugly tasting stuff, and called up a mighty burp. Hashim, open-mouthed, looked as if I had rapped his knuckles. The Wazir put down his cup, looking surprised. They got the message. We could go home.

* * *

I learned later that an enduring memory for Idie was how tired she often felt on these outings. Walking in the desert was like lifting a heavy weight with every step. Her legs were short; Hashim's and mine were long. While we idled along, she had to hustle to keep up. Climbing rocky hillsides made her leg muscles complain and her lungs shout for air. But she never stopped the hunt. She might have said, "Wait, I have to tie my shoelaces," or "Look, enough is enough, let's rest awhile," but she never did.

The truth was, I got tired too. The moral of this story is that something good came of it. We both learned how to put our heads down anywhere, under the shade of a small tree, at a dak bungalow, or in the car, and instantly fall asleep for fifteen minutes or so. Then, with total rejuvenation, we would get up and be ready to go.

* * *

On one trip, we arrived at a remote village of dung and straw huts in the middle of the night. We had been riding camelback most of the day and well into the night. Idie had asked repeatedly, "How much farther, Hashim?"

His reply was always the same: "It is near, Memsahib." When we arrived, Idie could not get off her camel. I lifted her down.

My bearer was with us. He had carried an alarm clock in one hand and a thermos, filled with soup for us, in the other. The clock started buzzing just after nightfall, almost paralyzing our camels. In addition, the soup had curdled in the hot sun, jogging on a camel. My bearer was a city boy and staggered away from his camel much as a bowlegged cowpoke would do, returning from a long day at the roundup.

The village headman gave us his one-room "house" for what was left of the night. We needed to get up at dawn so we could reach our designated shooting ground. Big rats scurried inside the "house," while the men sat outside, around a fire near our door, laughing and talking.

When bodily functions called, Hashim pointed toward a dark place at the edge of the village, wide open on three sides. Idie, flashlight in hand, took one look and said, "You're coming with me." One had to step among the clustering turds to get there

Back at our "house," the headman asked if the village women could meet Memsahib. Idie nodded yes, and they filled the room: dark skin, raven black hair, muscular bodies, fully pleated skirts, rings on fingers, bangles on arms. Whispering among themselves in the beginning, laughing loudly at the end, they stroked Idie's hair and fingered her clothing. None of them had ever seen a white woman, nor had Idie ever been "gone over" by women such as these.

Number One woman, holding Idie's hand, tried to rub the white off her arm. Others also tried unsuccessfully. I wonder, as they left us, giggling, and talking, if they were saying to each other, "How does she do that?"

* * *

During the hunting season, most Sunday nights were highly festive at the Chummery because of our Saturday shooting trips. Partridge were plentiful, so we usually managed to bring enough for a feast. Idie would whip up a barbeque sauce, becoming locally famous for it. The cook roasted the birds, and the halls of Ghiza Road rang with hunting stories told and retold until the early morning hours.

Then one day, Hashim came to the office with great news. He had just returned from scouting out the best places to shoot sand grouse. "There is a big buck antelope out there," he said; would the Sahibs go with him? Gene and I would have instantly declared a holiday, but Hashim needed time to prepare. We had to wait until Saturday.

Leaving before dawn, we drove ten or fifteen miles into the trackless desert. Five camels and camel watchers were waiting for us. Hashim had not mentioned we would have to pick our beasts. Grudgingly, we mounted up. We rode a wide circle looking for spoor. Hashim pulled up, pointed to the ground, and said, "Antelope tracks." I saw nothing but sand and pebbles. We rode on, and the sun became blistering hot. We sweated. Hashim pulled up again and pointed at the distant glare. "He is there, Sahib," he said. I saw nothing but desert.

We dismounted near a rocky depression. Hashim placed Gene on the ground a short distance away on the left, leaving me flat on the ground next to the depression. Idie was placed out of harm's way in the depression with the spare camels. We considered them stinking creatures, apt to kick and bite. She also missed the action. "Not fair!" she later stormed—and never forgave Hashim, or me, for putting her there.

Hashim and the two camel walkers rode off in opposite directions to ride a wide circle around the antelope. We settled down to wait. Soon there was nothing to see but glare. At last, the camels came into view, but no antelope. With some distance between them, they moved slowly toward us. Finally, the antelope appeared, running broadside to me about forty yards away. I fired one rifle shot. An antelope went down.

Hashim raced up, hurriedly jumped off his camel, and shouted, "*Shabash,* Sahib," or "Hurrah, well done!" He gathered twigs from scrubby desert growth, placed them around a flat rock and set them on fire. The liver was roasted and happily devoured by the camel crew, slicing off piece after piece with the short knives all of them carried.

Great jubilation greeted our return to the Chummery: Venison! The gang asked their friends to come and share with us. The house filled up; the table became overcrowded. Antelope are small, and the crowd was large. I was sure there would not be enough to go around. When my plate was served, I asked my bearer, "Will there be enough?"

He replied, "Not to worry, Sahib. Sahib such-and-such and Sahib this-and-that are having roast beef tonight. Their number one boy brought it. That's what they are being served; they will not know the difference." Apparently they did not.

* * *

Gene Graves went with Idie and me on another bird shoot and brought two cans of beer packed in ice in a wide-mouth thermos. I brought a spanking new Woodsman Colt 22 pistol, which I had not yet fired.

When we took a lunch break, Gene tossed an empty can about thirty feet from where we were sitting and said, "Take a shot with your new toy."

I loaded up, confidently expecting to tear gaping holes in the can. I emptied the magazine in its direction with ten or twelve shots.

Raucous laughter erupted. The can sat there, unblemished. I was dumbfounded. Though not an expert marksman, I was a fair shot with shotgun and rifle.

Sheepishly, I handed the pistol to Gene. He gave me a disparaging look and let go with another full magazine. The unblemished can just sat there. I would have sworn it was leering at us. Gene nodded when I said I thought something was wrong with the gun and I would have to take it back.

Then Idie spoke up: "Let me try it," she said.

"You?" She had barely ever touched a gun, let alone fired one. Hashim rolled his eyes. The coolies, with us to beat the bush, wrinkled their brows.

"Well, why not?" I gave the pistol to her with a full magazine.

Gene, Hashim, and the coolies all scrambled to get behind us.

Idie stretched out her arm, gun in hand. She pressed the trigger, and the gun began to jump; the can with it. By the time the magazine was empty, nothing was left of the can but a jagged piece of metal. Striving to muffle girlish giggles, she laid the gun down before me.

The coolies stared in disbelief. A woman had outshot the Sahibs.

Hashim came alive. "Shabash, Memsahib, shabash! Hooray!"

Gene and I were as mute as the stones around us. Idie had just fired a gun for the first time in her life. She never fired another one. The coolies seemed puzzled. I thought they might be thinking, "The Sahibs waste ammunition. Why do they not let Memsahib shoot for them?"

Later, whenever Hashim and I walked away, leaving Idie to knit or write letters, he always put the pistol down beside her.

* * *

Sometimes on our hunting trips, Hashim and I left her behind, in the custody of a native protector, but it was never easy. Where Hashim went, I went, and Idie went too, but she drew the line at wallowing in muddy paddy fields. On one unforgettable day, we left her on a desolate riverbank, way off the beaten track.

We never did that again. Hashim had promised a pleasant, motorized boat ride, up the Indus river to a place where thousands of ducks and geese fed in rice paddies. It sounded like a great goose shoot to me; Idie said it sounded like a romantic ride on one of India's great rivers.

Our motorized boat turned out to be a filthy native cargo boat, little more than a barge, with no "amenities" (bathrooms) and no place to hide from the hot sun. The boat's "motor" was a sun-blackened little man who poled us upstream for several uncomfortable hours. Sweating and seemingly unhappy, Idie's romantic thoughts were not making her smile.

The paddies were alive with ducks and geese. But they were all out of range. There was no cover, and the geese had posted sentries, big ganders outside the feeding flock. Having only ten shotgun shells with a heavy enough load to bring down the big birds, I had to get closer. Hashim said we should have brought a cow. "A cow?" I said.

"Yes, Sahib, geese do not fear cows. Hidden by a cow, we could have walked right up to them."

There was another solution, but it meant slithering in muddy paddies. Hashim and I left Idie alone with her protector, the boatman. We spent two glorious hours on our bellies in the mud. We got close enough for me to spend my ten shells and bring down six plump geese.

Back on the riverbank, strutting proudly, looking like little boys who had played too well, we laid the birds down for Idie to admire. She had always done that.

"That sweet Idie!" Relatives and friends always say. But oh my! Those tiny tapping feet, those snapping eyes—I wished for some of those relatives on that goose shoot!

Words with steel in them spilled out. Never again would she be left behind in some wild place with a protector who was half wild himself. Her fury made Hashim look for a place to hide, but there was none. As far as the eye could see there was neither tree, bush, nor large rock.

"I went that way," she stormed. "Hashim's watchdog followed close behind. I came back to the boat. Told him to get back on it and stay put. He just grinned. I went the other way, he stayed with me. The entire time you were away, that man was never more than two or three feet away!"

This was a new Idie. I had never seen her so upset, or furious. I was slow catching on, and she never said the magic word, but I finally got the message: there are no bathrooms on desolate riverbanks.

* * *

Idie heard from friends one day that a nice flat (apartment) would soon be available for rent near the Chummery. It would give us more privacy, so we decided to move, but continued our close relationship with the "boys."

News from the Bombay office told us Ed had suffered a heart attack and needed to return to the U.S. for treatment. Idie went to Bombay to help Faye pack. When she returned to Karachi, Idie flew back on British Airlines, just as the battle over Britain gained in ferocity. She told me she noticed a coolness in the attitude of our British friends in Bombay. We Americans were collectively referred to as "the second yellow race."

* * *

Late afternoon on Christmas Eve, the gang from the Chummery turned up at our place, bringing a large thermos filled with oysters from the Persian Gulf. A friendly ship's captain had brought them from his cold room. Would Idie make a cocktail sauce for these morsels, this gift from heaven? Of course, she would!

Someone hummed a Christmas carol and singing broke out. Caroling went on long into the night. When hunger came around again, Idie stripped our larder, including what we were to eat for Christmas dinner; our cupboard was bare. There were no grocery stores, butcher shops, or supermarkets in India in those days. The outlook for Christmas Day was bleak.

The gang would have dinner with their Standard Oil boss and his wife, who had heard from one of them about the looting of our pantry. She asked us to join them with their turkey, imported, of course. We thought of it as a thank-you. The turkey was served on Idie's large silver tray, as the boss's wife didn't have one. I don't believe I ever again saw a turkey served for dinner in India.

* * *

The ACCO policy on accepting Christmas gifts was severe. We were allowed anything we could eat or drink but nothing else. If we found money hidden in the bottom of a fruit basket, we needed to give it back; that's how bribes were paid.

Idie and I received several Christmas baskets of fresh and dried fruits and nuts (much of it from Kashmir). They were welcome, as fresh fruit was rarely seen in Karachi.

I violated company policy on one occasion, just before Gene left to go on home leave. At a small going-away party at the office, our cotton broker presented Gene and me with ornate silver pen and ink stands. I was delighted, especially when Idie said how much she loved the backdrop, set in a Kashmiri motif.

Idie's joy turned to anger later, when I told her I had discovered Pitu had been getting rich on company expense. Like the Persian carpets, the inkstand went into the closet.

What could we do about it? I remembered on our honeymoon, Idie had admired a gracefully shaped papier mâché beggar's bowl decorated with leaves and tiny birds. It was too expensive for us then, but this time a local silversmith from Kashmir crafted a replica of it with the inkstand silver. Idie said it was one of her favorite belongings.

* * *

Opening our front door in Karachi was like playing Russian roulette. It never stirred up any adventures for me, but when Idie opened it, something always happened.

Idie knew the unwritten rule: Memsahibs don't answer doorbells; "unclean" bearer boys do. That didn't stand in the way when she was doing a favor for Smitty, a new friend of mine.

"A friend will arrive from the up-country tomorrow afternoon," Smitty said, "and I don't want him at my office." Since I would be at my office, he wondered if Idie could receive him at our place and telephone Smitty."

No problem.

So, opening the door, Idie told me she expected to greet a dapper English gentleman and found herself eye to eye with a dirty, dark-skinned man carrying a rough walking stick almost as long as he was tall. He was barefooted and unshaven; his black hair was matted with cow's dung, his body smeared with ashes; and he wore nothing than a one white loincloth.

He was a *sadhu,* a holy man to Hindus, and an apparition of doom to Idie, she confessed later. Frozen into incredulity, her instinct told her to slam the door and shout for our bearer. Then the man spoke before she could holler. "Smitty sent me," he said, in a cultured British voice.

This was Smitty's friend? Idie said later she wondered what to do next and stared while the man quietly stared back. A promise is a promise. She had promised Smitty she would receive his friend.

When speech returned, she said, "Well then, come in."

She took him onto the verandah and offered him a chair. "Perhaps not," he said with a descriptive hand motion along his dirty body. Sitting on the floor, closing his eyes, he assumed the position of a Buddha in deep concentration. Leaving him there, Idie telephoned Smitty, who arrived in a few minutes.

Later, Smitty told us the man was British, born and raised in India, on a mission in the service of His Majesty's government.

Idie had met Kipling's modern prototype of "Kim" and had unwittingly played a cameo part in the "great game" of espionage. Colonel Creighton, in Kipling's book, was a secret agent in British Colonial India. My friend, Colonel Smith (Smitty), was known in Karachi as chief censor of civilian mail. He too was an important player in the great espionage game.

* * *

I suppose it was inevitable Idie would become friendly with the one Japanese man in town. He was a kind old gentleman who sold toys and curios in a shop in the port area of Karachi. Idie liked to admire his trinkets, as well as the view of the harbor. All activity in it could be clearly seen from where the old man sat in his shop. Idie's puzzle caper began there.

I was a nut about puzzles, so Idie bought one for me. A simple thing, four or five little sticks fitted together into one whole. She gave it to me with all the Chummery gang looking on. They were as nutty about puzzles as I was.

It came apart easily, and much to my chagrin and the delight of Idie and jeering onlookers, I could not put it back together. Having whipped me, the devilish thing soundly thrashed all the others, except Idie. When offered a chance to "have a go" at it, she modestly declined, saying demurely, "I am no good at puzzles."

If little pieces of wood can squeak, those did, as we college-educated non-achievers gave up for the night and left them unassembled. Idie confessed later she was alone the next morning and started working on the puzzle. The old man had shown her how to do it; she wanted to put it together as a surprise for the gang when everyone got home. But, alas, she had forgotten the key, how to lock the pieces together.

That night, we men, having nursed bruised egos all day, again attacked the devilish thing. Still, we could not put it together. Unable to restrain herself any longer, Idie finally spoke up. "I have changed my mind," she said. "Let me try." She paused for a moment as if in deep study and then, picking up the sticks one by one, deftly slipped them into proper alignment. The room was silent, all eyes riveted on her busy fingers, and when she made that all-important final twist to lock it together, it was done. There it sat, fully assembled.

Bedlam! Idie had done the improbable. How had she done it?

"Ah, by watching you all," she said modestly, "I just figured it out."

Three days later she owned up: when she failed to assemble the puzzle that morning, she returned to the shop where her Japanese friend gently guided her fingers, again and again, until she could have put it together blindfolded.

End of story? Not quite. Idie had been unknowingly fraternizing with the enemy. The storekeeper was a retired admiral in the Imperial Japanese Navy, who was monitoring traffic in and out of Karachi harbor. He was arrested and interned as a spy the day after Pearl Harbor was bombed.

* * *

Life changed for Idie and me, and so many others, when the United States declared war on Japan. President Franklin Roosevelt called American company CEOs, with Americans working overseas, to Washington, D.C. Will Clayton was one of them. He worked with several war agencies, including those tasked with procuring strategic materials for the U.S.

A plan to "loan" overseas employees to government agencies allowed Americans already overseas to work for the Allied war effort. Cotton was needed for blankets and uniforms, mica sheets for radios and radar, talc for electronic equipment, and beryl ore as an alloy with copper for fighter plane bearings, special tools, and later the atomic bomb. I already had contacts with influential Indian citizens and British military personnel and became a conduit for messages between Allied forces and their spies.

PART III
THE WAR YEARS 1942–1945

Living in a Tent

SIXTEEN

UNNECESSARY PERSONS

February 1942 — Bombay

The war in Asia came closer to India when Britain lost Singapore, a strategic military base, to the Japanese in February 1942. All people considered unnecessary to the war effort, or not directly involved in commerce, were evacuated from India. Idie insisted she wanted to stay with me but was told by the U.S. consulate that if she did, both of us would be among the last to leave India. If she left with other Americans, I would have first priority because I had a wife in the U.S. Idie shrugged her shoulders and halfheartedly agreed to go. She told me about this incident later:

"We wives, mothers, and children of American men in India had been on a U.S. Navy freighter for a few days, becoming friends and learning to follow the captain's rules for blackout at night. Our route home was circuitous to avoid German U-boats in the waters between India and Africa.

"Suddenly, our worst fears came to life: we were awakened in the dead of night and told to assemble on deck—no exceptions. The woman in the cabin next to mine grabbed her hat on her way out the door and remarked, as she stood next to me on deck: 'I cannot believe I am going to meet my maker in this purple hat with the droopy paper geranium.' The crew had been told that there were German U-boats in the water around us. We all stayed very quietly on deck, even the children, until the captain thought it safe for us to go back to our cabins, although sleep was hard to come by."

* * *

The only way for me to know if Idie was safe was by cable from the Houston office. Confirmation of her safe arrival did not arrive until March 25. Postal mail was disrupted and took even longer than before. In order to keep busy when not at the office, I took several weekend excursions to keep from worrying.

Hashim asked me, on behalf of a friend, to shoot a crocodile that was terrorizing a small village some distance from Karachi. Women washed clothes and bathed in a stream near the village. The croc, swimming silently underwater, would surface in striking distance and snatch them off the riverbank.

We went there, lying on our bellies on the stream's bank in 110-degree heat. The croc appeared, after a miserable hour or two. My shirt was sopping wet; Hashim, however, never seemed to perspire.

The croc floated, showing nothing but his two eyes, offering a one-inch target about twenty-five feet away. Being more than ready, I raised my gun. Hashim urged patience.

"Shoot now, croc will sink, dead or alive. Soon he will get out on other side of water. Shoot then. Hit spot behind eyes. Break spine. We get croc."

So, we waited, watching the croc's eyes slowly make their way across a short expanse of water. The heat did not let up, flies were buzzing and stinging. Finally, the croc pulled himself out of the water and settled down, as if to soak up sunlight. Hashim whispered, "Shoot now, Sahib. Shoot carefully. Behind eyes."

I aimed carefully and gently pulled the trigger. That beast, all five or six feet and hundreds of pounds of him, exploded off the sand, powerful tail and hind legs jetting him out over the water, closing over him, never to be seen again.

"What happened, Hashim?"

"Sahib hit but hit wrong place."

* * *

In the off season, Hashim and I walked through brush and across plowed fields, checking the partridges' new crop. Walking single file on a narrow, grass covered path one day, Hashim suddenly lurched into me, almost knocking me flat. For the first and only time in our association, I was angry enough to choke him.

Hashim dove into the underbrush, trying, I thought, to escape a shouted reprimand. He emerged cheerfully carrying a five-foot-long cobra he had just killed. It was the only snake I ever saw while shooting, a cobra I would have stepped on had Hashim not knocked me away. Hashim had probably saved my life, and I had wanted to choke him!

* * *

March 17, 1942 — Karachi

My darling Idie: how often we wished time would stop, so we could carry one moment with us throughout all eternity. Now, I wish we could put the clock back so you would still be here. Then, I wish all the harder time would fly, the war would end, and you would be with me.

At last, the Yanks have come. The Chummery boys recently had a group over for dinner, but I was at the Chinese restaurant with Tiger and missed it. Do you remember our American pilot friend and his outlandish stories? It looks good to see so many Americans on the street.

Had a late breakfast on Sunday and a lot of gab with the boys. I went through our things again and found the old Rice football pictures. I took them to the Chummery, where a good time was had by all, presumably at my expense. Art wanted to see the yearbooks and asked what you were called before you became Witt so they could find your picture. Someone asked who my girlfriend was before you came along, so I showed them Mary Lou.

Written comments by the pictures about "Scrap Iron" and "Hurricane Harry" almost started a riot.

I must try to do a little work now. Bless you, dear one. I love you – Harry

* * *

April 1, 1942 — Karachi

Darling Idie: Ralph and Van both received their cables in the evening of the 24th. Mine came the next morning. I was so happy to get it! I can breathe easier now that you are safe. I keep hoping to get a letter from Cape Town every time the boy brings in the mail.

Standard Oil people have been coming through here on their way home. Had some from Calcutta, Madras, and China the other evening, so we had a poker game.

Easter holidays are here, but without you, I do not care much about it. Time was when your sunshine made the very air joyous. It isn't that way anymore. I won't tell you again how much I miss you.

Love you, Harry

* * *

    I couldn't help grinning from ear to ear when I heard Ed Waddell would be returning to India to manage the Metals Reserve wartime agency in Delhi, after consulting with Mr. Clayton. How I wished I could work with him!
    Ed arrived unexpectedly in Karachi one day, bringing my first letter from Idie. I could not have been happier. He had sent a cable from Cairo three days before but arrived ahead of it. I was at the Chummery when Ed's note came, saying he was at the hotel. If I had not known his writing, I would not have believed it.

Business was dull as ACCO was following a cautious policy. Before seeing Ed, I had decided to return to the States, spend a while with Idie, then do whatever I could for the war. There seemed to be no question, but I would be sent right back, even if I joined the Army. To see Idie, even for a short time, would be worth anything that happened later.

Ed's coming made a difference. On a commercial mission such as his, I could become immediately useful. My contacts with native merchants could enhance his new work, expediting the movement of strategic war materials brought by air from China to India and then flown to the U.S. There were all too few people who knew anything about India.

A broker came to the office to see me, but not on business. As a father, he wanted to thank an American for the consideration being shown his son in America. His son was in a R.A.F. training unit in Terrell, Texas, and had said that our people were doing everything possible to make the English lads happy. The father seemed grateful. Though not surprised, I was proud to hear our people were doing their part. The man's son also told his father that Dallas was quite spiffy.

May 1, 1942 — Karachi

Idie dear: your Cape Town letter arrived the afternoon Ed left. I was glad to get it—thank you! It was beat up like it had been through a war of its own. I am glad we can cable back and forth as I feel some of your letters were lost.

I was feeling sorry for myself the other day, then the next thought, like yours on the ship, was one a friend gave me long ago: "The Lord giveth and the Lord taketh away."

You went, Ed came. Be sweet – yours always, Harry

* * *

Ed returned to Karachi days later. I found him in the bathtub when I got home from the office, lustily singing. He stayed until Monday morning, working every minute. I managed, without much effort, to steer him into the Chinese restaurant on two occasions. We had a merry time trying almost everything they sold. Ed was doing a grand job at work, much to the surprise of many. They found it hard to understand how he managed, with apparent ease, to eliminate red tape. He had just finished one part of his work and was about to begin something else, traveling to small villages in the Punjab to procure minerals.

About this time, Hal was promoted to the position of ACCO boss in Bombay. He would not release me without cabling Houston. They left things to Hal, who decided I should stay where I was. I wanted to join Ed, but I sensed an open break with Hal would not gain anything. I gave up the flat and moved back into the Chummery. I was surprised to discover how little I missed having the car. Riding a bicycle to and from the office has helped me with energy and weight loss.

The "boys" and I helped, as best we could, at opening night for the Anglo/American Canteen. I fried hamburgers, although they could not be *pucca* (the best) because all the doings were not available in brands the Americans were used to. The canteen seemed to answer a much-felt need. The next planned project was a recreation room for the troops where they could write, read, listen to the gramophone, and play various games in congenial surroundings.

> July 17, 1942 — Karachi
>
> Darling Idie: Hal called and said he had received Houston's cable suggesting we close the Karachi office. If Ed still wants me, I will join him. His work keeps the army going, so I suppose it is just as important as the army. I will be two- or three-weeks clearing things up here. There is a court case between ACCO and some cotton merchants, trying to cheat us. It is possible they may get away, but I have done the best I could.
>
> As you probably guessed, I am glad we are closing. Think I would have been ready for a straitjacket if I sat around doing nothing much longer. Will cable the moment I know my plans.

I know you are wondering why you left. The news during the past few weeks must have answered you, but in the final analysis, my darling, is you left for the best of all reasons. While I am lost without you and miss you more than words can say, I am still glad you are back home.

It will probably be a long time before you return to India. I think we must prepare ourselves for a long separation and make the most of it. Nothing could make me happier than to have you with me again.

Sending you love and a prayer that I may see you soon.
Your Harry

* * *

Ed came back to Karachi before receiving my letter telling him we were closing the office. He seemed happy to hear it. Characteristic of Ed, I went to work immediately. It was of no importance to him that I still had to close the office. I made the rounds with him and officially became his Karachi representative. After listening to Ed about the things he wanted done, it became clear I knew too little about what was going on. The only thing to do was to go to Delhi and study the files.

Ed then left for Bombay, after making me the Special Representative of the Defense Supplies Corporation, Department of Commerce, Washington, D.C. Really sounded like sumpin!

ACCO did not lose anything on the sale of office equipment when we closed. There was a good demand for it. The U.S. Army took about half of it, and I had no difficulty in getting rid of the balance.

Mr. Macy, the American Consul in Karachi, paid me a very nice compliment when he heard I was closing the office and joining Ed. He asked what I would do for an office and then suggested I sit across from him, in his office. It was mighty nice of him.

Deciding to stay was not the easiest decision. I wanted to see Idie badly. I could have taken the next ship, but I knew I could spend only a short time with her; then I would be drafted into the Army. I had a long conversation with Ed and then decided the work I would be doing was of utmost importance to the war effort.

My flight to New Delhi provided no seats, only boxes of freight. I slept most of the five hours with a "chute" for a pillow and a wooden box for a bed. We ran into heavy rain and did a lot of bouncing around. The pilot tried to get above it and then below it, but since neither was possible, we just bounced through it.

I had barely arrived when memories of Idie's and my one day in Delhi came rushing back. I focused my mind on the job before me and went to the American Missions office and then City Bank, where they were helping Ed get organized.

When the U.S. Army set up branch headquarters in New Delhi, something like a gold rush developed. Everyone from buck private on up rushed to employ cheap labor. One story I heard was that a black private was sitting outside his barracks, watching a black Indian boy polish a pile of government-issue boots. The boy's wages were no more than a few cents a day. A sergeant came along and asked, "What's going on here?"

"Oh, Sarge, us Sahibs don't do no work," the G.I. replied.

The U.S. Army brass was outraged. Tantamount to slave labor, they said. An order was issued: U.S. Army personnel must pay local employees no less than the equivalent of one hundred U.S. dollars per month. Consternation broke out among British officers, thinking that such a wage for menial labor would wreck the Indian economy. They insisted that the U.S. revoke the order or leave India. The order was revoked.

* * *

August 20, 1942 — Karachi

Dearest Idie: I am back in Karachi for a few days. enjoying the new work. It seems to grow every day, but I still think I will be able to work myself out of a job before anyone expects it. Presently, all I do is make reports and see that others do likewise. When this routine is standardized, there will no longer be a need for a troubleshooter in Karachi. Ed may dream up other things for me long before I find the end of this one.

We were all excited yesterday. The rumor was that the Allies opened the long awaited second front, and my telephone buzzed continually. I am now supposed to know what is going on all over the world, particularly in regard to the war. All highly secret stuff is supposed to be my dish. It turned out to be merely a large commando raid, but it was good excitement for a while.

My life is quiet; there is little chance of it improving until you return. I still see my quota of movies, have a weekly poker session, and that is about all. Most of the learning relating to the new job is over, and ACCO business is practically completed.

Well, back to work—Love you, too much, Harry

* * *

My work grew as Ed sent me letters with more things to do. I was grateful I had not experienced any problems, except for the monsoon. The rivers were on a rampage, the canals were overloaded, and a great deal of damage had been done. The railroads completely stopped running for a week. It took two weeks before they could resume. The only connection with the Punjab was the narrow-gauge across the desert, which made shipping materials very difficult.

With the office closed, Gene was undecided about what to do next. He would need to go to the ACCO court case, as would Hal, but I knew I would have trouble getting them both there. The magistrate finally became angry with the lawyers on the other side and told them to finish with me.

I hardly recognized Karachi. A new Chinese restaurant opened every week, as well as several cafés, patronized mostly by troops. A nightclub had opened too. I noticed the gym was not as crowded as it used to be on Saturdays.

* * *

I found an unexpected source for laughs. When new fellows asked me how long I had been in India, I said five years. They invariably came back with, "What did you say?" I would repeat it and they would shout, "*What*—five years?" Most were homesick soon after they arrived but felt differently later on.

I took another trip to New Delhi, this time via Lahore. My companion was an old employee of Spencer & Co. We settled most of the problems concerning the war and the world in general and became quite chummy.

I had a full day to waste in Lahore before I could get the next train, so I strode over to the sitting room but found it packed. People were sleeping on benches, overflowing to the floor. It did not seem a pleasant place to squat. I had a so-so shave from the R.R. barber, then ate the biggest breakfast I could find in preparation for a long day. After leaving my baggage in the cloakroom, I hired a taxi and went touring.

When I returned to the station to wait for the 8:30 p.m. train, my companion was British, returning to Bombay after a shooting holiday in Kashmir.

We arrived in Delhi at eight the next morning. I found out Ed had come from Bombay the day before. Scattered papers on too many tables to remember were in his room. Many people competed for space in another small room, but the work got done. I watched and then tagged along to the secretariat and army headquarters. At night, we drank vodka and burgundy and talked over past, present, and future. Had a roaring good time.

The fast of Ramadan came while I was in Delhi. Ed and I went to the big mosque; it was quite a show. People of all descriptions lined the road for blocks. Picture the devout who came to wash and pray, the beggars seeking alms, the sideshow wallas seeking their fortune, and sightseers, like us, who came to satisfy curiosity. A hobby horse merry-go-round entertained little children, some in rags and some in silk.

A small, wooden Ferris wheel with four tiny cars resounded with noise and a great deal of pleasure. Vendors of fried foods did a roaring business. The papers reported fifty thousand people in attendance. When we got back to the hotel, we asked Ed's boy, Abdul, to tell us about the ceremony.

He acted out four movements-standing, bending, bowing, sitting—called "Ek Kakad," which is considered one movement. After either clasping hands as we do in prayer, or opening them in a begging gesture, they implore Allah's mercy as the ceremony ends.

SEVENTEEN
STRATEGIC MATERIALS

October 1942 — Up-Country India

In my role as the Special Representative of the Defense Supplies Corporation, I was responsible for checking reports from the engineers in the up-country provinces of India, where they suspected deposits of mica, beryl ore, and talc.

I also traveled to small villages in Rajputana, organizing procurement and shipment of those materials to the U.S. as quickly as possible. I was the first American buyer to pay local villagers for quality beryl and soon became known as the sahib who would pay good money for rocks.

* * *

In October, I took a ride on a narrow-gauge railroad to Assam. My companions were Lieutenant Mueller of the U.S. Air Army and a young English couple returning to Calcutta after their home leave. Mueller had flown with the R.A.F. for a year and had recently been transferred back to our army. He liked England very much, especially the blackout. "Boy, that black out was really sumpin," he said. He was full of stories.

He told us when the mending pile stacked up, the fellows wore a frayed shirt on a date with their best girl and made sure she saw it. Invariably, the girl offered to mend it, and the shirt went back into the drawer until it should be needed again.

There were special outhouses near the officers' quarters for bathing but with no hot water. The Americans never got used to it. Mueller once mentioned this to a girlfriend, so she invited him over on a Saturday to take a bath. He said it was marvelous.

A tile bathroom with plenty of hot water and a warm room! This became an almost regular Saturday visit. He was making eighty dollars a month and about forty of it was used for room and board, leaving little for partying. That is when the English stepped in. If the fellows did not have money to get into town, the girls would come out and pool their resources with the guys, and the party went on.

In some ways, Mueller was a kindred spirit because he liked eating at every station. We had our second breakfast at Aligarh, trying each of the four courses as if it had been yesterday since we had eaten. We played hearts and casino, at which I was very lucky, winning both. We also read the usual trash.

We arrived in Allahabad at eight-thirty in the evening. Since Mueller and I were destined to fly on the same plane, we went to the Adelphia Club, an eating place for transient pilots of the Ferry Command and then to our quarters.

We slept on cots, under a net, with several men to a room. Most of the guests were just passing through and young enough to enjoy themselves. It felt like returning to college.

I was up at seven thirty for breakfast, only to find the others had long since eaten and departed. This being India, however, breakfast was still there. It consisted of pomola, oatmeal, French toast, eggs, coffee, guava jelly, butter, and water without asking for it.

I walked to town, about three miles away, and enjoyed the lovely spreading trees, green grass, and fresh flowers. Saw the University of Allahabad and home of Nehru.

Spent most of the next day looking for people to work with. I finally got everything settled without finding all the people I should have found. New fellows came in late, all young and full of beans, ready to go.

One had his hair cut by the local native barber. It looked awful, he said. He tried to talk his buddies into a haircut. Surprisingly, he succeeded.

"Cut it shorter," one onlooker yelled, but threats from the chair ranged all the way from cutting off the barber's ears to cutting his hair. The barber was a different man when it was all over.

I spent the following day near the phone, waiting to hear that the plane was ready. News came I would get away the next morning. I was glad to be on with the job.

* * *

I left Allahabad on the morning of October 14. The countryside was beautiful from the air, the usual patchwork design but more varied. Those fields were green, a pleasant change from the parched brown of Karachi.

I fell asleep for a time and awoke to find we were sailing over mountains. Some were heavily forested, others bare and rocky. One snow-covered one stood high above all the others and sparkled in the sun, like a great diamond.

We passed over many rivers. They seemed to sprout up every few miles, switching back and forth like a corkscrew. Occasionally, a snowcap peeped over the outer ranges of the Himalayas. Tea plantations became more numerous. A group of buildings, including living quarters and a processing plant, were always located at one end of the garden, and then, long straight lines of shade trees with squatty tea plants below. One garden after another passed by, connected by the crooked country road and the almost miniature railway. Tiny bridges spanned wide rivers, with the jungle crowding in wherever there was no tea.

We landed about noon. Even that was interesting: coolies were working nearby, all under parasols. Imagine several hundred Indian coolies, almost naked, each one under a parasol!

I stayed in the same place as my pilot. The house was built in the middle of a tea garden, shady and cool but not luxurious. Spent the afternoon working, then saw a double feature movie.

My bunkmate was a fellow from Georgia. A well-mannered, soft-spoken little man with wife and child at home. I enjoyed him because his way of talking reminded me of Idie, and because he was interested in India. I think he enjoyed me because I could tell him a few things about India and because I left him a tin of candy for his sweet tooth.

Most of my second day was spent writing a report—that is, as much of it as I could concentrate on. The fellows next door had trained in San Antonio and spent the entire day with intermissions for food and reliving days and nights spent with girlfriends.

* * *

I started my long trek back to Karachi on October 16. It was the most uncomfortable, and yet the most interesting part of the trip. It began in a car if you could call it that. It was close to falling apart, and the driver insisted on driving on the wrong side of the road. He was roundly cursed many times. I exerted much willpower to bear it in silence, thanking providence a little too often for narrow squeezes.

It was nearly dark when we started. The road was gravel with plenty of holes, barely wide enough for two cars. Our lights were poor so we could not make good time, even with a madman at the wheel. I was not sorry. It had been a long day, beginning at six. I had accomplished a great deal and was tired in a satisfied kind of way—the way you feel when you look back over the day's happenings and cannot find anything undone that should have been done.

A cool breeze was just strong enough to ruffle the leaves of the tall shade trees protecting their brood of tea plants. A few fireflies began to buzz, then more and more, until they looked like a great milky way transposed from sky to tea garden. It was one of those nights I shall always remember and be sorry Idie was not there.

As twilight blended into night, we passed fishing parties of natives trying their luck in the ditches and small ponds. Rivers had recently overflowed, leaving fish in fields and streams not usually having them. Big bunches of straw were tied onto long sticks and lit to make blazingly bright torches. The fish were attracted to the fire, and the fishermen pulled them out of the water in homemade straw baskets or handwoven nets.

I finally boarded the train to Delhi. I could have flown, but part of my job was to ride the train, another narrow-gauge antique. All day, the first day, I had a compartment to myself. Soon after dark, people began to pile in. Those seats are hard! We slept six people the two nights of the journey in the usual four berth compartments, with the usual amount of luggage Indian travelers carried. I did not enjoy that part of the trip, but looking out the window helped, as grain was ripening in the fields, trees were green, and the rivers had more character than the muddy trickles we were accustomed to in Karachi.

I changed trains three times. Each time was a mad scramble for the few first-class carriages available. Ed was waiting for me at the station. We got up at three in the morning and took off at 5:30, my first trip in a flying boat. The first part was smooth but later became rough. I read and slept all day. Monster spray covered the windows every time we landed or took off.

Our first stop was on a lovely lake in Rajputana. It was cold, as the sun had not been up long. We left the ship in a launch and strolled around the office while the boat refueled. Ed and I thought we saw a flight of teal (ducks) but could not be sure. We were told the lake was full of fish, but the ruler forbade them to be caught. Also, it was full of crocodiles that could not be shot.

We made it to Calcutta just before sundown, driving into town in the B.O.A.C. bus, then taking a taxi to the hotel. When we checked in, Ed realized he had lost his briefcase. Ed, without that briefcase, would be like a professor without his notebook. We spent an hour looking for it, then decided to take a dinner break. The desk clerk stopped us as we headed into the restaurant and told us an American officer had used the taxi after us and had brought the valise in. Halleluiah!

* * *

December 28, 1942 — Karachi

Dearest Idie: I will not tell you about Christmas. You know what it is like here. I missed you more than I have ever missed you, but that is natural this time of year.

I tried to get some geese for the lads here. I got stuck just beyond Mirpur Sabro. There were nine coolies at the time, but they could not push us out. They did not really want to as they were having such a good time making faces at themselves in the shiny part of the headlights.

Finally collected about twenty-five others who did manage to lift us out. I gave them five rupees, and Hashim begged me not to give them more because they would dig the hole deeper for our return trip. He was right. On the way back, I had to follow the canal about five miles before I could cross. The coolies were waiting but disappointed when I detoured. All the bridges were washed out on the camel trail. I came back with a new record: returned empty-handed.

Hope your Christmas was a happy one. All those yet to come will be much happier, especially if we can share them. Bless you, my darling, I pray that we may be together soon.

All my love, Harry

* * *

I continued to travel throughout India in 1943, procuring and shipping strategic materials out of Karachi to U.S. war factories, as well as coordinating shipments of materials flown from China to Assam, then transferring them to cargo planes bound for the U.S.

January 19, 1943 — Cawnpore

Dearest Idie: for the first time in my life, I am living in a tent. Not bad either, but there are things you would not appreciate!

I left Karachi Saturday morning and had a day in Delhi, reading files. I expect to stay a day and a half here, then will go to Bombay for a day or two and return to Karachi. Next will be Rajputana. I am enjoying the travel but wish you were with me. I think of you all the time.

I meant to cable you about settling the court case, but I forgot. It is done. We got back five thousand more than we spent. Ed has promised to tell you about it.

The pouch is closing, have to say goodbye. Love to all,
Harry

* * *

Ed returned to the States, and I took over his job as Special Representative of the Metals Reserve Company under the Board of Economic Warfare (BEW) and the Reconstruction Finance Corporation (RFC).

In February, I felt it necessary to write a comprehensive letter to the main office of the Metals Reserve Company in Washington, D.C. I also sent a copy to the National City Bank of New York in Bombay, informing them of the difficulties in procuring beryl in the native states of Mewar (Udaipur) and Ajmer–Merwars.

Most of the beryl found in that area needed to be blasted from hard quartz and feldspar. The workers had no power tools or pumps to dry out the open pits in monsoon. Without the power tools I was requesting, I expected a drastic curtailment in production. The only available explosive was gunpowder.

I also requested clarification on trade agreements between competing entities. I was anxious to have a free hand in India to negotiate terms with people we knew. Delay occurred when the notorious Marwaris (a south Asian ethnolinguistic group) entered the beryl fields and bribed miners to falsify their reports. We had experienced something of this between Major Crockshank of the Geological Survey of India and an entity in Naziabad. Both were offering the same price and the same terms, but the miner falsified statements from each party in the hopes of getting a few rupees more from either one.

We eliminated the possibility of this recurring by making Futshally and Co. our only buying company for small quantities in the whole of Ajmer–Merwars and Mewar.

* * *

On one trip, Andrew Corry, our geologist, and I traveled by jeep to Rajputana and got completely lost. There was supposed to be a mine in the vicinity, but nobody seemed to know where. The villages were four or five miles apart and in each, we picked up a native to show us the way to the next one. Invariably, they complained their head spun because of the tremendous speed. This, on bullock cart tracks! I thought it would be better if the guide sat in the front seat, but that was not possible. We stayed lost most of the time.

Our party also included a major in the British army who was a geologist, plus an old Mohammedan and two clerks. The feudal system was still alive. Villages were built as a part of the old Rajput forts and castles; people lived under the walls and walked to the fields every day. Most of the land belonged to a headman, basically a feudal lord.

The picturesque villages had incredibly narrow streets. Most were not wide enough for our car, so we circled the village. Mothers ran to bring their children to see it, the first for many of them. In most doorways, we saw women sitting at primitive spinning wheels, as well as a steady stream of women carrying jugs of water on their heads, going to the central community well. All of them wore silver ornaments around their ankles and in their hair.

It was after nine in the evening before we got back to where we were staying. An Indian dinner was waiting for us. We hoped we might be too late to have to accept it, but luckily, they did not try to force any of their sweets on us, so it was not too bad. We were tremendously hungry, and that helped.

The next day, we moved on to another mine but over an easier country. As the commissioner was due, we could not have the bungalow. We ended up in a new bungalow of a Marwari and were quite comfortable.

Next to the house, a company of the thief caste was camped. Every night they went around the village, stealing. In the morning, around eleven o'clock, the police came to take their boodle away, whip a few, and then wait for the next day to do it all over again.

Some of the women danced for us. They were about as dirty a crowd as I had seen, but they were graceful. One wore a deep purple skirt with a maroon border and jacket. She had bells on her ankle and wrists. While two men beat crude drums, she and the other women whined their type of singing while dancing. We stood on a balcony, looking down. As they whirled and twisted, I was reminded of a large flower opening its petals, then gracefully folding. When they had finished, I tossed them a handful of small coins. Two little girls caught them. Not even one coin slipped their fingers.

A headman lamented his religion allowed him only one wife at a time. We sympathized. It later developed there were no limits to the number of dancing girls he could have, and he had a few. We saw the favorite, quite pretty. Many of our days exploring turned out like that.

The plan was to go to South India, then back to Karachi. We were surprised to be officially informed that Ed had resigned. We did not know the reasons why.

* * *

March 22, 1943 — Bombay

Dearest Idie: this letter has been a long-time a-stewing. I made notes for you but never could get them into a letter. I did manage to write four or five hand-written pages while in Bombay but didn't complete them. My last trip kept me away nearly five weeks, and I find it difficult to write until I become somewhat stationary.

I miss you so much that I would do almost anything to get back to you. Then, I begin to think about this war and my work. It is much bigger than personalities. In the next three weeks I should know more. Be sweet, my darling, I'll see you as soon as I can.

Did you think I had forgotten March 3rd, my darling? On March 3rd, I was on my way to Mangalore, on the Malabar coast. I sat in an old rambling house, thinking how nice it would be to live in such a place. There was a large compound, bright with flowers and many trees. Tall palms, mangoes, and papaya were in every yard. There is a strong Portuguese influence. The people are friendly and much happier than most, though no better off financially, probably worse.

Thinking of you always, Harry

* * *

The most surprising aspect of the trip cropped up in Mangalore. I was accustomed to seeing coolies say their prayers as all good Hindus do first thing in the morning, wash to the tune of correct mantras, cook food, and draw the water before going off to work. But in Mangalore, they did not. They rushed to find out what the New York cotton market had closed at the night before!

All the Indians I knew loved to gamble, especially those who never managed a square meal. In Mangalore, they ran a lottery, in which a ticket could be bought for as little as a *pice* (smallest Indian coin). They had been cheated so often that a reliable check was necessary. Opening and closing rates of the New York market were considered infallible and not subject to manipulation. Several thousand rupees a day passed through this lottery. One fellow set himself up as a broker and got a daily telephone call from Bombay, after the quotation was received by wire.

* * *

My next train travel began in Tiruchirappalli, leaving at midnight, with a change at four in the morning. The connection was late, and I had to wait an hour on a platform with the usual crowd of food and cigarette vendors, smelly coolies, loudly talking wallas and squalling brats.

My one day in Cochin was wonderful. I wanted to stay longer and rest but didn't. I found a club overlooking the sea, with fishermen manning big nets. A lovely, lazy spot but I couldn't be lazy. I took my first rickshaw ride and found it enjoyable. Surprisingly, the coolie did not seem to have any difficulty with my weight.

From Cochin, I hired a taxi to Quilon. We crossed the backwater several times. It was lined with tall palm trees, bamboo and other vegetation that is always a pleasure to see after Karachi's bleak desert.

After this trip, I went back to "Trichy." I was invited to visit Sriringam Temple, ten miles away. It featured a museum and library, which I enjoyed. Among the old daggers, knives, and shields, I was intrigued to find daggers designed to be used with a clenched fist. The idea was to fight with your fists, concealing a six-inch dagger.

I also saw some very old books, shelves of them, being scanned by men who looked nearly as old as the books.

Most interesting of all was the ivory. It was believed to be hundreds of years old. The work was beautiful and depicted the love life of their deities, nothing being left to the imagination. I couldn't help coveting one exquisite box covered with carved ivory panels.

As I was leaving, the temple elephants came out to greet me. They were enormous animals with great tusks. One walked up close to me, knelt, raised his trunk, and blew out what was called a salaam to the illustrious visitor. That was my cue to pass out baksheesh. I would gladly have given my pocketbook and all in it to get the brute to move a few feet away. I held up a four Anna piece. The elephant took it in his trunk and passed it up to the mahout on his head, trumpeting again. This time to say thank you, I was told.

* * *

April 1, 1943 — no place given

Dearest Idie: I wrote a letter to Mr. Clayton, saying I thought the work was slowing down and I wanted to go home.

Today I am a man! And how do I know? Why, I found three gray hairs! How long do you think it will take me to become a distinguished gray-headed old gent?

Went to the Macy bungalow for dinner a few nights ago—it was like walking into an American home. General and Mrs. Hind were there. Both remembered you and asked me to send you their greetings.

I hope by the time you get this, Mr. C. will have said, "Come a running."

Love you, Harry

* * *

It was a long time before I heard back from Mr. C. In the meantime, everyone was telling me what a wonderful job I was doing and how important it was in winning the war. It was really because of the people I knew that I could do so well. Ed and I were still communicating with each other; I wrote him a letter about my intentions not to wait for a reply from Mr. C. but to resign and go back to Idie.

Ed's reply was that neither he nor the company he was now working for (the Metals Reserve) had any objection to my resigning and returning to the U.S. He also told me Mr. C. would reply soon, so I waited for his response. Then, I received a cable from Mr. C., making it clear that he considered it important I stay. I cabled Idie the bad news, while Macy acted pleased. It was flattering to know that my fellow workers did not want me to leave, but I hoped never to have as much trouble getting a job as I did in getting rid of that one!

I decided to write BEW, saying I would remain indefinitely, provided Idie could join me. Otherwise, only so long as it took to find a replacement within six months. I suggested Idie be employed by the company, as I thought her transportation could be arranged by them.

* * *

In May, Andrew Corry and I spent a few days exploring Jodhpur, staying with the Rao Raja Hanut Singh, brother of the ruling prince. His house, he told us, was forty-two years old, and it looked like it on the outside. Inside, it was modern and beautiful.

My room was large enough for twin beds, three large chairs, a desk, and a dressing table with a huge circular mirror. The bathroom was tremendous and very modern.

Hanut's room was also his office, and since his family was away, we spent most of our time there. He was one of the world's best polo players and collected old hunting prints in England. They were set in the most beautiful frames; silver, about four inches wide with a delicate sari-like border.

There were many other rooms, all furnished in simple elegance, including a billiard and trophy room. The prince had several leopard, bear, and tiger skins, of which he was quite proud. A high-caste Rajput prince who lived like a prince.

He was building a new palace but also experiencing shortages of material because of the war. Since it was unfinished, we could see it all. Once it was occupied, that would have been impossible. Besides the usual large banquet and business halls, with beautiful cut glass chandeliers, there was also a large swimming pool, squash court, and theater complex for stage productions or movies. Even a children's garden with an aviary!

We paid a short visit to the fort. We started late and had time to see only part of it. Built five hundred years ago on top of a high hill, its walls drop straight down for perhaps two hundred feet. It had never been taken by an opposing force. The last walk had to be done by foot, a hard climb, even over the newly paved road. During the old days, it must have been almost unapproachable.

At the side of the last big gate, I saw a large stone plaque set into the wall with the hand imprints of many women who marched on their way to cast themselves into the fire. I remembered hearing about the custom of *suttee*, in which a widowed woman must burn herself. Some handprints were pitifully small, probably made by child brides who were too young to know they were married. We were told the women were doped and then worked into a feverish pitch before they went up.

The old cannons and swords caught my interest, as did seeing the earliest known machine gun. It was a double row of small cannon (ten barrels) mounted on a special gun carriage. The first broadsides from such guns must have caused panic and consternation in the ranks of the enemy.

* * *

August 3, 1943 — Karachi

Dearest Idie: I was going to be home for Christmas. What a sad illusion. I should have said some Christmas. Macy says it will be about 1949. He has a new name for me—Indispensable! I had hoped for March 3rd, but it is now certain I shall not even make my birthday in August. Someday, I shall tell you all the developments and reasons behind them.

Today is one of the not-so-good days. There was a letter from OEW (Office of Economic Warfare) saying you could not come out by air, telling me what a great guy I am and what a tremendous contribution I am making to the war effort. It also outlined new work soon to descend upon me.

That is all very affirming, but it fell short of doing anything about my request to stay here until Mr. Somebody-or-Other arrives. They make it tough on a fella. There is no question as to the importance of the new work, and with my background, I am the logical one to do it. On the other hand, there must be others who can do it.

I try to see the problem objectively. I have been careful not to let my own interests govern decisions about the work to be done. I have to be fair about our sacrifice as compared to those of others. I find them small indeed.

When and if I do get back, I realize, and you must too, that we shall not have much time together. So, darling, be prepared to see me only to lose me again, should I return.

This letter isn't vey cheerful but neither am I. Hope it does not pull you down. There is a flat available at 3 Ramsey Road, which I shall move into if I stay. Be sweet. Miss you as much as anyone could.

All my love, Harry

* * *

Some of my difficulties in getting back to Idie had to do with the reorganization of U.S. war agencies in Washington. Several agencies merged to make better use of men and materials as the war progressed. Metals Reserve joined the Foreign Economic Administration (FEA) during the summer. Then, in September 1943, Mr. Clayton, the new Assistant Secretary of Commerce and War Property Administrator, sent me a cable, requesting a conference with him in Washington, D.C.

You better believe I hurried up the gangplank of a ship leaving Bombay before any more changes could occur. I got off in Panama and went to the Officer's Club, where I collapsed and was taken to the Naval Hospital. Diagnosed with malaria, I remember someone coming to visit me. I asked him to let my wife know where I was, but Idie never received the message. She told me later that secretaries from the State Department had called her, looking for me.

She said: "I don't know where he is. He works for you. Why don't you know where he is?"

They traced my steps backward, but it took some time. Idie, ever resolute that my guardian angel would take care of me, accepted Mr. Clayton's invitation to go to Washington and wait. She had been given a room at the Hay-Adams Hotel, plus passes to a session of Congress and other sights.

I was still not well when I left Panama to complete my trip to Washington, this time in a military plane. I was admitted to the 194th Station Hospital in Miami, Florida, with acute tertian malarial fever. I stayed there for ten days, finally arriving in the capital around October 24. What a celebration Idie and I had!

Many people seemed to want to meet me and hear of my experiences in purchasing and handling beryl ore under primitive conditions. They were also interested in my contacts with influential Indian citizens and with American and British officers.

Although I did not know it at the time, U.S. scientists had been working to enhance beryl's chemical properties to become beryllium, which could aid the flow of uranium neutrons to produce atomic fission, a step in making the first atomic bomb.

In November, Idie and I traveled to Houston for Thanksgiving. I received a letter from the Acting Chief of the Industrial Minerals Division, and I answered, confirming I would return to India but before mid-January at the earliest, as I was still under a doctor's care for a third bout of malaria. I also asked for a passport for Idie.

On December 18, 1943, a memorandum from the Associate Chief of Metals and Minerals confirmed I would transfer from the Metals Reserve Company to the United States Commercial Company (USCC). My duties would be to supervise the shipment of strategic materials, notably, mica and beryl ore, through the Port of Karachi. I would also negotiate purchasing those materials in India.

* * *

In the spring of 1944, Idie discovered she was pregnant. I saw her struggle as she faced another difficult decision in our married life. Hugging her tightly, I then stepped back to let her think through the option of traveling in wartime to India, or going to Tucson, Arizona, where her mother lived with Idie's sister-in-law and her young daughter. Her brother, Ernest, was in the Pacific with the Navy.

After much thought, Idie made the decision not to accompany me to India. Although pleased with our good news, I think my forced smile betrayed my unhappiness with what could be another long separation from Idie.

On May 3, 1944, I checked in with the Army induction station at Fort Meyers, Virginia, because I had been living in the U.S. for several months. I was given an Occupational Deferment for necessary government work in India.

I left Tucson in late May, expecting to travel extensively in the up-country.

EIGHTEEN
BACK TO INDIA

May 31, 1944 — Miami Beach, Florida

Dearest Idie: it seems hard to believe letters are again the order of the day. We can almost say the baby came by correspondence. Tried to call you but could not get through, so sent you a telegram. Hope you have it by now.

The trip was not too bad. Pretty rough from Tucson to Fort Worth but smooth the rest of the way. Rode as far as Fort Worth next to an American Airlines official and enjoyed listening to some postwar dreams for travel of tomorrow.

I arrived more or less on schedule. Do not know when I will leave for India, perhaps day after tomorrow. When I know, I shall not be able to call you, as we are restricted to the hotel as soon as we hear we are leaving. This place was a luxury hotel during the boom days. It is not what it was, but still comfortable. The food is good and cheap.

Everyone who leaves here is given an identification certificate with an army rating based on the amount of money you make. I am classed as a major. It is only a safety measure which ensures treatment as an officer if one falls into enemy hands. We must attend lectures, which can be done in one day.

You know how I love you—Harry

* * *

My flight was more pleasant than I expected in wartime. A flight clerk passed out cold fruit juice, ice, water, and coffee. Then, good box lunches. Time passed quickly.

I went first to Karachi, then to Delhi. busy all the time. I stayed in the FEA bungalow with three other fellows. One was a college history professor at a Minnesota college, one was a professor at Southern California, and the other attended Oxford, where he directed and sang in musical productions. All three were musically inclined and were also good at languages, frequently filling the air with French, Russian, and Arabic. If the conversation had not come down to earth, I thought I would have to talk with the mali.

I managed to arrive without my bag. Had with me the camera, shaving things, and one of change of khakis that came back from the cleaner too late to get into the big bag. Fortunately, I had enough to get by, especially since my suitcase with three suits was already on the way.

I told Idie that if I stuck to the program, I would be traveling constantly and could not mail letters regularly. I planned to write and send several at a time. I asked her not to worry if she did not hear from me often.

June 16, 1944 — Delhi

Sweetheart: I have been eating lots of mangoes and wishing you could have some. Curry and rice taste good again. I have eaten both for lunch nearly every day since I arrived in Delhi.

We professors live a quiet life. Every other evening, guests come for dinner. We cover a broad field of conversation and nearly always put forward complicated solutions to various problems. We have dinner between 8:15 and 8:45. All of us are quite sleepy by ten and go to bed by eleven if we can get rid of the guests.

There is no news of my lost bag. My possessions are surprisingly small now, and I am amazed at how little I am bothered about it. I had a couple of things made, so I wonder what I will do when the bag arrives from Karachi. With the work I am doing now, I do not need anything more than what I have.

Thinking of you constantly. The girls in the office are hoping you could send some nail polish, if it is not too much trouble.

Miss you. Love you, Harry

* * *

The work of procuring and shipping strategic materials had just begun. It would take some time before I could really get going. I needed to focus on that one job and let everything else go. It would be tougher than I thought, with no idea how long it would take. There was also a good possibility I would need to visit Nepal.

I was surprised at how well I was feeling, suffering nothing other than the heat. Even the rapid change of food and water had not affected me. For that, I was thankful.

One day, I left Bombay without any notice. Consequently, getting on the train was a struggle. I finally ended up in the oldest coach on the railroad. It was really a second-class carriage with one of the bars painted out to make it first. Having no pictures on the wall was a dead giveaway.

Railway stations had not changed. All the wallas and their wares were still present. Neither had any of them lost their voices, so the noise was familiar.

A Bengali man and I started out alone. He had more than his share of luggage, but since I had nothing but a small canvas bag, we were not overcrowded. At midnight, two young English officers got on with all their worldly possessions: tin trunks, eats, mosquito nets, handbags, water bottles, etc. They were nice young lads but a trifle too British for me, in their attitude of India and the war.

I arrived in Kodarma early in the morning. I stayed with Frank Watts, who would soon return to the States. He was staying with Mr. and Mrs. Watson. Watson was an American manager of an English mica mining firm with a French name. His wife was French, charming, and a good cook.

Watson and his predecessors had done well. There was a large master bungalow where the Watsons, Watts, and Knuckey, a Britisher employed by Watson's firm, lived. Many other bungalows dotted the landscape and were also occupied. I accepted the guest bungalow and reigned there all alone. I especially enjoyed the bathtub. It was nearly six feet long and fit me perfectly. I needed it after the dusty train ride.

Mrs. Watson raised chickens and turkeys. Nearby villagers brought her their choice vegetables and fruit. Arbor seats with brilliant bougainvillea climbing over them decorated the front yard. One wall of the verandah held a collection of knives, swords, and shields. It made an interesting display.

Just across the road there was a ten-hole golf course. I went one round with the others on my first evening there. The course was hard on the golf balls, as there were plenty of trees, boulders, and paddy fields. I did better than I expected and enjoyed myself.

The surrounding country was lovely; Kodarma forest began just a few miles away. It was not dense, but covered with trees and in some places, long grass. Terraced paddy fields had taken over the cleared areas. Agriculturally, this area could be very rich, but cultivators had not yet learned to use fertilizer.

The forest was considered one of the best for hunting, harboring leopard and tiger, sambar and hill deer, wild fowl (chicken) and green pigeon. The green pigeon fed only on berries and so was felt to be good eating.

Villagers would not enter the jungle at night because of the big cats. During the day, they entered only in twos and threes, never singly. There was a hill I wanted to work but could not because the natives refused to go, even in numbers.

I expected this trip to become a wild goose chase, but it developed into a most profitable venture. We located a site for beryl that could solve the difficulties we had elsewhere. I hoped to get into production immediately, so that we could make our quota, even with Washington red tape.

* * *

I made a new friend in Bhilwara-Mewar State. He was Irish American, someone who had lived in India too long. He came for a short visit and never left. Most of his waking hours were spent talking. If no one was around to listen, he talked to himself. This chatter resembled a broken Victrola record, as he repeated and repeated. This was partly due to his long association with simple villagers. He once told me a man could go nutty after spending a lot of time alone in the villages. I wholeheartedly agreed.

He liked alcohol in most of its drinkable forms. Even with the high cost of these beverages, getting himself into a mellow frame of mind was not expensive. Then the world took on a rosy tint, and he became fluent on many subjects.

He was partial to conversations about judging his fellow man. We once discussed the question of tyrannicide. Is a priest justified in telling a man at confession that his soul was not in jeopardy if he killed a tyrant? Such a sacrifice would be for the good of most. He regretted some humanitarian priest had not sanctioned the sacrifice of Hitler.

Other discussions gave me a better understanding of history. For instance, the reason why some of the notorious figures of history had their own private Father Confessor was because, according to him, the church had not laid down fast rules. Decisions were left to the individual. With questions so deeply rooted in theory, and with him unwilling to take a definite stand, we arrived at few answers.

He knew the idiom of the villagers better than his mother tongue and loved to use it. Unconsciously, he had absorbed the caste system. He saw himself on the top shelf and his manner of talking with villagers was adjustable, according to their place in the scheme of things. Every conversation began by asking the name and caste of the person being spoken to. Bengalis sometimes received particularly rude attention, whereas the local village chief got the polite salaam. Poor caste men usually found themselves called sons of pigs before the conversation had progressed very far, just to let them know where they stood.

He relied on an Indian proverb which he said had served him well: When he was speaking to a person of the thief's caste, he would ask, "Are you a thief?" If the man said no, the answer would be "Then you are not the son of your mother's husband."

He refused to drink bottled soda because the bottles were dirty, but he drank from most village wells, ate village food, and drank village milk. The wholesome fear of eastern diseases which we had, he had none. He was perhaps 99 percent Indian in the way he did things and 100 percent American in enthusiasm and energy.

He took up the study of geology as a vocation and became a good amateur geologist. That is how I met him. We had him roaming the hills, looking for the kind of stones we were interested in buying. He found some fine specimens, although their occurrences were rare. His enthusiasm was amazing. On the move constantly, there was a wanderlust in his eyes and itching powder on his toes. A real tumbling tumbleweed.

Time was an abstract thing without any significance in his life. Never on time, he talked the hours away in Indian fashion. From lowly coolie to biggest Burra Sahib, it was against his principle to pass anyone on the road without stopping for a chat. This dubious virtue could be an irritation, but all things considered, it worked to our advantage.

That man was Father Lyons. Don't get the wrong impression; he was a wonder for our work, and I knew of no one else who could do it half as well.

* * *

My second day in Bhilwara was spent with Father Lyons, bouncing over the countryside in a jeep. Since the top of the jeep was being repaired and the monsoon was on full blast, we stood a good chance of getting wet. Lyons was driving. He was wrapped in a sheet, which soon became soggy, while I carried an umbrella. Hanging on was no easy task! We lunched off corned beef, cheese, and orange juice while sitting under a railway culvert with a ceiling just high enough for the jeep. It was the only dry spot we could find. After we were pleasantly wet, the rain stopped, and the sun came out.

We found some good specimens, so the trip was successful. We drove on to Gaya so I could catch a train. It was beautifully clear when we started and then, after twenty-five miles, a great black cloud drifted over our heads and opened its doors for the deluge. We stopped at the nearest dak bungalow to change clothes and begin again. Since I had only one change of clothes, history repeated itself within the next twenty-five miles. You can imagine the state of my things by the time I reached Bombay.

* * *

July 18, 1944 — Bhilwara, Mewar State

Dearest Idie: I started a letter yesterday but because I had not taken a bath in four days, I decided to do something about it. Afterward, the bed looked so good I didn't get around to writing. This morning, I was industrious, almost to the point of gentlemanliness. I was immediately sorry to lose my beautiful week-old beard. Next time I have such a beauty I will make a special effort to send you a picture.

We are working steadily. Being in the open is grand. Driving a heavy car can be hard because of the mud, water, and occasional boulder strewn on the road, but it is as enjoyable as could be expected without you.

Have received none of your letters. There are probably some waiting for me, as there has hardly been time for them to reach me. Hope you are well and a little better reconciled to the way things need to be for now. I hope it will not be too long before I can get back to you.

All my love, Harry

* * *

    I stayed in Udaipur three days, most of which was spent exploring with Menke, a geologist. The night before we left, the British political agent came to see our strange monstrosity of a car and informed us we would never reach our destination, as the monsoon was on—or didn't we know? We described the specialties inherent in the car, but he was insistent. He was almost right.

Menke and I arrived at the Gangapur dak-bungalow at about six o'clock. The *chowkidan* (ethnic cook) said he was a fine cook, but the only thing he had was a small chicken and rice. We ate his curry and rice at midnight and felt we were lucky to get it, after only six hours of preparation. It was not very good either.

We stayed two days, then moved into the fort at Duala. It had been built three hundred years before and looked like it. Not the most comfortable place to stay, but I felt I could make it my headquarters if I needed to stay for a while.

The fellow who lived there was a Rajput. Every year at one of the maharani's festivals in Udaipur, he would behead a cow with one blow of his sword. I saw his very old Damascus steel blade; it was a real honey.

We went hunting and saw a big black buck. He got away, and I was glad, as he was magnificent. A doe and fawn were with him, and he would not leave them, even when we finally began to throw dust in his eyes with the rifle. He was fast enough to leave the two behind, but he deliberately slowed down when the fawn tired. I also noticed plenty of black and gray partridge in the surrounding fields, and quail.

* * *

I learned, in Naziabad, Rajputana, that eclipses of the sun were bad medicine for the Witts. They could cause all manner of misfortunes, such as missing black partridge, getting stuck in the river, and other, not amusing things. There was an eclipse one day while Menke and I were working in the field. I decided that if I ever heard another one was coming, I would go to bed for the entire day.

We started at ten in the morning. By eleven we were stuck in a river with a shifting sand bottom. It took about five minutes to sink enough to get the differential and axles well imbedded. We looked for the usual drove of coolies to pull us out, but there wasn't a soul in sight! This was the first time I had ever stopped anywhere in India in broad daylight, when inquisitive coolies did not surround the car.

There being nothing else to do, Menke and I made ourselves as comfortable as possible on a large rock in the middle of the river. We played cards while Gulab, one of our boys, tramped the remaining two miles to the nearest village for coolies and bullocks. Eventually, one of the other Indians with us brewed up a pot of tea.

Gulab finally came back with a few coolies and four bullocks. The heavy car didn't budge an inch. Gulab returned to the village for more. He found four more bullocks and two coolies, but they still they could not budge the car.

By the time the eclipse had passed its peak, the villagers had said their prayers and were convinced the world had not ended. They came to our river to bathe. Gulab announced to all present that *bidis* (locally produced cigarettes rolled in leaves) would be available to all industrious souls willing to push. In true Indian fashion, the bidis were demanded first, followed by a thirty-minute smoke, and laugh fest.

Fifty coolies surrounded us, laughing at the sahibs' predicament. Not wanting to be left out of the festivities, Menke and I each lit up a local cigar. The natives had never seen one before, so we gave them one. Then our fun began. They passed it among themselves, peace pipe fashion, each taking a couple of puffs. They coughed after each puff and made the same remark, "*Bahut mazbut!*" (very strong!).

When the bidis ran out, we got as many men around the car as would fit, whipped up the bullocks and got the same result as before. Every coolie had a different plan as to how we might get out. Finally, a couple of the bullock drivers, who were cultivators, took Gulab and trotted away, coming back with a half-grown tree to use as a lever, raising the wheels up on top of the sand. They succeeded in getting the wheels about half out when six more bullocks arrived, making a total of fourteen. Not an inch of progress could they make.

It began to look as if we had presented the river with one fine car. Day was ending, and the clouds seemed close to opening. A good, hard rain would turn the river into a torrent. Work on the wheels continued, and the next time all fourteen bullocks pulled, we began to come out inch by inch, amid much cheering, laughing, and fond patting of the bullocks. The fellow who thought up using the tree as a lever put the strutting peacock to shame, cutting capers all over the place.

As we started to leave, Menke gave the coolies a couple of packs of cigarettes—Camels, in a box with bright colors and a picture of a camel. They silently held them in cupped hands. But what were they? They had never seen anything like it.

"To smoke? But the sahib is joking. How would one smoke such a big, bulky box?"

Menke opened a pack and passed cigarettes around. As they lighted up, their vocal cords loosened, and we left the whole crowd laughing happily.

It was six o'clock by the time we left. With customary foresight, I had waded around the car barefooted all day and turned up with the finest set of blistered feet you ever saw. We returned to Bhilwara to reconsider our itinerary.

* * *

My next stop in Rajputana was Jaipur. I spent most of my time looking for stones, greatly missing Idie. How she would have loved seeing the cut and uncut ones! Around fifty thousand karats of uncut emeralds were on the table at one time. Only a fraction of that amount would be kept after cutting. There were also bags full of diamonds and sapphires, both blue and star.

Emeralds are just a high-grade piece of beryl, the stuff I was buying by the hundred tons. Gem quality was found in only a few places, however, and in very small quantities. None of the mines we were working at produced gemstones.

The fellow we had come to see was a Parsi. He owned a few businesses, rug weaving, brass, and silversmithing among them. He also owned a wonderful museum, containing many old Moghul relics. His specialty was dealing in precious stones, chiefly cut ones.

I arrived back in Delhi on the last day of July. I walked briskly into the office and began to sort the mail. "Yes!" I shouted, finding two letters from Idie. She remarked that some of the words in my last letter had been cut out by censors, especially when I named places I had been. One letter had a stamp on the inside of the envelope that read: Tucson, Arizona, July 1, 1944. Other people were reading my mail!

July and August proved to be busy. I almost forgot my birthday in August, but Idie remembered.

August 14, 1944 — Tucson, Arizona

Dearest Harry: I had a landslide yesterday, receiving five letters! It was wonderful. I knew you said you would not be able to write or mail regularly, but I was anxious to hear. I am so glad, at last you have received something from me. I am feeling better every day, but when the heat comes up in the afternoons, I crawl in the back room and stay there until the cooler hours arrive.

The war news sounds better, but it will still take time. How is your situation? I am sure you will not be able to finish your work within a year. I would love to be surprised but will not be disappointed if you need to stay longer. You are always welcome here, you know!

Tomorrow is your birthday, and how I wish I could say, "Happy Birthday!" in person. We seem to be apart so much on celebration days, but I do not know anyone who has spread their honeymoon over the years as we have. Your last visit home meant so much to me and I often think of our sweet hours together. I long to be with you and talk with you, instead of spiritually, as I do now. Nothing can take away the wonderful memories of the years we have been together, or the plans for years to come.

I love you, my sweetheart, now and for always, Your Idie

* * *

On August 16th, Eric Beecroft, Acting Special Representative for the FEA, sent me a letter informing me that my official headquarters would be changed immediately from Karachi to New Delhi.

One evening before leaving, I was invited to dinner and ate my first peacock. It was nearly all breast, as tender and juicy as any bird I had ever eaten. I remarked to my hosts, "I know where my next Thanksgiving turkey will come from."

When I moved, I gave my gun to Hashim, thinking, *I am probably making a breach of British law in India, for it is stingy about giving natives permits to carry firearms.*

Another surprise was waiting for me, my lost bag had been found! I shook my head in disbelief, as I had become used to not having things and was not particularly interested in getting them back.

* * *

Once I arrived in New Delhi, I could see the fellow in charge was pathetically short of help and about to fall ill with his long hours and worry over not having someone with whom to talk through decisions. I gave up a trip to the northwest in order to help Eric, thinking I could take it later. Sitting still for a change felt good. I was thinking I would buy a small ranch when the war ended, settle down and never stray from it. Then I decided I'd better ask for a raise.

One day, I was invited to the home of George Merrell, the first secretary to the personal representative of the President of the United States. He had been there for about five years and knew how to handle his job. Most of the time he was in charge because there was no one else to occupy the chair. We became good friends.

* * *

On August 22, Eric Beecroft wrote to Mr. James McCamy, Executive Director for Areas under FEA, recommending reclassification of my job to Acting Special Representative. Eric was taking a leave of absence, and I had become his principal assistant in the central office—this, in addition to my work in the field. I assisted Eric with a variety of problems in procurement of materials and administrative management. I was pleasantly surprised to see that Eric had included, in his letter, such things as my seven years of business experience in India, my specialized commercial knowledge of the strategic commodities, and my versatility and effectiveness with the natives.

* * *

August 27, 1944 — New Delhi

Dearest Idie: this has been an uneventful week. Am steadily busy but am also impatient to get away again. Beecroft, who is Acting Special Representative in the absence of Fischer, is going on a trip with McCamy, who has just returned from Washington. Unless I stay, it will be impossible for him to leave.

Bet you always knew I'd make good. Guess the local boy has nearly reached the top of the ladder! Acting Special Representative, that's me!

Had my first letter from you in some weeks yesterday. Since the baby seems to be growing, you probably realize he is coming. Think I shall call him "Buddy." I cannot imagine you being anything but trim and slim. Now you must sleep on your back. Guess I should rush back home to see for myself.

Miss you terribly. Hope you continue to do well, Harry.

* * *

Andrew Corry, along with Paul Johnstone and Bill Bissell, joined me on a trip to Patan State, north of Jaipur, to inspect a possible mine site. It was thirty miles beyond the end of the road, nestling in a valley amid boulders and sandy cart tracks. High on a hill, an old fort looked down, as if it could still withstand charge after charge. I was sorry we did not have the time to visit it, especially since it was intact.

We stayed in the state guest house. Its condition indicated the Raja of Patan should have been on the lookout for a rich heiress. It was just a big old barn made of stone with a few rickety chairs and *charpoys* (frames strung with rope to make a bed) carried in for guests. The others hadn't seen anything of the up-country, and they seemed to enjoy themselves.

Lots of monkeys ran wild in the village. When we went to bed on the roof to keep cool, we were told to take everything movable downstairs so it could be locked up, or the monkeys would carry it off. We didn't do that, nor did we lose anything. But the next day, we saw a tottering baby get its bottom smacked by a monkey while playing in the village street. It seemed the monkeys often swatted little kids on their fanny.

We stopped at the village well to take pictures and found an old fellow whose job was to fill the skin buckets as they reached water level, singing a song of encouragement to his bullocks. Each time the buckets reached bottom, he would sing that the buckets were full, the bullocks could now pull. It was late in the afternoon, with lengthening shadows. The sight of the old village and the picturesque men and women, with the domineering fort in the distance, made a thrilling scene I would always remember.

The man whose property we had gone to inspect brought along his Mohammedan cook, and we ate one of the finest Indian meals ever: curried baked chicken, potato curry, peas curried, tomatoes curried, mutton and peas pilaf, and a sweet rice and fruit.

We had a rifle with us, and the half-brother of the Raja (another of those wrong-side-of-the-blanket fellows) came along with a shotgun. We were short on cartridges, so I made a resolution to let the others shoot. Paul shot a partridge, missed another, and then another. Soon after he missed a second time, a big black buck ran across the cart track.

I then reverted to primitive instinct, jumping out of the car, jerking the gun out of Paul's hands, shooting, and missing. That great big fellow stood there, wagging his tail at me while I shot two perfectly aimed bullets well over his head. After that, I behaved better, and let them do the missing. We had twenty shots. I hit three of them to make sure we brought something home. When we got close to Delhi, I gave the guns to Paul, and he got a peacock with one and missed the other two.

We left Patan about midday and drove into Jaipur, arriving about sundown. Six miles out, the old Amber Palace and fort come into view. The sun was setting; the clouds were silver-lined, painted in every color. This palace was a massive, impressive site. It was built on a high hill, with a tremendous wall all around.

We could only spend one day there, but it was enough to give the others a good impression of the area. I decided to put Jaipur near the top of my list of interesting places to see. We drove by the bazaar several times, taking pictures. Do not think of this bazaar as an ordinary, dirty side street. These were main streets, bisecting the town, a good sixty feet or wider, as straight as any at home. They were all clean, and Ganesha, the elephant of good luck, being a special favorite, had small shrines built in his honor on almost every street corner. All gateways and doors had his small image above them. Streets leading off these main intersections were narrow, and most business was done on the main streets.

We spent the day in the bazaar, especially in two shops. One of them belonged to the man I had come to see (the agent for Standard Vacuum as well). My favorite shop was the Gem Palace. I had already seen everything in the place, but I always got a kick out of it. The others were amazed at the number of beautiful things. A new necklace had just come in. It was a string of pearls, five long strands, and each single pearl was a perfect match in size, color, etc. It was the most beautiful thing I had seen in a long time. The asking price was 85,000 rupees.

* * *

In September, I became the Chief Disposals Officer for the Disposal of Surplus U.S. War Property, under the FEA banner. Part of my job was to cooperate with officers of the U.S. Army, such as the Commanding General for the Services of Supply, the American Commissioner, and representatives of other agencies who shared responsibility for property disposal. I could now negotiate, with directives from Washington, with Indian government officials charged with administrative responsibility for property disposal.

Idie wrote to me in October, telling me that her "red war shoes" were wearing out. Leather, rubber goods, and cotton materials had been rationed by the U.S. government in 1942. They could only be purchased with a coupon book and in small amounts, three pair each year.

October 13, 1944 — no place given

Dearest Idie: Your letters are coming through quickly. The last one took about fourteen days. The time varies a great deal. It is good to get the news so quickly.

I haven't been away for five months yet, but it seems longer, even with the traveling. I have covered over 25,000 miles since I saw you. I expect to go to Kashmir a week from today. Will write you later about the work. It is coming along beautifully, and everyone here and in Washington is greatly surprised at our successes. They just do not know my friends.

All my love, darling, Harry

NINETEEN
KASHMIR ADVENTURES

October 16, 1944 — Traveling

Andrew Corry and I left Delhi in mid-October to explore the back country of India, looking for strategic minerals. A merchant from Jaipur had told us he knew where there was a mountain of beryl. Andrew, who was supervising the extraction of beryl ore from quartz and feldspar, said he thought it could be a promising area.

We left in the jeep at six a.m. with my bearer, Mohammed. We had eaten a light breakfast before leaving, but by nine we were ready for another. We stopped at Parry's Hotel in Ambala. The food was good, even the coffee. A couple of Army wives and the usual troop of native children, playing outside, were fascinated by the jeep.

The country between Ambala and Amritsar was flat and monotonous, but as the day grew older, roads became jammed with bullock carts and the usual dog, goat and pedestrian traffic, a pageant of people and things. Dhoti-clad men dozed on top of bullock carts, numerous scrawny dogs loafed by the road, and straight-backed women in colored cotton saris walked gracefully, balancing belongings with careless ease on their heads. In the still atmosphere, dust churned by feet, hooves, wheels, paws, and tires hung in a cloud around each group of travelers.

Progress was slow, hot, and dirty, but joyful too, as we merged into a stream of humanity going about the important business of living.

At three, we ate lunch at the Amritsar railroad station. After studying the map, we decided to cut off seventy miles by bypassing Lahore and going directly to Sialkot. One small stretch on this road looked like it might be trouble, but we had confidence in the jeep, so off we went. For some miles we rolled along at a wonderful clip, and then, our grand road suddenly turned into a *kutcha* (inferior) track. Jolting in a laboriously slow manner, I took the first turn that gave promise of a good road, and the jeep floundered on a well-camouflaged stump. We were stuck, with one wheel spinning merrily in the breeze a foot above ground.

Even in such isolated spots, help is readily available. It took only a few minutes to find coolies and a pair of water buffalo, but oh, so much longer to get the job done. Each one of the coolies had a different idea on how to do it. They squatted in a semicircle beside the jeep, noisily debating. Andy and I had a few ideas of our own, but we didn't even get a hearing.

While Andy struggled against perverse discussion, I sat in the shade of a bush, whittled, smoked my pipe, and wondered how long it had taken me to learn to allow coolies to exhaust their thought processes before attempting to say anything. Andy was still a beginner, but he finally gave up. When the headman came over to tell us it was impossible and the coolies were going back to their fields, we passed cigarettes around. When the cigarettes were at finger burning length, we suggested how it might be done. In a matter of minutes, we were back on the road.

Sundown crept in and still no decent road. My eyes wandered from the track to the petrol gauge and back again. I knew we had little left and expected to hear a dying cough from the engine. Suddenly, just as it had disappeared, the *pucca* (good) road materialized.

It was eight p.m. before we reached Sialkot, still looking for gas. Imagine our dejection to find all the pumps empty and a complete ban on sales to anyone except high military authority! Eventually, after making rude noises over the telephone, our tank was filled. We were warned to turn back as there was no petrol ahead, but feeling confident, we kept going the next day.

We were impressed by the great number of lights in Sialkot. I remembered Diwali, the Festival of Light, was that day. Everyone who could afford it had a light of some kind in their home or shop. There were many electric lights, but the greater number were clay receptacles, too small to hold more than a thimbleful of kerosene. Beside a door, on a window ledge, or a balcony, these little pinpoints of light were a cheerful sight. Singularly, they made only a dot of flickering light in the black night, but together, they gave Sialkot a romantic atmosphere. Andy had never seen a Diwali and said the town looked like a fairyland.

One tiny temple was the most outstanding. It was covered with tiny pinpoints of light, every spot capable of holding a small bowl had one of the clay lamps winking in the night. A superlative miniature among towering coarser things. What loving hands must have dressed up this small place. What prayers must have been sent heavenward to make Sialkot a place of pure fantasy.

Our host for the night was the Mountain View Hotel. It was Parsi-managed and comfortable. Dinner was good and well served. So ended a good, full day.

Our tea arrived at six a.m. the next morning, and we were on our way at dawn. Our only sightseeing at Sialkot was the large milestone near the edge of town. It carried two interesting captions. One side read: "The wayfarer has come from the scorching plains where the dust riseth as smoke from the furnace." And on the other: "The land whither ye goeth is a fair land of hills and green valleys and clear running water." True in every respect.

The sun topped the horizon, and in a field close to the road, a wrinkled old Muslim knelt with the sun to his back, face to Mecca, saying his prayers. It was such a familiar sight that I almost passed him unnoticed until his words began to knock around inside me: "Allah, Il Allah …," and the rest of that means: "Allah, the omnipotent, is great. There is no other but Allah, and Mohammed is his prophet."

We had no delay at the customs barrier. A shivering little man took one look at the jeep and said he was mighty sleepy, as he had been on duty all night. He opened the gate and passed us on. Jeeps were no novelty to him.

From the barrier all the way into the city of Jammu, red bunting and gaudy signs proclaimed a royal welcome home to the traveling Maharaja. "Long live our gracious ruler" and "Great happiness to our beloved Maharaja" were the most popular.

We did not stop there. The guidebook has the following to say about it: "The ancient city of Jammu is a picturesque sight, with pinnacles and temple spires, capped by golden balls and cones, glittering in the sun against the purple background of the hills. Each hilltop was once the possession of a leading family, which fortified itself against aggression in the bad days of old."

We ate our second breakfast at the Udumpore dak-bungalow. It was a large building situated on a hill overlooking the rolling country through which we had passed, and a view of the road ahead of us, complete with formidable mountains.

From Udumpore, the road zigzagged up to seven thousand feet and crossed the Katni Pass. It was a lovely drive, terminated on the other side by a mountainside thickly covered with fir, spruce, and pine. The sun seldom broke through, reminding me of the redwoods on the California coast.

We drove at a snail's pace to keep the sweet aroma with us as long as possible. It was delightfully cool. A trickle of water from a hidden spring tumbled along broad ferns lining the road. It was tempting to linger, but we knew other delights lay ahead.

At Batate, on the Chenab River, we had lunch in a small bungalow built like a Swiss chalet. The *khansamah* (a cook specializing in smoky spices) promised food in thirty minutes. He did that, serving us tomato soup, mutton cutlets, fried eggs and potatoes, a sweet omelet, toast, and coffee.

The tiny dining room was all windows, looking over the valley and up to the snow-topped peaks of Pir Panjal. In the garden, cosmos and zinnia were blooming in great profusion. The khansamah had so many on the table, we had to remove them to have room for our plates.

Since we ate in the European kitchen, the Hindu cook was not likely to get baksheesh, so he took white stones and spelled out "Happy Day" on the ground near the jeep. He got his four annas.

From Batate we started another long climb, finally crossing Banihal Pass at eleven thousand feet. It became a monotonous climb, winding around one mountain for twenty miles, looking at the same barren hillside. Andy and I took our shirts off to get a little sun but as we approached the top, we had to bundle up. The pass is a tunnel, 660 feet long, cut through the top of the mountain. At each end a Kashmiri soldier was on guard.

We arrived at dusk; the sun had set a few minutes earlier. It was cold and black inside the tunnel, but the opening at the other end was the deepest of blues, with the stationed sentry making a wonderful silhouette.

We stopped, despite chattering teeth, for our first look at the vale of Kashmir, spreading out below; then we went on to Upper Munda for the night. It was about eight thousand feet up, and the wood fire in the fireplace was most welcome. Shortly after enjoying our meal, we were snoring away between blankets.

The beauty of Upper Munda was not apparent in the darkness of evening, but the morning brought a sight to behold! The bungalow was built on the side of the mountain facing the valley. The mountain rose two thousand feet and towered above us, almost straight up. The slopes blazed with color from scrubby trees and bushes. Autumnal paint brushes did a great job. In the distance, the valley poplars had turned from green to deep orange and brown. They speared upwards, out of the valley, like welcome land markers. The fields were clean, waiting for spring planting.

It was our intention to get off by eight, but tea did not arrive until 8:30. I was not unhappy, as the bed was mighty comfortable. Rain had fallen during the night, and clouds hung close on the mountains. The valley below was absent in a misty veil, and the wind blew bitterly cold. The sun finally topped over the mountains and drove the rain away. Then we drove on, as I had no intention of facing a cold drizzle in an open jeep!

When we arrived in Srinagar, I devoted the day to showing Andrew and the mine owner something of the city. We climbed Old Soliman, and I rested twice as often as Idie had done. We enjoyed the view of houseboats on the canal, the winding river far below, and the houses squeezed together.

We stopped for a late lunch and visited the emporium. The emporium was a government-operated market for Kashmir products. All the larger shops had branch stores here, and one could buy all his Kashmiri things in one place.

Janki Noth, an ex-supervisor of the emporium, went with us, so the prices we paid were about right. First, we visited the shops, asking the price of the things we wanted, then putting them aside for Janki to buy. He often found flaws and took us to other shops where he found better things. He always got at least 50 percent off the asking price. He kept the blanket man running around behind us, carrying the blankets, for about two hours. I wanted to give in because I really wanted them, but Janki would not allow it. Eventually we paid the price he set. He was the most economical part of our trip.

* * *

November 5, 1944 — New Delhi

My darling Idie: the Kashmir trip was a wonderful experience. We were away eighteen days and visited everywhere you and I had so much fun together, except Gulmarg. The scenery was magnificent; I am hoping the photos will be good.

We went about seventy miles north of Srinagar, all but the first day on ponies or by foot. Most of the time we were at around eight thousand feet but spent little time in snow. It is still early, although one pass did have about a foot. Fortunately, we brought plenty of blankets and accumulated long underwear, woolen khakis, and fur-lined walking boots.

We were quite a crowd. There were about thirty pack ponies and eight riding ponies plus coolies, bearers, etc. Sometimes we stayed in rest houses, but mostly camp was set up beside the river. We slept in tents and ate under the stars. The camps were most enjoyable because of the great log fires.

I didn't shave for eight days and now resemble a cross between a shaggy bear and a wild goat. Non-shaving accounts for the bear part; non-washing, that of the goat! The river was really cold; I am still a sissy about it. Andrew Corry had several baths in the river. That sounded like a friendly rap on death's door to me, so I sat close to the fire and tried not to notice. Even the sight of him splashing away sent chills through me.

This letter is meant to break your long fast of news and let you know I am okay and feeling as healthy as ever. I did not gain or lose weight, and with all the walking I did, I think it downright sinful not to have shed a pound or two!

Two letters were waiting for me. I was mighty glad to have them. It is good to hear Buddy isn't giving you much trouble. You do not tell me all, so I cannot know how troublesome he is.

I think I told you I was going to ask for a raise. It begins November first and will amount to about sixty or seventy dollars more after figuring out the living allowance.

All my love – Harry

* * *

December 3, 1944 — Tucson, Arizona

My darling Boy: Another year is almost over, and the Christmas season is upon us. I started decorating and wanted to share the fun with you. It really is such a pleasure to open trunks and get out the pretty things we purchased together. We plan to have a tree as big as we can get in the house.

So, you are going to get a raise! I presume it will go to your expenses in India. I am going to try, after Buddy is paid, to live on a strict budget. It seems I have spent a lot, but there has been a need. Guess you will have to do the saving in the family.

Sweetheart, I know you have asked me a couple of times if Dr. Smith can tell us when Buddy will arrive, but Dr. Smith says he is no gambler, so you will just have to be patient. Sorry, neither can I do it. He said last Friday when I had another examination, it would not be before Christmas, so you might just as well settle down until January.

Have the best Christmas you can and know that my thoughts are with you. Your Idie

* * *

That December, the ACCO office received the news that Will Clayton had been named the First Assistant Secretary of State for Economic Affairs in Washington, D.C.

As Christmas edged closer, we invited a house full of dinner guests to Rajpur Road. I promised to take some of the fellows on a shooting trip, as they wanted to get something for Christmas dinner. We decided to go to Jaipur, with its lovely wild country.

Greg Hewlett and I shot some peacock, and three of the girls from the office came over early with a box full of cellophane bells and other decorations. We had a very small tree with cotton and mica for snow. It was hastily done but served the purpose. Walt Hand, the boy from Alabama, played Santa and dished out candy bars and fruit. He made a very good one, wearing a suit made by Sheikh (from the office), who copied it from a magazine. Hewlett mixed some eggnog, and we all enjoyed it.

Somewhat later, I took what I supposed would be my last Christmas shoot for years to come. I could not see Idie and Buddy being so tolerant as to allow them. Gregg Hewlett and I decided to visit one of the mines on the southern border of Jaipur State. I claimed it was an outing for Gregg, but it ended up with me shooting as much as he.

The country was a thick jungle, covered in rolling hills. Tiger, panther, sambar boar, and blue bulls were known to frequent that area but were protected for the Maharaja to hunt. We saw none of that wildlife, but we did see a tiger's tracks when we exited the mine we had gone to survey. The tiger must have been a tremendous fellow!

I took a few moments at sunset to sit on a small hill. I watched the geese circle, and I listened to them honk their way into the fields for the night. They were only about a hundred yards away and circled all around me, three bunches of about a hundred each. I suddenly felt one with nature, a sense of peace enveloping me.

TWENTY
NEW BEGINNINGS

January 1, 1945

People in the office were telling me I was probably already a papa but had not had time to hear. The new year began with cold rain and wind, making me wonder what the weather was like in Tucson. Some of the nicest things in my Christmas box, sent by Idie, were the packages of noodle soup I could make with hot water and eat at my desk.

I jumped out of my chair on January 17th as I read the cable from Ruby that Idie had given birth to a baby girl on January 13th. "Hallelujah!" broke whatever silence there had been in the office as everyone crowded around my desk, slapping me on the back.

> January 15, 1945 — Tucson
>
> Sweetheart: you have a very sweet little girl. So, Daddy, you now have two sweethearts to love you and receive yours in return.
>
> I hope you like the name. I simply could not name her anything else but Harriet; especially after I saw her. She was so much like you at my first glimpse.

As for me. everything was normal and took the average amount of time. It was much easier than I expected, and I fooled everyone. At my age, people do not usually get along so well. When the doctor told me I had a girl, I was shocked. I sent your dad a night letter (a letter sent at night at a reduced rate for a.m. delivery).

Your New Year's Eve letter arrived shortly afterwards, perfectly timed, and a real joy, as if you had peeked in on us. I am sure your prayers and thoughts helped me.

Will say bye for now and write a few more lines tomorrow. Harriet and I send Daddy and sweetheart all our love – As always, Your Idie

* * *

January 18, 1945 — Delhi

Dearest Idie: Ruby's cable arrived last evening, and I could not be happier-except if I could be there with you. Thank you and please tell the little girl who has come to our house I am mighty happy she has arrived. Tell her too, she is the luckiest little girl there is, having you for a mother. I think deep inside, I wanted Buddy to be a girl. I hope you are not disappointed. Our last letter seemed to indicate that you had decided it must be a boy.

People in the office say they are happy for us and are full of congratulations. The girl who works with me, Virginia Willis, has been visiting the APO every day, looking for the cable. She was guessing what Buddy would be and tried to get me to express a preference. Whenever a letter arrives, everyone gathers around my desk to hear the news. Right now, others are beaming almost as much as I.

I know you will write everything just as soon as you are able, but I find it difficult to be patient. The cable didn't say, but I assume she arrived the day it was sent, January 13th.

My darling, only you know how much I wish I could be there with you. Please tell little Harriet I will see her and you at the earliest possible moment. Ruby's cable says, "Idie Baby fine." I pray that you both are superfine.

All my love to you both, Harry

* * *

As happy as I was to be a new papa, I knew my work had to keep progressing. The next ruler of the native state of Kapurthala had lunch with me and some others at Rajpur Road. FEA was using his Delhi house as a dormitory for six or eight men. He was talkative and well-mannered (in the Western sense). He and his wife, a nondescript English lady, had traveled in Europe and visited America. He spoke glowingly of a cook, a southern negress, who prepared Mexican dishes and barbeques he liked very much. He thought New York a wonderland, especially the shop "where you drop in nickels and all sorts of things to eat pop out."

We served them an Indian lunch that I thought was quite good: pilau of almonds, chicken curry, shami kabob, vegetables, poppers, etc.

After lunch, I put on my shooting togs and drove out to Palwal, about forty miles along the Agra road. Our boys who had been living in the Kapurthala house had to relinquish it to a person within the regal ranks and wanted to have a party. If they could persuade me to supply the meat, a large party (probably fifty people) could materialize, otherwise they felt it ought to be restricted. I was easily persuaded, telling them to invite anybody they wanted.

I took some new arrivals with me, and an Indian Christian clerk named Peter. We picked up a local shikari and went out after buck. We found two fine herds, and I got off three shots—all misses. Finally, just before dark, a lone one came sailing across the cart track we were following. It was natural for the jeep to follow, so across the fields we went.

Heading for rough country, the wise old fellow soon lost us, and we bogged down in the soft earth. We sent the shikari to bring help from a village only a couple of hundred yards away. By the time he returned, night had settled in. He came back empty-handed, as the village was Hindu, and they refused to come because we were shooting. It wasn't a big job to jack up the wheels, but it took time. We arrived back at the bungalow around nine o'clock.

We retired immediately after dinner, to be ready for an early start. We were off again at daylight; into the denser country they call jungle. We were searching for a blue bull, the largest of the Indian antelope, also called a *nilgai*. It was cold, driving on cart tracks so early in the morning, in an open-air car. Thankfully, my lace-up boots were comfortable, just the thing for these trips. We saw a buck but let him go and continued our search for the bigger bull.

We picked up one teal before entering the jungle. It was difficult to see more than fifty yards in any direction. By midday, Kapurthala's party began to look like a small affair; one teal wouldn't feed many.

At twelve thirty, we spotted a herd of deer, and I managed to get one small buck. That was better. A few minutes later, a much larger buck came along, and we started after him. We were almost within range when the biggest wild animal I have ever seen came charging across an open spot, accompanied by crashing jungle. It was a blue bull, weighing at least a thousand pounds. I still had buck fever, as I have no other explanation for missing such a tremendous animal. Not only that, but I missed him five or six times! He soon lost us. I felt mighty small.

Around one o'clock, we spotted a whole herd of bulls and cows. They are not protected, as they ruin crops and grazing land, so it is okay to shoot them. Out of this bunch, I dropped a cow, and the party's success was assured. She weighed around three hundred pounds.

Getting this great pile of meat on the jeep was quite a job, but we finally did it and arrived back at the bungalow for lunch about three.

At four thirty, we went out again. This time, we returned with two small *chinkara* (Indian gazelle), a dove, a partridge, two sand grouse, and four peacocks. We made it back to Delhi in time for dinner.

The cow went into the party pantry along with the peacocks. We gave one buck to the Rajpur Road servants and another to the secretary to the personal representative to the President of the United States. We ate the other one for lunch the next day, with the assistance of a great number of people.

The party was a tremendous success. I became the butcher for a while, showing the cook how to prepare the steaks for grilling. One of our servants got some mesh wire and iron rods for an outdoor pit, and I made a sauce with chili powder. The pit was beautiful after dark; the steaks and sauce were wonderful. They had a sixteen-piece G.I. band and ninety-four guests. There was an indoor, open patio in the house: a wonderful party spot.

* * *

I was pacing the office when Eric Beecroft's authorization to return home for consultation arrived. Eric was on business in Bombay at the time. He planned to leave after returning from Bombay and then come back to India the latter part of April.

I knew I was scheduled to go home for a couple of months after Eric got back, but I also knew the best laid plans were often changed. I hesitated to tell Idie because I doubted Eric could return quickly, as the wheels turned slowly in Washington. I frowned as I scribbled a note, thinking it might be well into July before I could leave. The next letter on my desk was a surprise. It approved my title as Acting Special Representative while Eric was away.

* * *

I seemed to keep celebrating Harriet's arrival with parties, occasioned by the successes of Sunday shoots. On one, I was able to bring back that blue bull I missed the previous week. He was a tremendous rascal, but overconfidence got him. He only trotted when he should have run! He was so big we could not get him into the jeep trailer, so we butchered him there.

We got this fellow early in the day, and before the evening was finished, someone shot another. Then we did have our hands full! It took two hours to skin and dress each of the brutes. Peter was with us; he sure was tired at the end of the day. He was amazing; anyone else would have been in the way.

We saw a very large herd of deer, possibly more than a hundred. We counted fifteen bucks; the remainder were does. We did not shoot any as they took off across the fields, a beautiful sight. Peter said it was once not uncommon to see several herds of five hundred each. They must have wrecked the crops.

* * *

Idie wrote when she found a free moment, reflecting the joy and stress of a first-time mom. Some of her letters contained stories of things experienced by other families in the U.S.

March 3, 1945 — Tucson

Dearest Harry: Today I am thinking of you on our special day, remembering again that first wonderful night. I hope you can feel my hugs!

My brother has been wounded. He says he is all right but will have war souvenirs for life. It took several letters to get the whole story, and we still have some questions.

It happened during the return raid of the Japanese on Saipan. Little did we think the pictures of the bombing of Saipan in the newspapers would affect us. Ernest has been under strict censorship, and it has been difficult to get the whole story. When he comes home it will creep out. We hope it will be this spring.

Love you, Idie

* * *

March 3, 1945 — Delhi

Dearest Idie: another March 3rd, and this time there is another of us. It has been a long time since the first one, but it hasn't been nearly enough, as you make the days worthwhile. Everyone here, mostly me, is looking for that first picture of Harriet. When do you think we could expect it?

I am as busy as I have ever been. Things should quiet down, as Eric expects to leave tomorrow. We are busy getting memos ready for him to take to Washington. He seems sad at going, afraid he might not be allowed to return.

Just wanted to say "Hello!" and that I love you, Harry

* * *

We had lots of visiting firemen during those days. Rajpur Road was more crowded than ever, with people moving in both directions. Representative Dirksen of Illinois (Republican) was in town for the stated purpose of investigating civilian war agencies. He covered it all in a general way. We did our best to show him what we were doing with the taxpayers' money. Since his stated job was to "investigate" civilian agencies, we were a bit worried, but he was a pleasant and informed visitor. His schedule included a visit to the Holy Land for Easter.

March 13, 1945 — Delhi

Dearest Idie: You can never know how much I appreciate the pictures of you and Harriet. I was happy to see both of you looking so healthy. I am well, working steadily and going about the same pace until the visitors leave.

I suppose I should try to re-impress you by signing this with the new title of Acting Special Representative (of the Foreign Economic Administration). I do not know if the title of Special Assistant to the Personal Representative of the President of the United States goes with this job or not, so maybe I should wait and do my impressing when I see you again.

All my love, Harry

* * *

We Americans, no matter what agency we worked for, were always glad to hear about good happenings within our community. George Merrell, once Secretary in charge of the mission and now "Commissioner" was given a great honor. His Excellency Viceroy Wavell and Lady Wavell ate dinner in George's home. For all practical purposes, Viceroy Wavell was Emperor of India, never going to the home of anyone. The news that he would go to George's was most exciting for his entire household. I, too, was invited.

Ruth Merrell, George's sister, was my secretary then, and she kept me amused for the ten days before the party. She was proud of George, then excited, as the plans progressed, and finally, just scared for fear everything would not go smoothly. She had to practice her curtsy, find what His Excellency's (H.E.) favorite drink and dish were and, above all, decide who should sit next to him and to her. Of course, George did all the deciding, but Ruth had fun planning.

Peter and Mrs. Humphreys arrived first at the party. We all had a couple of quick drinks to get fortified, if necessary, but it wasn't. The Wavells were very pleasant. George and Ruth met them on the verandah and brought them in to be introduced to us. We formed a line, the girls curtsied, and we shook hands. His Excellency asked for an old-fashioned and she, tomato juice. Dinner was served soon afterwards. I sat next to Mrs. Humphreys and across from Lady Wavell.

Lady Wavell had a charming personality. She wore a simple black dinner dress with a ruby and pearl broach; he dressed in a dinner jacket. They seemed completely at ease, and the conversation flowed easily. It was after eleven when they went home, a new record.

* * *

April 2, 1945 — Delhi

Darling Idie: I met the Maharaja and Maharani of Jaipur the other evening, who were among the guests at a dinner party hosted by George Merrell. George told them I had taken some pictures of the Maharaja's state while I was traveling, and I should take their pictures for the reel as well. So, I am now invited to Rambaugh Palace, to shoot a tiger and to take their Highnesses' picture. If I can get away for the three or four days it would take, I shall go.

We went to see some Indian dancing after dinner the same evening. Jai and Asesha (only to George and Ruth) had to leave early but we still found it interesting. I am learning what some of the movements mean, and that makes it much more fun.

Much love to you, sweetheart, Harry

* * *

The "new" job was not really new. I had been doing the work for some months, without the title or the salary. It seemed Washington agencies were trying to catch up with themselves. The correspondence I received from Washington also told me there was a move within the agency to keep Eric from returning.

I thought it would be better for the office if Eric did not return, but it put me in a difficult position. If Eric did not come back, I would need to stay longer. On the other hand, if Eric did get back, I wanted to leave because I found it trying to work with him. I knew if I stepped out, some of the people in Washington would ask why I hadn't said something sooner; maybe they could have done something about it.

I sat back in my chair and thought of Eric's great desire to come back. If they did not let him return, he would be terribly hurt. Then again, such personnel problems were getting to be almost commonplace, and I could not allow them to bother me anymore.

* * *

Opening the mail in the office sometimes made me step back and take a deep breath. One envelope in particular caught my attention in April because it was postmarked Patiala. When I pulled a card out of the envelope, I saw it was an invitation to attend the New Year's Durbar in Jaipur, a formal assembly of nobles called together to mark state occasions. *What will small town Texans think about this?*

George Merrell and Ruth, plus two bearers, picked me up at three p.m. in George's car. We spotted several large black bucks just inside the border of Patiala. One was a magnificent animal with beautiful long horns. Prancing around and kicking up his heels, he was showing off for his females.

At the customs barrier, two ADCs (administrative assistants) from the palace waited to guide us the remaining distance. They were tall, bearded Sikhs, very handsome in their military uniforms. A few miles from the city, we passed an old fort built in the time of Aurangzeb, called Bahadur Kila. Built on a hill, with walls receding up the slope. It was in fine condition, even showing us the old cannon protruding from the walls. We passed several beautiful parks, as His Highness had an active interest in horticulture. He was hoping to visit California when the war ended. I thought he should also include the Rio Grande Valley.

It was ten of seven when we drove through the gates. We were scheduled to have drinks with His Highness (H.H.), but he had gone directly to the home of the Prime Minister, where we were to have dinner. Other guests were Lord Wavell, his wife and daughter, a British major general's twenty-year-old son, and a U.S. Army major.

At the Prime Minister's house, H.H. formally introduced us to his wife, his sister and her husband, and some ADCs. His Highness's title was longer than my arm. He was my age, perhaps six feet seven, and slender, with an athletic frame. Known as an excellent cricket and tennis player, he was informal with us, dressed in a regular British Army uniform.

He had two wives: the first one his father picked and forced him to marry; consequently, he seldom saw her. The other was said to be a love match; she was with him at the party. She wore a silk print sari and a bracelet of three or four rounds of small emeralds with alternating seed pearls.

We had a couple of drinks before dinner with the usual small talk. One guest asked H.H. which jewels he would wear to the *durbar* the next day and he said he did not know. One of the ladies said he must wear diamonds. He then asked what preferences people had, so I asked what he had besides diamonds. He laughed and said at this durbar, it was usually either diamonds or emeralds. I said emeralds were my favorite, and Ruth agreed, so it would be emeralds.

A buffet dinner was ready, consisting of various curries and salads, Indian sweets, and fruit. While having coffee, H.H. did two or three card tricks for us, and then a poker game was suggested. I tried to say no gracefully, but when I learned the chips were valued at only one and two rupees, I stopped struggling. This was my first poker experience with a Maharaja and Maharani, so the lesson was not very expensive.

The talk and humor were typical. If you got caught bluffing, you were laughed at. Her H. and H.H. included. They were both pretty good, she was better than him. I lost, but George won.

We returned to the palace at midnight. My lodgings consisted of a small sitting room, large bed, and tremendous bathroom. It was furnished in a Victorian style, not by any means luxurious or too comfortable. The bathroom was one of those things you can take a few laps around in the morning before breakfast if you don't want to go outside. We were there only a short time, so my room and the corridor were about all I saw. Things from China and Japan were displayed in the hallways; gifts, I supposed.

The durbar was scheduled for eleven a.m. The night before, I had asked H.H. if I could take pictures, and he said yes, as many of whomever and whenever I wanted. I scurried around while the show was on, and finally ended up with a full roll, most of them under the tented marquee.

The throne was a white marble pavilion, small and delicately carved like some of the buildings in Agra and Delhi. Extending well in front of it, a tent had been put up for protection against the sun and rain. The sides were left open, held up by silver poles.

Promptly at eleven, the Patiala hymn rang out. H.H. and party moved slowly down the red carpeted walk. The procession was led by a group of bemedaled and beplumed ADCs closely followed by H.H. and royal regalia. H.H. walked underneath the royal parasol made of gold brocade, carried well above his head, followed by the chief fly whisker, holding a horse tail whisk, set in a silver handle. The Prime Minister and cabinet followed.

When H.H. reached the throne, he remained standing. The royal salute boomed from a cannon in the distance; his four brothers bowed before him and offered their gifts. After each offering, a one sentence chant was recited by the two gold bearers who stood with H.H. All other nobles and servants of the court then passed by, making their offerings.

Near the end of the tent, one dancing girl and three men with instruments sang throughout the ceremony, which lasted exactly one hour. About 150 nobles were present, all carrying swords with jeweled handles, dressed in fine brocades.

H.H.'s jewels were fabulous. His breast was covered with emeralds, some an inch long and a half inch wide, all deep in color. He wore, at his waist, a carved emerald, perhaps six inches long and two inches wide, and on his left side, a diamond, at least two inches across. Around his turban, hanging in scallops, were diamonds about the size of my little finger.

Regrettably, we received the news of President Roosevelt's death immediately after the durbar and rushed back to Delhi. We had intended to stay the remainder of that day and possibly the next. I was sorry to miss the other festivities, but what we did experience was certainly a treat.

* * *

April 29, 1945 — Delhi

My dearest Idie: we have just heard the news that the war in Europe may be over. People here have accepted it calmly and are awaiting confirmation. I hope it is true, and the war in the Pacific will collapse soon too. It has been a mighty long time in coming.

Eric is having a great deal of trouble getting back. If he does not make it, I shall have to stay here for probably another six months. Thinking of the future, how would you like to come out with Harriet, if it were possible? I do not know how long I will have to stay. It is worth thinking about though. I am not looking forward to this separation continuing longer, as I know you do not either.

I am well and keeping busy. Sending all my love to you two, Harry

* * *

May 3, 1945 — Delhi

Dearest Idie: when you receive this note, May 10 [our wedding anniversary] will have come and gone. This one will be different because Harriet has arrived, and you are not so alone.

I am losing count of the May 10's spent away from you, but the memory of ones together has not faded. I think our anniversary on the ship going home is the nicest remembrance of all, next to our wedding day. Do you remember the evening when the sun was setting on one side and the moon rising on the other, and we were together?

Someone said, on our wedding day, that he hoped in five years' time, I would be as happy as he was five years after his own wedding. This is our sixth, and each year adds to my happiness. As I grow older, such words as love, devotion, confidence, and trust take on new meaning.

Thanks, darling, for the many years of happiness you have given me. May there be many, many more – Harry

* * *

May 11, 1945 — Tucson, Arizona

Dearest Harry: your little sweetheart and I celebrated our anniversary by looking at pictures of you. Imagine six anniversaries, and we have only been together for three. It was a pleasant day and I enjoyed it by remembering those wonderful moments, vividly recalling minute by minute, getting off the boat on the 8th until we left for Kashmir on the 10th.

And then, the wonderful times afterwards. I am more grateful each time I think of our wedding trip. Thank you, my dear one, for the marvelous life you have made for us, the love you have given me, and the companionship we share.

Your letter about the trip to Patiala arrived yesterday. I am so glad you were able to go. It sounded very colorful and most enjoyable. Isn't it a shame you were called back so quickly! My, how we girls would have enjoyed seeing those remarkable jewels!

My sweet, your letter about Harriet and me traveling to you was a surprise. I know whatever decision you make about your work will be for the best. Even though we would be happy to come as soon as we can, I realize it may not be possible. I want you to feel perfectly free in your decision. We are comfortable here and well provided for.

I do not think it wise for us to consider going if a war is still on and you work for the government. The uncertainty is too great, and I would rather Harriet did not have to travel yet. She is so well; I would hate to change her surroundings. That is not what I would like to say, but what I must say under the circumstances. So, for the future, my sweet, we will stay here.

Remember your two girls love you very much, Idie

* * *

A month later, I received a cable saying Eric would not return, and a new man was coming. He would leave the U.S. around the middle of July, so I would need to stay until he was settled. If he arrived by the end of July, I could leave by September. That meant I could almost count on Christmas at home! Some people did not like the news, but I thought it the best ever!

PART IV
WAR'S END

New Delhi Lights

TWENTY-ONE

VJ DAY JOY

August 4, 1945 — Delhi

I studied the cable I received from the State Department. The war was over in Germany, but Japan still threatened the Pacific. I felt sluggish after a tiffin party at Rajpur Road and shuffled the other papers on my desk. The many jobs I had been doing for Mr. Clayton were now funneling into dispersing extra war materials and preparing for a trip to Nepal on behalf of the State Department.

> August 6, 1945 — Delhi
>
> Dearest Idie: Wilcox is scheduled to leave the States today. He should arrive by the end of the week. Yesterday I moved to Curzon Barracks, U.S. Army. I am not yet finished, but got nearly all the clothes, etc., I intend to take. I went through everything and decided to get rid of a lot of worn-out clothes.
>
> Rooms in Curzon are comfortable, and the food is good. They are built in doubles with two people sharing a bath.

I will share with Paul Casey of the American Mission. I have a corner room; Paul is on the other side.

I think I shall be comfortable and wish I had broken away long ago. It was very expensive at the house, about double Curzon.

By the way, I haven't had a letter in the longest time! If Harriet Anne is going to take up ALL of your time, send her back. I can't take the competition.

All my love, Harry

* * *

News came on August 12th that the war seemed to be over on both fronts. Speculation ran wild on how soon everybody could go home. It would take much longer than most thought. People were happy but somewhat fretful of what peacetime employment would be open to them. My friends, civilian and army alike, accepted the news rather thoughtfully. They were all my age or older, married with families. The great percentage did not know to what they were returning.

One of the most capable army men I knew, a lawyer, was in the process of changing from one firm to another when he joined the Army. He quit one job and did not have time to take the other. Another, a civilian, had worked for a large Hollywood studio. He said he could not bear the thought of going back into such a screwball game, but he might have to because his war agency job was temporary, like so many others. There were some who were irrepressible and wanted to celebrate with vim and vigor, but they knew what they were going back to.

Wilcox arrived with his secretary, as planned. When I met the plane, I found Wilcox charming and capable, probably the kind of man we should have had in the office all along.

I thought his secretary would probably not be very popular. I had dinner with them the first night and they came to Curzon for lunch the next day. They had the usual beginner's fear of the water, the food, the insects, the natives, and all. He seemed a polished apple, and she, a hard manageress of his affairs. He hoped to get me to stay longer, but with the war over, I did not see much point in it.

August 16, 1945 — Delhi

My dearest Idie: yesterday was filled with events long to be remembered—the official news of the surrender by the Japanese, Wilcox arrived, and birthday for me. It was a hectic day, one I had wished was right where it is now, in back of me. I suppose there is truth to the saying everything comes to he who waits—and helps himself.

All the monuments, fountains, and drives are lit to celebrate V-J Day. Some large fountains are ugly in daylight but, at night, with lights are completely transformed. Wish you were here so I could tell you, in my best guidebook language, what every building houses.

My present plans are to stay in Delhi until the first week in September and then proceed to Nepal for about three weeks. With the breaking up of the war theater, transportation may be difficult. We should be prepared for the journey to be more time-consuming than before.

I asked the Houston office for a statement of our account and have now received it. You have done some work on the house, bought a car, and had a baby. I think we are fortunate to be so much in the black. I did not expect to end up with anything close to that number. I am anxiously waiting to be with you again, Harry

TWENTY-TWO

AN EXTRAORDINARY BIRTHDAY BASH

September 1945 — Rambaugh Palace

As Wilcox and his secretary settled into the office routine and became more familiar with India, an invitation arrived for me to attend the Maharaja of Jaipur's thirty-fifth birthday celebration. A full week of festivities were planned but I knew George, and Ruth Merrell, plus some others from the Office of Missions, could only take off four days. I enjoyed seeing the expression on Wilcox's face when I told him about the celebration.

I rode with George and Ruth, in George's official automobile. It is not for the fainthearted. George and Ruth were in the back seat, and I was up front with a new Muslim driver. All went well until we reached the outskirts of the city. After that, I saw terror in the street and felt fear in my heart.

The driver stopped the car, unfurled a small American flag on the left front fender, glued one hand on the horn, and floored the gas pedal. Flag whipping, we barreled through narrow, crowded streets. Neither speed nor honking let up until we approached Rambaugh Palace.

I was point man, expecting I don't know what to crash into the windscreen at any moment; the happily grinning driver having a ball. Near miss after near miss, grazing bullock carts, people scattering like a covey of petrified quail.

Good Old George sat less perturbed than a serene Buddha. Ruth, ashen faced, simply closed her eyes, and hung on, praying, I suppose.

Turning off the main road, the driver—reluctantly, I thought—slowed to a stately creep toward the palace, where we received a royal salute.

Two handsome, superbly mounted Rajput cavalry soldiers with long, unsheathed swords in hand, guarded the gate. We paused briefly. Both cavalry officers raised their swords, flat blades facing us. The beautiful horses, proud heads erect, politely stepped sideways as we passed on into a wide, well-manicured garden in front of the palace.

Rambaugh is not a storybook palace. No high walls, no spires towering over it, but it is a splendid, luxuriously furnished modern mansion. Built on a terrace, it overlooks a fountain pool and expansive lawn, bordered with cedars and other decorative trees and bushes. A large fountain in the center of the pool erupts at regular interludes, sending a tower of water forty feet high while small jets arched streams of sparkling raindrops. We dubbed it Old Faithful.

The terrace became the gathering place before meals, and sometimes late into the night, energizing the lighted fountain. The best way to describe those evenings is to repeat Ruth's words: "Isn't it romantic?" I guess it was, but I didn't find any romance.

Can't tell you much about the palace, as I wasn't there much. I drank cocktails, dined sumptuously, and slept in an elegant suite; the modern tiled bathroom being a special treat with no tin tub, no thunder box! (pull-chain toilet).

We attended a late afternoon cocktail party at the Old Palace, Chandora Mahal. We sipped our drinks and nibbled treats on a spacious covered verandah overlooking a stunningly beautiful garden, reminiscent of Moghul gardens in Kashmir. Jai, the Maharaja of Bikaner, and other Rajput notables were there, along with us commoners. We took turns shaking hands with our host, Lieutenant Colonel His Highness Saramad-i-Rasahai Hindustan Raj Rajendra Shri Maharaja Dhiraj Sir SAWAT MAN SINGHJI BAHADJR G.C.I.E., Maharaja of Jaipur.

Celebrating a Maharaja's Birthday

I don't remember any entertaining conversation. It was a gala occasion because of where it was and who was there, but low key. No glitter, no pomp, no ceremony. Most of the men wore military uniforms, but not dress uniforms. Jai and Bikaner are honorary colonels in the British Army. George and I wore bush jackets—mine a summer-weight khaki, George's a little more upscale. A sprinkle of women were present: English and American, sporting tea-time frocks, leaving their big hats at home. If Indian ladies were present, I missed them, a disappointment. Indian ladies bring elegance and a touch of the rainbow. The sari, I think, is the most beautiful of all feminine attire.

When Prithi Singh, Jai's aide, whispered to me that they would leave the party early, I, too, slipped away, down the terrace steps into the garden, chuckling at the thought that, while sipping and nibbling, I had walked on water. Water for the garden, the Stream of Life, flows out of the palace, under the verandah, and drapes in a wide, sparkling sheet into a pool below. Bouquets of cut flowers, in niches in the wall behind the falling water, form a mosaic of what is in bloom in the garden. All would be replaced at nightfall with small lighted lamps, transforming an already enchanting place into a dream world.

A shallow stone-lined canal, filled with fountains and perky water jets, carried the stream across a wide expanse of lawns, flower beds, stately trees, and flowering shrubs. I wanted to spend the rest of the afternoon there but couldn't. The party was over, and I had to stay with my group. I did take with me a new feeling of awe and understanding of what the Moghuls meant by "Paradise Garden."

I was expected to attend a garden party on the palace lawn. I don't like them and dodge them whenever I can but couldn't weasel out of this one.

Someone in our group said later the garden party ought to have a literary title: Jaipur's Garden Party in Three Acts. I'd walk a mile to go to another one like it.

Act One was very British, a mélange of dolled-up people standing around or sitting at round white tables dotting the lawn, a small band playing soft background music. "A charming scene," according to one Brit. I did my small talk, ending with an English lady under a wide, frilly hat and her escort. I was bareheaded, without a topee, as was George. The music took a break, and I thought the party was over. It was only a pause for Act Two.

A small troupe of native musicians and *nautch* girls (dancers) appeared. Approaching the table where Jai and George sat, they squatted and bowed, heads almost to the ground. Jai raised his hand. They began to make their kind of music, with one stringed instrument, several drums, and a bevy of high-pitched voices. Chit-chat ceased. My ears told me it was time to leave. My eyes told my ears to shut up and look because a nautch girl had begun to dance, and nobody misses that!

She was a picture of swirling color and erotic motion, richly garbed, compelling rapt attention. A tight-fitting bodice, tiny mirrors woven into the fabric, midriff bare, long pleated skirt swirling around bare legs, barefoot toes with tiny sliver bells on them, larger bells around her ankles, rings on her fingers, a loop of gold dangling from each ear. I don't have words for the dance, but Prithi summed it up: "It's all about love."

When her short performance was over, the girl came to rest in a brightly colored heap, head touching the ground in front of Jai. An aide handed him a soft leather pouch filled with silver rupees. He tossed it toward the girl. She caught it in midair.

What a great way to end the party!

Then Act One returned in full flower. I went into my quiet-slip-away mode. That's when Act Three opened with a terrified scream rolling across the lawn, instantly altering "a charming scene" into an aura of fear, bordering on panic.

In the unnerving silence following the scream, a man burst from the shrubbery, closely followed by a huge black bear, both running hard, the bear growling, the man screaming.

People scattered; panic took over. Upended tables, chairs, and tea fixings littered the lawn. I was on the fringe, out of it. Jai and George were on their feet, Jai, looking composed, George, holding his ground. The man stumbled and fell only a few feet from them. The bear pounced. Man, and bear rolled together on the ground. The bear was growling, the man silent. People made all kinds of sounds. Jai stepped forward and gave a sharp command. Man, and bear stood up, the bear towering over the man. Both bowed. Jai tossed another soft purse.

No doubt about it, the party was over.

Jai seemed elated, as he remarked, "Put one over on George." I didn't hear George's reply, but he looked a lot paler and wilted. Ladies, now wearing roughed-up frocks, searched for lost shoes and hats. They did not seem amused.

I will cherish the memory of this garden party, something a Texan could be proud of.

The next day, the beautiful horses were on parade, at a grassy field inside the walls of the old fort, along with Rajput soldiers who had recently returned from the war. They marched past Jai, Bekarer, and Jodhpur, each prince stepping forward to take the salute from the troops of his state. A small but impressive ceremony. A band played; flags flew. Jai made a short speech. I don't know what he said, as Prithi was not available to translate; he was on horseback.

Two cavalry units followed, one riding superb black horses, the other one on equally superb browns. Every horse, head proudly erect, was prancing as if he thought he were king of the walk. The riders were splendidly attired in blue uniforms: tight-fitting jodhpurs, puggarees (turbans) streaming behind, a wealth of brass buttons, highly polished tall black boots, unsheathed swords in hand.

A royal show to honor a prince on his birthday with pomp and ceremony!

His Highness's elite assembled in a massive sandstone audience hall inside the walls of the old palace to pay him homage. Elephants and a red carpet set the scene, a last gasp for princely India. Democratic India was just around the corner; there would be no princes. But princely trappings and ritual ruled that day.

Among other rich ceremonial parade adornments were several elephants, lined up in position in front of the building, their trunks gently swaying. Gold brocade, inlaid with precious stones, covered their backs and sides. Small silver bells dangled from silk tassels, and a larger silver bell graced every elephant ankle. Gorgeously turbaned and attired *mahouts* (riders) proudly perched on the shoulders of each one. A red carpet, coming from elsewhere in the palace, passed in front of the elephants.

We climbed narrow stone steps to a side balcony, overlooking the already full hall, filled with men only, sitting on mats covering the stone floor. A red carpet separated the elite from lesser mortals. The lesser mortals looked like clerks in business suits. The elite, sumptuously garbed in brocades and silk, included some graybeards, reminiscent of an earlier, opulent age. I wanted to mingle with them but had to stay put.

An instant before Jai appeared, walking alone in his colonel's military uniform, someone out of sight struck the stone pavement with a staff, sending reverberating echoes through the hall. Expectant, almost breathless silence followed, all eyes focusing on the elephants. Jai walked slowly past them, following the red carpet between his sitting people. Some gently murmured, and all heads were bowed, hands in salaaming position. Jai sat on his throne, a large, carved wood chair on a block of sandstone, well above the others in the hall.

Our nest on the balcony was too far away to clearly follow the colorful motion and conflicting sounds below, but I can tell you it was a solemn occasion. The elite, one at a time, approached the throne, making abeyance to Jai. Traveling singers, on the outer rim of the hall, made their kind of music. Bejeweled, silk-clad nautch girls danced, this time in sedate grace and beauty.

Jai made a short speech I couldn't hear and walked the carpet again. It was over, leaving me with conflicting emotions, disturbed by the thought, *The King is dead. Long live democracy. Will it serve India well?*

An hour before everything started, Jai had said, "There will be an elephant fight tomorrow." That sent a triple shot of adrenaline through all of us. Elephant fights, a favorite sport of Moghul emperors and Rajput princes, are banned in British India, so excitement was at fevered pitch. "It might not come off," Jai continued. "They have met before, and the loser often will not again face the winner."

"Never mind," Prithi whispered. "Fight or no fight, it will be exciting."

So, there I was, with Jai and a few others, standing on top of a stone wall, looking down into the arena, a walled-in dirt lane about forty yards long and half as wide. Open archways at each end of the four-foot-thick stone walls barricaded with six to eight inches of thick tree branches.

I remembered a phrase from some favorite writer: "The air was alive with electric energy; something big, perhaps dangerous was about to happen." That's the way it felt, two fighters in the ring, spectators on top of high walls, behaving like a bleachers crowd at a baseball game. His Highness's guests on our side, along with palace people, ladies wearing brightly colored saris and the commoners on the opposite side. Both making their kind of noise, our side politely squabbling over the size, strength, and degree of madness of the two brutes, picking their winner, betting large sums on him; the other side egging on the elephant handlers with rude, unprintable local jargon. The fighters, some distance apart in their respective corners, raised a ruckus. The previous loser had both hind feet chained to a wall near the far end of the lane; the champ was penned behind a low stone wall too high to climb over, but low enough for elephants to trunk whip each other.

Prithi said elephants are not naturally bellicose toward each other. They must be "conditioned" to fight, maddened to uncontrollable fury, the final stage of which was underway when we arrived.

Both elephants had been heavily doped for three days preceding fight day; the champ now a raging maniac, ready to fight anything in sight; the other, also mad, but not mad enough to blot out the memory of his previous defeat, needed more "conditioning."

Trumpeting challenge after challenge, the champ frantically attacked the low wall in front of him. He couldn't push it over, so lunged into the thicker, taller wall behind him and sent his trunk snickering up it, trying to reach the spectators on top, even trying to climb over the low wall. He pounded the top of it again and again, squealing, his great ears flapping.

Meanwhile, handlers raised a tumult around the loser. They shouted, beat sticks on circular brass pans, waved colored cloth in front of his gaping eyes, threw sand colored water at his head, and set off firecrackers under his feet. He fought back, trumpeting with rage, blowing dust at his tormentors. The chief handler approached Jai and told him the loser was as ready as he would ever be. "Release him, get him up, facing the champ across the wall," said Jai. One might say that was a "Let the games begin" signal, but it was more than that, as it told a small group of brave little men the time had come to put their lives on the line for their prince. From that time on, it was dangerous to be in the arena.

Three shouting, cloth-waving men lined up in front of the elephant while two others quietly positioned themselves as close as they could safely get to the elephant's shackled hind legs.

Angrily squealing, the elephant tried to reach the men with his trunk. He sucked up sand and spread it out, driving the men back. They quickly returned, the elephant stretching out his great body and trunk, searching for the men in front of him. At that moment, two other men darted in to unshackle the hind feet. The elephant whirled, sent his trunk out at one of them who dove out of reach as I gasped. The trunk hit the ground with a resounding thud, inches from him.

I can't tell you how long it took to free the elephant, his handlers surviving near miss after near miss from that lethal trunk. Glued to my wall-top vantage point, nerves jangling, I was as wild-eyed as the demented elephants; time became a forgotten dimension.

Unshackled, the elephant tore after his tormentors, chasing one into a small ground-level niche in the wall with his trunk unsuccessfully following him. Another man approached the elephant head on. He charged. The man dove into another hole in the wall, farther up the arena, to be immediately replaced by another. A cat and mouse game, aimed at gradually bringing the loser up to the pent-up champion. But the fabled elephant memory did not permit the loser to face the champ again.

Jai shouted, "Let him out!" meaning the big, arrogant champ, still trumpeting challenges behind the low wall.

It was a big risk for Jai. An open fight probably would mean death for one of the elephants and serious injury to the other. The great beast, his trunk and short tail straight out, charged wildly. But overeagerness cost him, as he only landed a glancing blow. Dodging and squealing, the loser slipped past the champ and took off at high speed toward the gate, over which we stood. The champ trailed by no more than a few yards, the two of them stirring up a dust storm.

Onlookers went wild, shouting, jumping up and down, telling the loser to stand and fight, urging the champ to kill the coward. For me, another sound drowned all the bleacher sounds—a heavy thudding of eight ponderous feet reverberating across the arena. The earth might not have shaken, but I thought it did.

The lead elephant slammed into the barricade not more than eighteen inches under my feet, splitting the top limb. Seconds later, the champ rammed into the barricade. One short step back by the champ, one more massive ram, and the loser was hurled off the ground and through what was left of the barricade.

The champ, not pursuing, turned back on the handlers still in the arena. The loser raced on for a short distance and jumped into a small lake. The last I saw of him; he was squirting water over his aching body.

I played hooky the next afternoon, our last day. I chose not to go to a fight between a panther and a wild boar, both trapped for Jai's birthday celebration. They would fight in a tall silo-like structure, with a walkway on top for spectators. I chickened out after asking Prithi what would happen.

"The beasts," Prithi said, "are kept in small cages, facing each other, on the silo dirt floor. They will not have been fed for three days, so they will be hungry and ferociously angry. It will be a great fight with blood everywhere, but the boar will win. Always does."

George and Ruth had to go. Ruth said it happened just like Prithi said it would. "It was horrible. I wish I had feigned a headache." I don't know what George felt.

We returned to Delhi the next day.

TWENTY-THREE
WHITE MEN IN NEPAL?

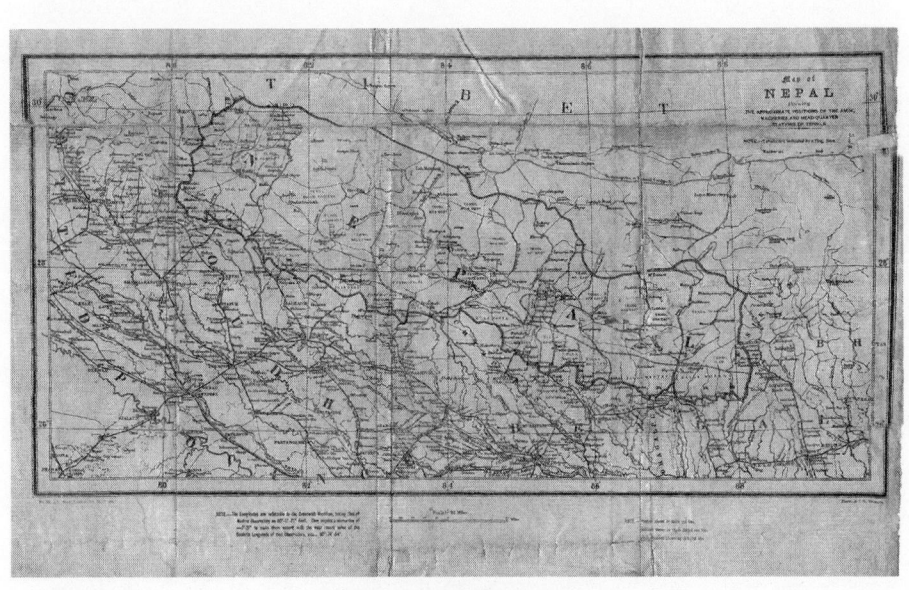

Map of Nepal in 1945

September 1945 — Nepal

I packed my bag again, as the long-awaited trip to Nepal was unfolding. I expected to be gone for two weeks to a month. I strode purposefully down the platform of the Old Delhi train station on the evening of September 10th, with my bearer, Syed Mohammed. I couldn't help whistling softly, finally able to follow up on an overture by Lieutenant Colonel K.N. Rana, the director of the Nepal Bureau of Mines, who wanted to supply metals and minerals to the American market.

The train had no dining car, but dinner was served at Hapur Junction in the railway station refreshment room. Upon arrival, an announcement alerted us that twenty minutes had been allotted for dinner. It included separate courses of soup, chicken curry and rice, a "side dish" of mutton cutlet made of minced meat, shaped in the form of a chicken leg, custard pudding, and hot tea. A formidable challenge under ordinary circumstances for either serving or eating in twenty minutes!

Tables dotted the dimly lit lantern room, their white cotton cloths giving welcome glimpses of reflected light. Barefoot waiters wore long white serving coats, divided waist high by red cloth belts. Their white tunics rose to a stiff and pointed crowning peak, giving an added appearance of height to medium-statured men. They moved rapidly from tables to kitchen and back again, casting long shadows on walls and floor and occasionally across one's table. There was no ordering; this was a take-it-or-leave-it dinner. Bringing course after course in rapid succession, waiters seemed not to walk, but to glide, their long robes playing a softly swishing tune, accompanied by slaps of bare feet on the floor. It made for an eerie atmosphere.

Food was bolted down, and the twenty-minute deadline was met. I heaved a sigh of relief when I returned to the reality of a train compartment. The engine tooted on time but sat another thirty minutes before pulling out.

After transferring early that morning from the main line at Lucknow to a less-traveled branch, I felt secure in thinking there would not be enough first-class passengers to fill my space, so I opened the typewriter and began to clack away.

People crowded in with accustomed fashion, carrying bedrolls, bundles, pots, and pans, the paraphernalia of country travel on Indian trains. We numbered eight adults and one baby, plus all the gear by starting time, in a compartment meant for four. Fortunately, several were short trippers, and we slimmed down to a comfortable three, two Hindus and one lonesome Texan. An odd trio with little in common.

The Hindus were a vivid personification of the great contrasts for which India is famous. They were as different from each other as I was foreign to them. The younger, clean-shaven, and neatly groomed in western-style clothes, was obviously a seasoned traveler with poised assurance. He traveled with a briefcase and good leather suitcase. He sat with his feet on the floor, jingling coins in his pocket, smoking English cigarettes. The other, a gray-haired elder, wore the traditional long tailed shirt, hanging almost to his knees, and thin cotton dhoti, exposing bare flesh from hip to toe. He was unshaven, and his belongings were wrapped in a cotton bundle. The old fellow seemed ill at ease and perhaps did not feel safe on the train. He sat buddha fashion with his feet drawn up on the seat. He did not smoke but chewed betel nut, the juice of which dribbled untidy brown stains from the corners of his mouth.

At stops for meals, the younger ate in the refreshment room. The older got his water from the segregated jug and ate only fruit and toasted grain off a little square of dirty newspaper. Most disconcerting of all, none of us spoke a language which neither of the others could understand. Even the Hindus spoke different languages and could not communicate with one another.

But the day was not entirely silent, nor was it devoid of activity. The monsoon was with us, though tapering off. Heavy clouds masked the burning sun most of the day, but frequent showers rolled by gusty winds played havoc, even inside our compartment.

Our venerable railway coach was in a sad state of health, not fit to travel. It rattled, leaked, and groaned. One window was stuck wide open, and the three of us together could not get it down. Old Buddha had preempted the space in front of it, steadfastly refusing to move, even when the wind tore away the newspaper he had been holding in front of the opening. He crouched, drenched, dhoti pasted to his thigh, and wryly grinned. He neither complained, cursed, nor tried to help himself. He sat, apparently content with the karma decreed for him.

When the door of the compartment blew open, as it did on occasion, the entire room was swept with wind-driven rain. It picked up accumulated dust already with us and turned the floor into a slippery brown mess. The door opened outward. The first time it banged open, the youngster and I jumped to close it. Buddha remained on his soggy perch. Fighting the wind, cursing the rain in two languages, we were slipping and sliding, finally shutting the door, but not before both of us lost our footing and were momentarily in danger of being thrown from the moving train.

When the door slammed open again, it remained so up to the next station. After the encounter with the door, the young man's aplomb wilted. All of us were streaked with mud and sitting buddha fashion with our shoes off. No longer present were the vivid contrasts. All of us were equally disheveled. Perhaps the old man was the most poised of all, if there was any poise in that compartment at all.

In true monsoon fashion, the squall hammered us for thirty minutes. One moment we were rushing along, buffeted by a sheet of hammering rain and then, with startling suddenness, the wind and rain were gone, and we were running through quiet paddy fields bathed in brilliant sunshine. It was another eighteen hours before I felt clean and dry.

On this branch line, all trains came to a rattling halt at stations thirty minutes to one hour apart. Poignant little dramas ensued around the third-class carriages. The noise began before the train came to a full stop as a wave of people gathered around the doors to each carriage. There were never enough seats or enough standing or hanging room. Pushing and shoving, too many were trying to get in. Those on the outside, carrying odd bundles, clawed and scratched their way forward. Those on the inside tried to bar the way, protecting their seat, or standing room.

The old and very young turned the spectacle into minor tragedy. Frightened and tearful, they wandered around the edge of the crowd, pleading for help. Many lost the fight. When the train began to move, and they were still on the outer rim, their voices shrilled with plaintive yearning. They wandered listlessly to a corner of the platform, dragging pitiful belongings, to await the next train. Some would wait another day, two days, or perhaps more.

The scheduled arrival time was four a.m. I was up and dressed. It was nine when we arrived. Like the old and very young at many a railway station, I sat and waited for a train.

The last lap was on a narrow-gauge railway, in an ancient train that chugged along at a maximum speed of twenty miles an hour over flat country. Paddy rice filled the fields, flooded from heavy loads of water dropped by the monsoon.

I saw fishermen casting circular nets for sardine-sized fish, flooded into the fields and ditches from nearby streams. Naked except for loincloths, they moved gracefully, pausing to watch the train go by. Net in hand, wet bodies glistening in the sun, they were a living picture of vigorous, primitive strength.

As I looked out the window, I was thinking time would soon slip further into ages past. Familiar scenes would be replaced with trivia of another dimension. It would not concern life on a railway station platform, for in the interior of Nepal, there were no railways.

The crossing would be into an isolated mountain kingdom, ruled by maharajas and princes, long closed to the free entry of western peoples and ideas. It was a country steeped in superstition and nurtured in eastern feudalism, an outpost of mystery. Famed Gurkha warriors, fabulous deities, and monstrous demons filled my thoughts. I fidgeted with impatience.

At Raxaul station, Subedar Sher Bahadur Malla was waiting for me. He would be my aide, guide, and companion on the trail to Kathmandu. Names, and connotations of names, are highly important everywhere in the east. The Subedar had an excellent one from all points of view. Subedar is an army rank. In the Nepalese army, it is said to be equivalent to Captain. Sher Bahadur means tiger, the brave one. Malla shows the Subedar is of the Malla clan, early rulers of Nepal. A name with an auspicious omen.

Sher Bahadur was a bright, cheerful young man. He spoke English well and was highly efficient. I had been at the Nepalese government's guest house for little more than an hour and had taken a most welcome bath, been served tea, and then been informed that Colonel Rana in Kathmandu had been advised, by telephone, of my arrival. Dinner was even being prepared. It might not sound like much of an accomplishment, but believe me, it was the equivalent of moving mountains. Maybe there was something to a name, especially in being a tiger!

The bungalow, though not elaborate, was substantially built and comfortable. It had running water, a large compound enclosed by a high stone wall, and an open verandah, running the length of the second floor.

From the verandah, I could watch a little engine switching narrow-gauge railway cars to separate tracks. The sun was sinking into dark monsoon clouds hanging low over the horizon, promising wet days ahead. The rest of the sky was ablaze with color. I saw a group of Gurkha soldiers walking toward the bungalow as a brilliant red and orange sun welcomed them home.

I was inside the door to Nepal! The next day I would begin the trek into the Himalayas. It had been a long day, but one salved with anticipation of adventure and the realization of a long-held ambition.

* * *

I awoke at six-thirty. Had I known what was before me, I would have slept longer. A train was to leave for Amlekhganj at eight thirty but was delayed while loading the heavy luggage of the Gurkha battalion. The troops then left for Kathmandu, and we pulled out at nine a.m.

Nepal had only one railroad, a narrow-gauge line, running from Raxaul to Amlekhganj, a distance of a few miles through the *Terai*. Terai means "moist land." It was relatively level, lying between India and the lower ranges of the Himalaya. Some of it was cultivated, but great stretches of it were swamp, jungle, and forest. Inhabited by elephant, rhinoceros, tiger, leopard, wild buffalo, deer, bear, and wolf, it also harbored many insects with malaria. Tribes who lived here were not affected by the malaria; they seemed to have a natural immunity to it.

Long before the announced starting time, Sher Bahadur was pacing up and down the length of the train, prodding coolie and passenger alike, urging haste. Loading the baggage went slowly. Arguments flared over where to put what—also, what and who could or could not go. Eight o'clock came and went, eight thirty, nine. Sher Bahadur became fidgety; exhortations became pleas and then threats to leave behind everything, and everyone not loaded. Loading was completed in short order.

It was a novel experience to see a man of the east so genuinely concerned at the passing of time. Dripping perspiration, Sher Bahadur exerted himself in an extraordinary manner to save every possible minute. An atmosphere of great urgency built up as he urged, negotiated, and gave orders. Experience had taught me that when a man of the east is worried about time, monumental obstacles lie before him. His one confidence to me was "We have a hard day in front of us."

An entire carriage was reserved for me, a fine and thoughtful gesture. On a narrow-gauge railroad, however, this does not imply a tremendous amount of space. The train was composed of five coaches, each having capacity for about forty people, packed sardine style. Not all who wanted could get aboard. When I suggested some come in with me, Sher Bahadur pretended he did not understand. Upon further insistence, he let me know quite clearly the suggestion was preposterous. When he oversaw a guest, that guest traveled in style, in comfort, and alone on the train. I had no idea where the Subedar sat. He would not even share my luxury.

Furniture in the car consisted of lower berths, three chairs, and a table. Curtains hung at the windows, the floor was carpeted, and there was a small washroom. However, this furniture was not built for people of outsized measurements. Berths were two feet too short for comfort and almost that much too narrow. The chairs sported heavily padded dome shaped seats, so when I sat, no part of the chair was visible behind my frame, and I kept sliding off. I moved to one of the berths. It made an excellent seat.

Our route was uphill. The overloaded train crawled at ten to fifteen miles an hour. Every village was a stopping place. Baggage, freight, and people were transferred, accompanied by shouts of welcome and departure, negotiations, and argument. Extra time was lost while the conductor chased third-class ticket holders out of second-class spaces. Hardly did we get underway before many were back where they did not belong. Most of the passengers were Gurkha soldiers, recently back from the war, I took the Subedar's word for it when he said, "They are rough fellows, these soldiers."

Our direction was almost due north toward the Himalayas, through a hunter's paradise. Sher Bahadur told me the Maharaja came once a year for a shooting expedition, in which the elephant played a key role. Nepal maintains large herds of elephants. When used in ceremonial and state functions, they are bedecked with jewels and gold and silver trappings. But they are also hard, productive workers.

I looked for big game but saw none. In its own way, the more mundane scene was equally fascinating. The paddy harvest was underway. It was largely women's work because it had long been the custom for Nepalese men to seek employment in India, where jobs were more plentiful and remunerative.

Villages were well kept, and most of the houses looked substantial. Their walls were bamboo frames covered with a fine red-brick mud which was dried in the sun. Doors and window frames were made of exceptionally hard sal timber. Roofs were of thatch, rising to a pyramid apex. Raised, hard packed-earthen platforms, usually with a roof over them, served as porches.

In the forested areas, enormous sal trees grew close together, with vines and limbs forming a dense, humid, almost impenetrable barrier. In many places, the sun never penetrated to the ground. With malaria ever present, few willingly journeyed across this fearsome country during the hot rainy seasons. More than once, natural elements of the Terai had turned back invading armies or left them ravaged and ineffective from illness contracted from drinking swampy water or insect bites.

Foothills slowly grew into full-blown mountains, slowing the train to little more than a crawl. It gave me an opportunity to peer into the jungle in search of wildlife. At times, the railway resembled a tunnel in the dense growth, so close as to be touched from the train. The only wildlife I saw, however, were a few chattering, black-faced monkeys.

Two large parcels, containing my lunch, had been prepared at the Raxaul guest house for eating on the train. According to Sher Bahadur, there was no suitable place to obtain food between Raxaul and Chisapani Garhi, which we would not reach before late afternoon. I am sure Sher Bahadur dined on deliciously spiced native curries. I did my best to persuade him to let me join him but to no avail. One package contained a whole roasted chicken and medium-sized boiled potatoes. The other contained three small loaves of bread, an apple, pear, and orange. An ample and quite delicious repast.

Buses were waiting when we arrived in Amlekhganj. One was reserved for first-class passengers. Regular army trucks had been pressed into service for the others, most of whom were Gurkha soldiers. The first-class bus was a Chevrolet chassis with a body built by Nepali craftsmen. It was converted into an adequate, if not luxurious, set of wheels. It had four partitioned, second-class sections, which took up the largest space.

The driver's assistant was chased out of his seat so I could ride in the cab. Sher Bahadur squeezed in on the other side of the driver, a very tight fit, but he made it. It was the first and only time I have ridden in a bus with the driver cramped in the middle! With his freedom of movement restricted, it was not the safest way to navigate a bus on a mountain road, but the driver did a magnificent job.

Nine men and one tiny woman occupied the first-class space. It was barely wide enough to run a bench down each side. When passengers were seated, there was constant jangling of knee against knee and sidewise rocking into neighbors. Being tightly wedged together gave the advantage of restricting movement to mild tossing, instead of throwing bodies, which would have resulted if more space had been available.

In the baggage cubicle, three mail sacks and three men rode in comparative luxury. With mail sacks as pallets, the men lolled, sat, and stretched out more comfortably than anyone else.

In the second-class part of the first-class bus, twenty-one people were crammed together. The job of getting all these people into confined quarters could not have been improved upon, even by circus clowns tumbling out of small cars. Benches ran the remaining length of the sides of the bus and across the front end, next to the baggage space. After the benches were filled by squeezing, pushing, and shoving, more travelers were crowded in and bunched together on the floor. A knee in a neighbor's back, a foot in someone's lap, shoulder against chest, no matter, as everyone wanted to go home.

Good humor radiated their ability to cope with the situation. Their acceptance of the situation, without major fracas, was an object lesson in oriental patience. There was no bickering or arguing; everybody cooperated in getting loaded and underway.

Luggage was roped to the top of the bus and covered with a tarpaulin. When fully loaded with passengers, heads half in, half out of the windows, and the unshapely mound of baggage stashed on top, the bus became a monstrous thing, unsteady over the road.

Sher Bahadur again urged haste. He paused long enough to tell me the last phase of our journey would be on a difficult mountain trail which he did not wish to make after dark. Each delaying minute made that more certain.

It took nearly an hour to load passengers, secure baggage, and collect fares. Loading passengers and securing baggage was overseen smoothly by competent people acting with long familiarity with the job. It was the collection of fares that took time: a fascinating example of the innate desire of people to drive a hard bargain. The fare was fixed, published in plain sight, announced repeatedly, and well known to everyone on the bus and in the town. Yet practically every passenger feigned ignorance, expressed surprise, and argued for a cheaper rate. All ended up paying the fixed rate, but time was lost.

It was afternoon by the time we pulled out of Amlekhganj. Purple monsoon clouds had gathered threateningly, giving the appearance of an impenetrable wall rising out of the road. As we progressed up the winding, rock-strewn road, their near presence became ominous. We passed through a long tunnel, and then our bus became part of that mass of wind and rain. I tasted my first monsoon onslaught in Nepal, it boded no good for the foot/pony-back trail waiting for us.

The rain first fell in slanting columns, so trees on nearby mountainsides were only partially visible. It turned into a steady hammering, rising to a crescendo of wild jubilation. But this was not its best. The downpour accelerated in volume until everything was obscured. Mountains, trees, and the front of the bus disappeared into furiously pounding water, whipping unmercifully at everything in its path. The purple cloud descended upon the road, and we were in it. Its power was startling, a reminder of the insignificance of humanity when confronting aroused nature.

And then it was suddenly gone. First came a slackening of the rain, with brief breaks in the surly, swirling clouds. Trees were briefly outlined in the sky, as if without support from roots. Dark purple passed on to be replaced by gray drizzle. How can a busload of people be suspended one moment in a torrent of driving water and tumultuous hammering, and then be ambling along the next?

When I could see the road, it followed a small river toward the Himalayan barrier which guarded the mountain passes into the Valley of Kathmandu. Before the downpour, water in the river was bright emerald-green, reminiscent of the Kishanganj in Kashmir. Enormous boulders hovered in the riverbed and on its banks, speaking of the power even a small river can generate. Thinking about the exploits of demons in Hindu mythology, it was easy for me to conjure up visions of a titan taking a handful of those stone monsters and tossing them down the river, like children playing jacks.

The road's end came five miles short of a spot where a washout obliterated any sign a road had been there. What was left simply ran up to an enormous pile of rubble and stopped. Consequently, our foot/pony-back journey began prematurely.

Coolies were waiting to carry the baggage. They huddled in the drizzle under homemade umbrellas woven with cane ribs and flat faced grass, then folded in the middle to form a pyramid roof over the head of the carrier. Since my store-bought umbrella leaked, I tried to trade it for one of the more suitable if bulky home products. The coolies knew when they were well off and refused to trade.

Each coolie carried about eighty pounds in a basket slung across his back. Short of stature, they looked hardly shorter than their loads, but it did not bother them. They staggered off in a happy chorus of shouting and singing. After slipping into my raincoat and waterproof boots, I followed the carriers over the mound of rubble and onto the road.

The loss of time became serious. Unloading baggage and distributing it among the coolies cost another hour. Simply looking at the formidable barrier of mountains in front of us was reminder enough that Sher Bahadur had been right. The day had proven to be a hard one, and daylight was rapidly disappearing. The hardest part still lay ahead.

Preferring to stretch my legs after the cramped bus ride, I declined the offered pony. This seemingly put Sher Bahadur into a quandary. He apologized for the rain; was the pony not all right? Why should anyone walk when there was a good pony to ride? He shook his head, giving in to save time, I thought.

It was an invigorating walk, even though the atmosphere was dank and humid. The rain increased in tempo until it became a steady downpour. It was relatively easy going, but perspiration soon had me as wet under the raincoat as I would have been without it. I discarded the coat and gave myself to the enjoyment of the elements. This too, seemed absurd to Sher Bahadur. I mused he must have had doubts about the man whom he was assigned to get safely to Kathmandu.

The hills around us became rugged; their seeming innocence seen from the railway carriage disappeared. Now they looked like their real selves, steep and rough, cruel to the unwary. The river had also changed. No longer was it placid but a roaring torrent, reminiscent of a muddy-colored demon, greedily licking everything in its path. Small waterfalls hammered over the great boulders, and a steel suspension bridge lay bent and twisted almost beyond recognition.

Small rain-born rivulets raced down the mountainside, tinting the color of minerals in the soil. A scarlet stream came rushing over the rocky hillside, transforming the bigger river's waters into an almost cheerful bright red, while only yards further up the trail, dirty black pushed arrogantly forward, becoming Joseph's coat of many colors.

Bhimphedi, a large village and the terminus of the motor road, was our objective. With still a mile to go, I mounted a pony to save time. There was no chance of reaching Chisapani Garhi in daylight. The stop at Bhimphedi was short, just enough to confer about what to do next and to catch our breaths.

Chisapani Garhi was two miles above Bhimphedi. The trail leading to it was little more than a pony track. It wound back and forth and up the mountainside, as if a great snake had dug a furrow in passing. While "winding" is the correct word, it does not draw a good picture of what the trail was really like. The angle of ascent was steep; the switchback was used but relatively sparingly. It seemed the Nepalese were firm believers in the axiom of a straight line between two points. It was a difficult climb for me. It was seemingly all in a day's work to the Nepalese.

We started in twilight, which is brief there, and we were shortly groping in the dark. Our progress was painfully slow. Bhimphedi is supplied by electricity from a dam nearby, and its lights began to flicker out of the gloom as we started the uphill grind. Sher Bahadur and I discussed the possibility of stopping at Bhimphedi. We decided to go on as we were expected in Kathmandu the next day and would not make it unless we reached Chisa Pani Garhi that night. What a temptation, however, to lay down our weary bones!

Before we left Bhimphedi, a telephone message was sent to the governor of the fort at Chisa Pani Garhi, requesting lanterns be sent down the trail to meet us, and another pony. As the sun sank lower, the temperature went with it. I was wet through from the rain, despite the physical exertion, and my teeth were chattering. My raincoat was miles behind with the slower coolies, and my lightweight khaki shirt and trousers were no match for the mountain chill.

Syed, my bearer, had borne up well. He had endured the unaccustomed food and insects, the cramming together and monsoon drenching, with something close to aplomb. Indian bearers of city sahibs do not often walk for miles on mountain roads or on twisting pony tracks. This trail came close to finishing him. Syed's pants were in tattered shreds as he limped manfully along in growing misery. There were not enough ponies to go around, and Syed had done five miles on foot before we started up the trail. He was undoubtedly reaching low ebb when Sher Bahadur slipped off his pony and forced Syed to ride. Syed complained bitterly at having to ride while the Subedar walked, but the tiger came out in Sher Bahadur, and he sent the pony off with a slap across the rump. I doubt Syed had ever been on a horse. He was suddenly so busy hanging on, his complaints ceased.

After fifteen minutes on the trail, I got down and suggested that Sher Bahadur also ride. Another problem. Neither Sher Bahadur nor Syed considered it honorable for them to ride while I walked. After a long negotiation, I convinced both of them it was necessary for them to arrive in less worn-out condition than I. Upon arrival, all I would have to do is rest; they would have chores to perform. They rode for the next fifteen minutes, while I struggled along in a disgraceful manner, thinking every step would be my last.

The lights of Bhimphedi kept us company for the first mile. When we reached the ridge where we would lose them for good, we stopped for a breather and a last look. At any other time, when less footsore, wet, and cold, we would have enjoyed a thrilling scene. The wild beauty was deeply impressive, even in our exhausted condition. The fast-flowing river sparkled with reflected pinpoints of lights. Bhimphedi nestled under ruggedly rising mountains; all else was hidden in the monsoon night. I looked in detachment, wondering if we had neared the halfway point to Chisa Pani Garhi.

A spring marked the halfway point. We stopped to await the arrival of the lanterns and the other pony. The lights coming down the trail were encouraging. Bobbing up and down in a now-you-see-it, now-you-don't fashion, they carried the message that we could now move more swiftly to warmth, a bath, food, and a bed.

When the lights and the new pony arrived, all were rested and ready to go. Had the new pony been given his head, he would have either galloped all the way or broken his neck. A spirited animal, he had not been ridden for several days and was a wild thing, ready to run. To keep him where the lights showed the way, the pony boy hung onto his bridle. Thanks to the wild spirit of this pony, the last half of the trail became an invigorating finish to an arduous day.

At about nine o'clock, we arrived at Chisa Pani Garhi, much to the relief of all. Chisa Pani Garhi translates into "cold water fort." It is well named, as the water had a polar chill in it, but it was also soft and sweet to the taste. An old fort stood there, guardian of the trail. In earlier days, it must have been easy to defend and difficult to take. It was built near the top of the mountain, and a clear view extended for miles in the only direction from which an attack could come. Before reaching it, one must pass through a narrow defile. We were as glad to see it as an invading force must have feared it.

The altitude was about five thousand feet, and the air was pure, and cold, a wonderful change from the hot, humid plains. After a warm bath, I stepped under the cold water for rejuvenation. It did the trick. I shivered again, although wrapped in a warm blanket. Dinner was a fine whole roasted chicken and medium-sized boiled potatoes. It was good to be in an unspoiled country, bone weary but still pleasantly so.

* * *

Early morning noises penetrated my sleep and fuddled my brain at six o'clock. Eager to be off, I jumped out of bed. And quickly jumped back in! Only half awake, my physical senses suffered a severe jolt. It was cold out there; my leg and back muscles were painfully sore. Rationalization came easy. Why not bundle up until the morning chill faded away? Yesterday was rough; why not take an extra hour of ease today?

Syed banished the thought. Having stationed himself outside my door at five o'clock, no doubt at the thoughtful suggestion of Sher Bahadur, he entered with bedside tea at the first sound of my stirring. He remained to lay out fresh clothes and announced breakfast in thirty-minutes.

It is unwise to record my early morning thoughts, especially when early morning is chilling. Grumbling in normal character, I muddled through with enough time for a quick look outside. No air anywhere compares with sharp, crispy mountain air, laced with tangy forest smells. I involuntarily breathed in great gulps, as if trying to store it away for recall in less invigorating circumstances.

Small wood cooking fires added their own private aroma to the blend produced by growing things. Bubbling teapots and jingling horse gear, as well as clanking of cooking pots against stone, made music to pace the growing activity.

Men and women divided belongings and stowed packs, while snorting ponies were saddled. Under a nearby tree, a group of Gurkha soldiers drank tea, their breath producing little vapor clouds to blend with steam from the teacups. Another group, packs on backs, were already moving onto the trail. Laughter and good humor floated from group to group.

On this fine day, mountain and tree, boulder, pony, and human stood out in bright splendor. Purple monsoon gloom and the gray haze of yesterday were a drab memory. Even the trail, so darkly wicked last night, projected a quiet image of rural charm.

To the people in the scene, it seemed a morning like all mornings and not to be frittered away in idle musing. Breakfast of scrambled eggs, toast, and tea was quickly served. We moved out immediately to the last stage on the trail to Kathmandu.

It was my good fortune to have the Peppery Pony again. Snorting and prancing, he seemed eager to warm up with a good hard run, but the trail was dangerously rough, and he had to be held in. What a great and zestful animal! He was a short-legged, wiry mountain pony, but with spirit enough for Pegasus. Long after the other ponies began to need urging, the peppery one continued to jog smartly, snorting with pleasure, head bobbing, tail switching.

Shortly after leaving Chisa Pani Garhi, the trail slanted steeply toward Sisagarhi Pass. It had little resemblance to a man-made thing. Narrow, strewn with all shapes and sizes of rocks, deeply cut by water erosion, it followed the course of running water finding its way to the river below. Always a difficult trail, one sees it at its worst during monsoon.

Villagers were responsible for upkeep of the trail in the area near their village. When the climb to a village was especially difficult, large stones had been cut into steps and set into the trail. They were wide, often ten feet, and sometimes closer to a hundred, leading up and over rugged terrain to a village perched on top of a mountain; then down the other side. Monsoon rains had dislodged many of those great stones, adding to the woes of unwary travelers. They would be replaced after the monsoon, and the holes would be filled.

As we were in a rested condition, the first hour was exhilarating with the changing panorama of the trail. Each of the Gurkha soldiers carried a heavy load of personal belongings. Somewhere on each person, a *kukri* (Nepalese knife) could be seen. Some carried it on their back or tied it waist high, with a brilliantly colored red or blue sash. Others stashed it in a basket or bundle, but all had at least one. In the hands of the Gurkha soldier, it is a symbol of death to the enemy. But it does not serve only as a weapon. A jack of all trades, it is a singularly important tool in Nepal, as is the pocketknife to a Boy Scout. It can also be used to behead animals for food and for religious rites or used to turn the red soil in a garden. I saw a young boy using one to husk corn and cut it from the cob.

To a heavy-footed plainsman, it was impressive to witness the sure-footed Nepalese men and women glide over the trail, even when carrying heavy packs. I slipped over large obstacles while they seemed to float without breaking stride. I stumbled over rocks and sloshed through holes filled with water; the Nepalese seemed unaware of impediments, carrying themselves with upright dignity fit for a drawing room.

The greater part of the day was on horseback, but we walked the downgrades to rest the ponies and to lessen the chance of a fall. Going down was always slippery, difficult for the ponies, even without a rider. Nor was it easy for this human traveler, unaccustomed to mountain trails. Feet not normally encased in heavy boots grew heavier by the hour. Yesterday's blisters evolved into raw spots of torn flesh aching for reprieve.

This trail was too rough for animal transport, so pack animals were not used on it. Goods entered Kathmandu either by coolie or electric cableway. The cableway required only two hours, but the maximum load per cable truck was five hundred pounds. All heavier goods went by coolie. Automobiles then in Kathmandu were carried in fully assembled by fifty to seventy-five coolies, straining under ropes and poles. Considering my own challenges, the carrying of fully assembled automobiles and electric generators seemed incredible.

I was told coolies preferred their loads in a basket with a wide, oblong opening at the top. A wide strap attached to both sides of the top of the basket ran over the shoulders and around the forehead. At first glance, it appeared head and neck would bear the brunt of weight and strain, but it became evident that with skillful manipulation, a balance was achieved, transferring the weight to back and shoulders. Our coolies were small, wiry, stouthearted men. Many carried long wooden staffs to help with the rough places. They were remarkedly strong, able to plod along with a steady gait which ate up the miles as fast as the ponies.

Some men and most of the women who could afford it, traveled by *palanquin* (a chair suspended by long poles carried by four coolies). Small children rode in a basket hanging from one side of a bamboo pole slung over a father's or coolie's shoulders, laughing along the way.

Near midday, the trail dipped into a valley of striking beauty. Much of it was under cultivation, green fields with nearly ripe paddy rice. Water buffalo, sheep and goats grazed in the uncultivated part, watched by small boys. In the villages, several houses stood alone in their own private fields. Houses were built in the same general oblong pattern with two or three floors. The ground floor was for animals, upper floors for people and food storage for man and beast.

A plentiful supply of cucumbers, pumpkins, and yellow corn was visible at all houses. Corn, tied in long, neatly trailing bunches, hung on the outside of upper stories of most houses, adding colorful decoration. A bustling, prosperous air permeated the entire valley as the harvest had been good, and winter was not likely to be unkind.

On the hard-packed clay porch of several houses, popcorn was being prepared in narrow-mouthed, wide-bottomed clay jars. The jar with corn inside sat over a slow-burning open fire. The open mouth was stuffed with long, thin bamboo, resembling chopsticks. The person doing the popping twirled the bamboo between the palms of his hand, agitating the corn. What an odd place to see this old standby of movies and baseball games! And what an ingenious way to pop it without the loss of a single fluffy piece.

Lunch was under a tree at the end of a meadow, where the trail again took us to the mountains. And what was my lunch? One whole roasted chicken and medium-sized potatoes. I wondered if it had come with us all the way from Raxaul.

Then the trail turned wicked. It was possible to ride most of the way up, but the climb was difficult; it was necessary to rest the ponies every few minutes. Even the peppery pony was stumbling. Neither man nor beast wanted to tarry, for the mountainsides were covered with dense jungle growth. It screened the narrow trail from any outside view and kept out fresh air. Dripping with sweat and panting from the humidity, all suffered from the overpowering sultriness. Human and beast had only one aim, to get it over with.

As we entered Sisagarhi Pass, the view on either side was well worth the toil, blistered feet, and sore muscles. The walled-in valley shone in brilliant sunshine. A lazy stream, shining silvery white, snaked idly through the fields. The distant mountain effectively sealed off the valley from outside eyes. At our feet lay the brown-colored dense jungle, its thick growth hiding whatever was inside as darkly as it kept those inside from seeing out.

To the north, the Kathmandu Valley spread out under a thin layer of clouds. The sun broke through occasionally to permit white and copper-colored roofs to spark a welcome. Pagoda- and dome-shaped construction stood out in bold relief. Beyond the city and across the valley, the massive ranges of the Himalaya reared up as far as the eye could see.

The trail dove steeply from the pass to wind down and merge with the white thread below, the motor road to Kathmandu, eight miles from the trail's end. We walked through dense tropical vegetation, hotter and more humid than the other side. It was a fast, slipping and sliding descent, for something new had been added: earthworms by the million. They slithered out of overly wet soil onto the rocky trail to be squashed by travelers or to expire of their own accord. A normal occurrence during monsoon, the slimy ooze produced a horrible stench that urged haste. Happily, the worst of it was quickly left behind.

We entered an area where women wood choppers were gathering wood for stoves in Kathmandu. By the time we were halfway down, their axes had stilled, and they were beginning the homeward trek, accompanied by a thrilling rendition of hill songs. High overhead, from some perilous perch, the song began with a sweet-voiced young girl. As the girl's voice died down, the song was picked up by a more mature voice near the end of the trail. A small boy joined in once, only to be drowned out by his elders. When it seemed the song was over, a deep-throated male answered from the next ridge, and the women picked it up. The song shuttled up and down the trail, as if some unseen conductor were giving signals to bring everyone in at exactly the right place. A stirring climax to an arduous day on a rough trail.

The trail ended about fourteen miles from Chisa Pani Garhi, on the floor of the Kathmandu Valley. A touring car was waiting to take us to the guest house. It was an old model, but a Rolls-Royce could not have been more welcome.

* * *

What a tremendous relief to shed heavy boots! That was action number one. Action number two was the greeting of Subba M.R. Bhandary, Controller of His Highness's Household. He called immediately, saying I was some days late. He also asked what kind of a trip I had experienced and placed himself at my service.

"The trip was very interesting," I told him. "My every want was amply provided for. I am delighted to be in Kathmandu and am wondering if a parched traveler could have a cup of tea?"

Tea came quickly but the controller could not join me at once. His father had died nine months before, and according to caste custom, he had to observe a full year of mourning, during which he must abstain from numerous habitual practices. Among them was giving up tea drinking and being able to shave only once a month.

The abstentions in no way detracted from his charming personality. Our first visit was short, but long enough for him to tell me Kathmandu got its name from a temple built about three hundred years ago from a single great tree. The Sanskrit word for wooden temple is Kastamandup: "kasta" means wood and "mandup" is temple. In Hindi, the word converted to Katmandoo or Kathmandu.

As soon as my baggage arrived with clean clothes, I stepped into an oval tin tub of hot water. Being too short by some feet and none too wide to fit my frame, this bath was still sheer luxury. Weary stiffness faded.

Later in the evening, Major K.N. Rana called on me to pay his respects and outline a tentative program for the next two days. A truly delightful man, short of stature, broadly built with a round face and a personality that flowed from a pool of innate good humor. The high admiration I felt for the Nepalese people gained a notch, even at so brief a meeting with this good man.

* * *

I met with government officials over several days to discuss Nepal's request for twelve army trucks through the FEA disposal program, and to investigate the possibility for Nepalese businessmen to open an export-import business in quartz crystal with the U.S.

September 22, 1945 — Kathmandu

Dearest Idie: this is a hasty note to let you know I am okay. Major Rana just left my room after a long conversation. He offered to arrange, and to accompany me, on a trip to Lhasa, Tibet. It would take fifteen days each way, so I had to say no, even if it meant crossing the roof of the world. This was a most flattering gesture, and the second one I have received since arriving.

The first was the offer to take me out of Nepal by the trade route lying in the heart of the country. This I have accepted since it means the loss of only a few days. NO OTHER EUROPEAN HAS EVER BEEN GIVEN PERMISSION TO TAKE THIS ROUTE. I am looking forward to it!

See you when I can, my sweet, all my love, Harry

* * *

On September 24, Lieutenant Alfred D. Brown, an expert in quartz crystal, arrived in Kathmandu. I was glad to see him and smiled warmly when we heard we were invited to visit a quartz mine in the Lamjung area, taking the route described earlier by Major Rana.

We left Kathmandu on October 1, with an entourage of about fifty people, including coolies, cooks, and pony boys. Steep slopes and intermittent rain made progress slow, and we were also challenged in keeping coolies because the Hindu Dussehra Festival was approaching. It celebrated good over evil, and much like our Christmas, was a time for good eating and wishing one's neighbors well. Camp was often set up after dark and dinner preparation took hours.

I scribbled notes and kept a daily journal for a report I would write for the State Department, recording the rugged terrain through which we would travel, the geology of the region and a section for general interest. I also wrote daily to Idie, even though I could not mail it.

Walking the trail on the first day, we saw little traffic, except local people bringing in yarn for spinning, firewood, or grass to feed animals. I spotted tiny villages built near the top of the hills, people seemed industrious and friendly. Old men and children sold peanuts and cucumbers while women wove fabric on handmade looms. Cargo out of the valley seemed limited to homespun yarn in white and blue, probably for Tibet, as this is one of the old established routes. Women traveled with the men and carried equally heavy loads.

Brown and I usually rode ahead of the cohort, leaving Major Rana to be sure all went well behind us. We came to a spot where a landslide had washed away the road. The earth was soft, and we half slid, half walked while the horses followed. At the base of the hill, the trail reappeared and led us to the village where we were to meet the major.

When we entered the town, we became the center of a curious crowd. A policeman wanted to know where we were going, and why. We told him we were traveling with the major, who was behind us. Our crowd of onlookers soon lost interest and moved away.

The view was magnificent. Looking back over the trail from which we had come, Kathmandu stood out dimly. In front of us were folds of tremendous mountains. In the center of this panorama, and far below, a tiny river wound around the base of the hills. We camped nearby.

* * *

We began the next morning with a steep ascent. For a short time, we rode but then had to walk. If there is such a thing as the devil's highway, this is it. We were cautioned to ride as much as possible because landslides had washed away the road further on and we would be forced to walk. The ponies could not carry my great weight up the steep slope, so I walked. I congratulated myself on the foresight to have hobnails put on my boots. It was a hard climb, and I was grateful to get back on the horse, a welcome perch!

We wound around the top of the hill, our visibility good everywhere except down, as the clouds were below us. After some time, we started down the other side. If the first side was the devil's highway, then this was his brother's. Nowhere could there be a worse strip of Mother Earth. It was also the monsoon's path, cutting deeply into the trail. Some stones on the path were round and slippery, others were shale with vicious cutting edges. To get the ponies down safely, one pony boy led each animal, with another hanging on to its tail.

We passed through a number of villages, all built near the top of the hills with steep approaches where the trail had been made into rough stone stairways sometimes two miles long. In the course of that day, we had started at 5,500 feet, climbed to nearly seven thousand, then descended to our next campsite at 2,200 feet.

* * *

Early the next morning, Brown and I left to scout for green pigeons. We found a flock, and I shot one for dinner. By early afternoon, we had arrived at a suspension bridge over the Trishuli River, which led to the village of Trishuli Bazar. Brown and I walked across the suspension bridge in step, the first two white people ever to do so!

The town was one street wide, built on several levels up the gentle slope of the hill, and about one city block long. We became "museum pieces" as great crowds gathered to stare at us. All traffic stopped. No one was allowed to get within ten feet of us. The crowd got as close to us as possible and seemed to enjoy looking at us.

We camped about a mile from town, on the riverbank, and waited for the coolies to arrive. Brown and I took the opportunity to bathe in the coolish water. It moved swiftly, giving us somewhat of a massage. I felt like a new person afterwards. The coolies lagged behind, carrying sixty-five pounds each. Camp was once again set up after dark.

Surprisingly, dinner was a wonderful chicken curry. Wonderful, because we had been eating roast chicken for lunch and dinner every day since we started. Breakfast usually consisted of fruit, eggs, leftover chicken made into croquettes, native bread, and tea. Lunch was always cold roast chicken, potatoes, and more bread. Dinner was often roast chicken or game we shot, fried potatoes, rice, bread, and tea.

Three coolies deserted that day, going home for Dussehra. This time the ponies were staked next to the camp and a guard set, as leopards were common in that area.

* * *

We were up early on October 4 and on the trail by 7:30 a.m., struggling with the rough terrain, unable to ride almost all day. We saw more traffic, people carrying fruits, rice, and leaves for cattle fodder. We followed the trail around and through the river after lunch, then up and down. It began to rain gently, then a lot. We could only do seven miles that day. A goat had been given to Rana at the last camp, and it was slaughtered for dinner. The cook beheaded it with one blow from a kukri. An efficient, merciful way to kill.

We were well into difficult country but saw houses situated on several levels of the hill on which they were built. There was not enough flat country on which to build more than one or two small houses. Paddy patches went right up the base of the mountains.

* * *

The coolies were slow in leaving camp the next morning, partly due to the desertion of several of them. I decided to go ahead, noticing villages were becoming less numerous, and paddy fields seemed smaller, but I saw considerably more corn, lemons, guavas, and oranges.

I traveled pretty well, making a short descent to the suspension bridge and then climbing again. On the way up, I kept thinking the top would be reached around the next bend but there was always another.

When I reached the first pass, I stopped and took in a fine view, my first uninterrupted one since coming to Nepal.

I met a Gurkha soldier who had served in Italy and Germany. We rested together, and I told him what a fine place I thought Nepal was. He told me, in the GI language he had picked up, "Americans, good, Italians not so good, Germans, very no good."

I walked all day and felt better than I had in months. Camp was set up by a snow fed river, cascading by our tents. Dinner consisted of fried trout and fish curry. What a treat!

Local dignitaries came to meet with Major Rana and to show him samples of quartz crystal from nearby mines. They acted like kings, owning much of the land and leasing it to those who worked it.

* * *

Occasionally, we would spend a day or two in camp, to lay-in new supplies, let the ponies rest, and allow Major Rana time to visit zinc and copper deposits. Brown and I realized the trip would take longer than we thought, partly due to the disappearance of coolies and monsoon landslides obliterating the trail.

When Major Rana returned to camp on October 6, he brought a large wild pig that he had killed. It needed to be properly butchered before bed, so it was another late night for the cook. We did have fried wild pig for breakfast the next day, and it was excellent!

* * *

The next day, I again left camp ahead of the others and enjoyed an easy walk beside a trickling stream that fed the Ankhu River. As the group caught up, it became apparent we would need to cross the river and then climb what looked like a small hill. Up we went, very steeply to the top. From there, we looked down on the swiftly flowing Buri Gandaki River. Camp would be set up beside it for the night. Brown and I went to the river for a bath, this time with soap. It was very cold, but also refreshing.

Inside Nepal at Last!

The bustle of the camp was something to see. Our tent always went up first, then the major's and then the others followed as best they could. The coolies were becoming more experienced at this point and did a more efficient job, but never without considerable noise and confusion. After the tents were up, various cookfires were assembled. They were a cluster of rocks with a few sticks of wood underneath. They did very well with what they had, but it took forever. It was invariably dark and almost past dinner before we could have any tea.

* * *

Our next day's trek took us to Khan Chok, where Major Rama and Brown visited a copper site, and I spent the morning working on my notes and report. Near lunch time, several flights of cranes flew over, close to several hundred, flying very high. They had just cleared the snow peaks from Tibet and would not stop until they reached India. When I first saw them, I thought they were geese because of their flight pattern.

On October 10, we walked what we thought was twelve miles, but the local people said we had traveled only eight. We were never quite sure how far our next camp would be, nor how far we had come. Distance was measured in *kos*. A kos is 2.2 miles. The trail had been laid out many generations before as an avenue for trade between the villages of Nepal and Tibet, as well as for military travel. Without instruments, it was difficult to measure distance. A man took a green leaf from a tree and started walking. When the leaf withered, the man stopped, placed a stone on the road and called it a kos. He then picked another leaf and started again to make the next kos. There seemed to have been no revisions in the system since that effort.

This area was famous for wild fowl and pheasant, but we didn't see any. I was able to bring down some pigeons for eating. Major Rana said he saw a pheasant, so I went after it, slushing across wet fields and wading in the small stream, and was almost in range when the bird took off. I managed a long shot and it dropped. My first pheasant, only it turned out to be a big old owl. The coolies were delighted, cutting off the beak, declaring it magic against snakebites. Scratch the bite with it, and healing takes place.

* * *

I left camp early again, on October 11, walking five pleasant miles downhill. The country was heavy with jungle growth, lasting about a mile and a half, then opening into rolling green meadows. Even the paddy fell away. The trail was a narrow cow track, but good.

For two days, on our way from Chepeghat to Udaipur, our compasses behaved badly at 3,300 feet. They pointed north when we knew the direction was west. Major Rana, Brown, and I went over our schedule with the maps. Originally, we were to complete the trip in fourteen days, but we had consumed eleven and were not even halfway. The coolies could not keep up. They were paid but felt forced to work because they wanted to go home for the festival. We camped early, hoping for an early start.

We got on the trail by seven fifteen the next day, hoping to reach Lamjung or nearby, so we could release all the coolies. I learned our group was a tremendous drain on village economics; each man required two pounds of rice per meal.

Following a mountain stream to the top of a mountain, we rode around it for the next three miles. After walking down to Taru Ghat, we crossed the Marsyangdi River on a suspension bridge. The trail was moderately good to this point; then it became a poor track through paddy fields and goat tracks, sometimes only six inches wide.

* * *

Hooray! On October 13, we made it to Lamjung, near the mine sites we were to inspect. We were six days behind schedule! It was a good thing we did not know the real state of affairs, or I would never have agreed to such a long trip.

We decided to make Lamjung our headquarters for a few days, as it was a somewhat larger town than others nearby. The camp personnel could celebrate Dussehra there, and sufficient food would be available for us. Religious celebrations and feasts happened every day.

Some letters and newspapers arrived from Kathmandu. FEA had been disbanded and the State Department had taken over part of its functions. I thought a number of our people would be gone by the time I returned.

On October 16, the Nepalese camp members insisted Major Rama perform the traditional well-wishing ceremony, in which the eldest male member of the family blesses all the younger ones. Celebrations and animal sacrifices were performed. Brown and I were given the honor of performing the sacrifice of a water buffalo. We both tried with the kukri but were only partially successful, slaughtering our animals, but not with one blow.

* * *

We were able to get back on the trail that day and branched off the main road, taking a much less frequented path. Ups and downs all the way, sometimes crossing streams with big boulders, sometimes in the jungle, and in paddy fields, on and off the horses every few hundred yards. We traveled from yesterday's 3,100 feet to 5,400. I tripped and stumbled most of the day, but I felt good.

I topped a hill and saw a Dussehra procession was just finishing. The entire village was out in force. The village elders immediately came to see what they could do for me, but they couldn't understand a word I said. I was surrounded by the usual crowd, but this time with more reason, as I was the first white man to visit their village. They would not allow me to sit on the ground but took me to the durbar-palace of an ancient chieftain. It was slightly larger than the average village house, two-storied with a thatched roof. A long Tibetan horn was produced, and a salute, plaintive and long, was blown for me. In order to show I was to stand at attention, one of the elders took my hand and placed it at my cap.

The people of the village wanted to give us some of their small stock of goats, milk, rice, and fruit. We paid for most things, but they wanted to give us everything. It was touching to see them come, dragging their unwilling goat, or toting a basket of rice. They gave their particular salaam with both hands, bowing almost to the ground, seemingly honored we would take what they offered.

We were unable to move the camp for two days because no coolies were available. I kept busy with Idie's letter and my report. I looked like a shaggy bear, without a shave since the beginning of the trip, and no chance for a haircut either. I enjoyed the beard and decided to give the Delhi office a few moments of fun by wearing the moustache when I got back.

* * *

The trail became more difficult from Lamjung to Manjung as we trekked down a steep hill, then climbed along a ridge to another steep descent, scrambling down crabwise and sliding our feet sideways to get to the bank of a river that fed the Marsyangdi River.

I paused as I surveyed the crude bamboo bridge over it. Tree limbs were overlapped and tied together, meant to form an uneven platform, but it was in fact a pile of round limbs, swaying above the torrent of rushing water. This was a time of indecision when I knew fear. I could not jump over the river, and the frightening thing was the sound of furious, foaming water rushing down from the heights, attacking great boulders in the river.

As I wallowed in this dark thought on my side of the river, a small girl with a bundle on her head came to the other side. She stopped and looked enquiringly at me. I stepped aside. Then the little girl, balancing the bundle on her head, chin held high, bounded joyfully across the "bridge," seemingly unconscious of danger. What should have been evident from the beginning, became crystal clear: cross, or lose face with my Nepalese friends. It was not a pretty performance, but it gave them a good laugh.

* * *

From there, going became even more difficult. Manjung is built on top of the highest hill in the country, 4,200 feet above sea level, with a foot path to get to it. We stayed at the house of a chief, a two-story clay structure, painted, as all the houses, were for Dussehra.

Everyone in the village came to see the white men. These lookers were very persistent. We were their first white visitors, and they hung on every move we made. Sometimes it was difficult to find any privacy. It was partly our fault because, at the beginning of the trip, no one was allowed near us. We discouraged this, as we were as curious about them as they were about us.

It was eight thirty before the few coolies we still had arrived. We each had a cup of Ovaltine, made with condensed milk and hot water. It was wonderful! The chicken curry was ready about ten, and then we fell into bed.

* * *

When we arrived at the site of the quartz mine near Manjung, village dignitaries and mineral scouts for Major Rana brought forty pounds of crystals for Brown to see. From this large selection, he found many of the specimens too small to be considered, but he did choose three or four pounds to take for laboratory inspection. We also taught villagers how to dig and where the best results could be obtained. That delayed us until eleven a.m.

The village chief tried to persuade us to stay and rid his village of a pair of panthers that were stealing buffalo calves. We were so far behind schedule that we could not stay.

Challenges erupted every day in our trek from Manjung to Buli Buli. The distance was reported to be twelve miles on trails only a few inches wide and covered with dense undergrowth. When we completed what we thought was twelve miles, there was only a cowshed waiting for us. Buli Buli was still four miles away. The rations had already been issued, so there was little food. Breakfast at Manjung had to sustain us, as lunch on the trail had consisted of two oranges. Dinner was popcorn and one small cup of Ovaltine each.

That trail was as difficult down as it was up, a footpath with many obstacles. We received a different report at every village as to how far away Buli Buli was. We stopped at dark and sent scouts to see how far away we still were. The trail was dangerous enough during the day; Rana was concerned for the coolies. There were cows at the shed and a roofless structure that served us well for the night after our one small tent arrived.

* * *

Once in Buli Buli, a subedar (warrant officer) from a nearby village came to pay his respects. He was an old pensioner, who had retired at the end of the last war (World War One). He wore his old uniform, well kept, with three medals won in France. He walked with a stick, but looked smart, with military bearing. He salaamed the major, shook my hand and gave us the first correct information we have yet received.

We arrived at the designated campsite on a bluff beside the river, surrounded by mountains. A wonderful discovery was the large pot full of live snow trout waiting for our breakfast. We stayed there a couple of days so Rana could visit a brine spring from which Nepal obtains its only indigenous salt.

I stayed in the camp while Major Rana and Brown visited the spring six miles north. They found it was not large, and only producing small quantities of salt annually. A recent landslide had covered it, so the major searched for a new rumored outlet. Upon finding it, he recommended a water geologist be employed to investigate the site to see if more could be produced. Otherwise, Nepal would have to import salt.

After a fine lunch of fried trout, vegetable curry and rice, I walked about half a mile in search of pheasant. Hunting dogs arrived to help. They got the scent of a fox and took off; we never saw them again. The subedar said the dogs were meant to tree the pheasant. I told him I preferred to shoot them on the wing, and he said, "But they fly very fast." He shook his head, wondering, I thought, why I should take a chance on a flying shot when I could take a sitting one.

One of the Nepalese with us had planned a bear hunt and an opportunity for us to see native dancers. Brown and I followed him on a footpath over the hills and down to the riverbed, as usual. The rain came down in sheets and we were soaked, even wearing raincoats. It became apparent by three p.m. we could not continue the hunt.

We spent the night in a house lent to us by someone who, like other families in the area, had two houses, one on the top of the hill for summer and one in the protected valley for winter. In the shelter of the house, pulling at my pipe and watching the rain, I mused that I must be a fair-weather hunter, as I did not care for the soaking, difficult trail.

The dancers came from the Gurung community, known as fierce fighters, as well as graceful dancers. Three men and two women dancers, four drummers, and a chorus of ten performed for us. The whole troupe consisted of sixty performers, but the courtyard was too small to accommodate all of them. They danced some of the Mahabharata, one of the two great Indian epics. The entire performance usually takes around a week of long nights to complete. The dancers wore bright costumes; the women sported pigtails and jingle-bell anklets. A lamp was hung up on a pole with an umbrella attached to it so we could see them.

The next day we set out for Baglung Danda and then Falang Kot. The trail took us over a small mountain, then down the other side and across a narrow valley. The last two miles included a steep, slippery uphill climb. We camped at 6,300 feet, cold and wet.

The Kidam Khola River was at the bottom, but there was no bridge. It was deep and fast moving. The ponies swam through, but Brown, Rana, and I climbed the bluffs lining the river on a game trail. The last sixty yards became what the major termed a "monkey trap," meaning we climbed straight up, ladder fashion, hand over hand, We then joined the ponies and rode through paddy fields, eventually climbing the hill to Blangkot on winding stone stairways.

The site for the camp was a good one, set up in the front yard of a woman mendicant. She kept a fine vegetable garden and we cooked some of her radishes, popcorn, and bananas in the fire as we waited for the coolies. For dinner, we ate beans, pumpkin, mustard greens, and okra. A fine change from the meat and fowl diet that we had been on for so long.

The mail caught up with us there. Major Rana received a letter saying Lieutenant Brown needed to report back to the U.S. Army on November 1. Impossible! He couldn't get word to them either, which would mean a good Army chewing out.

Major Rana cut the camp workers to the bare minimum. Walking down was the usual difficult job but it should have been easier. The river had flooded into a tremendous lake. We sloshed through flooded paddy fields to get to the next campsite.

Rana and I talked about business opportunities for Nepal while waiting for the coolies. He wanted Nepal to drop her veil of deep secrecy and allow publications like *Harper's* to carry stories about her. He could have lived an easy, luxurious life but chose to work hard. He was the means of our entry into Nepal and wanted others to come, but not sightseers. He wanted workers.

* * *

We spent the night three miles away from our intended camp at Pokhara because the weather was terrible. Morning brought sunshine, and we made good time, arriving at our designated site just in time for a serenade by three flute players. A wandering minstrel and his son also showed up, as did everyone in the village.

They gathered on the maidan. Spectators were fifteen to twenty deep in a circle around us everywhere we went. As we were the first whites to arrive in Pokhara, and Major Rana was a representative from the durbar in Kathmandu, everyone nearby came to see for themselves.

Rana visited the governor and arranged for horses and coolies to be at the camp the next day at seven a.m. We walked through the town, built in the shape of a great T. The streets were the usual rough stone pavement, and most of the houses were made of clay, with a few of stone. The bazaars seemed to have more goods than any of the others we had seen, including some luxury items and cigarettes. Our audience was still with us when we retired at 8:30 p.m. No one did any work, as practically the entire population of Pokhara were outside our tents all day.

We were ready to break camp at six a.m., but no ponies or coolies had arrived. By nine thirty, Rana gave orders to commandeer all ponies in Pokhara and all coolies necessary for us to get on our way. The owners would be paid but would not have the use of their horses for a few days. By ten thirty, we had twelve ponies and enough coolies. We left the tents and heavy gear but took our personal baggage plus emergency rations, usually carried by nineteen coolies. Rana then cut the camp personnel from twenty-one to eleven.

The trail was wide, rocky, and steep. We took a wrong turn at one point and went an extra mile, winding up short of where we wanted to be at the end of the day. We were in a village where one man owned five houses. He made two of them available to us. It was interesting to see women smoking cigarettes but not the men.

* * *

We followed a ridge in the morning, enjoying another fine view. Masupuari, which is over twenty-one thousand feet, stood out in bold relief, perhaps fifteen miles away, over three folds of mountains. We stopped at Naukot, where breakfast was prepared on the parade ground, under lovely shade trees. The cooks preceded us, but it took them two hours to prepare. Time was a foreign word; no thought was given to it in their language.

Rana received a letter from the governor of Pokhara, apologizing for his people's failure to bring the ponies and coolies. There was also a letter from Kathmandu advising us that the British minister had returned from Delhi and requested the Prime Minister to recall us immediately, without allowing us to proceed any further into the interior.

We made it to the trail's end on November 1. Hallelujah! We had walked steadily down for the first three miles after our last hard climb. Going over a streambed did not seem nearly as bad as others at the beginning of this trek.

The Terai stretched below us. It was an impenetrable-looking jungle with flat, sizzling hot Indian plains stretching out beyond what I could see. Butwal was just under us at the foot of the hill—the end of thirty-two days in the forbidden hinterland of Nepal. It had been an incredible experience, but I was glad the trek was over, and I could make my way to the U.S.

TWENTY-FOUR

HOME AT LAST AND AWAY AGAIN

November 5, 1945 — New Delhi

Dearest Idie: after twice as much time as anticipated, I am back in Delhi. Nepal was fascinating but perhaps the most difficult of all the trips. I feel I am in the best physical condition since leaving Rice. Nepal is all hills, and the trails over them are steep. I have about one hundred typewritten pages for you but cannot send them until I finish my report, as I must occasionally refer to them.

I plan to go to Bombay for ACCO work for a few days, provided I get the Nepal report finished. I will then return to Delhi for about a week and scoot for home. I hear from others that a delay of two to three weeks is happening in some places. If so, I shall take a ship. They are talking twenty-one days to New York. I am trying to wrangle a high-enough priority to get home for Christmas.

There were three letters waiting for me, the last one dated late in September. Nothing yet in October. Hope everything is all right. Glad to hear the baby is getting along well. Am mighty anxious to see you both. The young rascal will be almost a year old. You must wonder how she got there and if you really do have a husband tucked away somewhere.

As usual, I stirred up something of a hornet's nest, much to the delight of the Nepalese and discomfort of the English.

Love you very much and hope to see you very soon – Harry

* * *

I made it to Bombay without postponing the date more than twice. A record! It was good to see the place again—it hadn't changed much. It was a melancholy drive through Bandra and over the well-remembered ways Idie and I had traveled. The policeman on the corner where we turned to go up to Pali Hill seemed much the same, as did the tall palm beside the apartment in which we were married, but more tired and battered by the winds.

I stayed at the Taj Mahal Hotel. My room looked out over the harbor, and how I wished Idie were with me, sharing the thrilling sight of a full, high moon in a blue sky. In the foreground, the Gateway to India was a magnificent play of light and shadow with small fishing boats gently moving on the quiet harbor water. A little way out, big ships sported winking lights. Across the harbor, barely outlined, were the islands in the deeply blue water. On the land side, the ever-present clock tower was still telling the time from Ballard Pier.

I went to the cotton market and had lunch at the Indian club, meeting with a group of brokers and mill buyers. The market was in an unhealthy state, and I did not believe ACCO would reopen immediately. Mr. Fleming, chairman of the board, would not like the slant of things as they were.

I returned to Delhi and focused on completing the 109 pages of my report for the State Department.

It was December 6 before I could leave and fly to Karachi, beginning a convoluted trip home via Cairo, Tripoli, and Newfoundland. I arrived in New York at 1:30 a.m. on December 14 and left later the same day, arriving in Washington, D.C., at eight a.m. on December 15.

I relaxed as I surrendered my job at FEA, after being debriefed. I took a deep breath before reporting on my trip to Nepal to the State Department. I asked for serious consideration to be given to my recommendations for the U.S. to assist Nepal in her efforts to industrialize and develop her mineral resources.

I had hoped to meet with Mr. Clayton but learned he was vacationing at a guest ranch near Tucson, of all places! A State Department official suggested I meet with him there.

On December 18, I practically danced onto a train car bound for Tucson, anxious to see Idie and meet my little daughter. Christmas was especially joyful when Idie's brother was able to return to Tucson in time for the holidays.

I caught up with Mr. Clayton at the guest ranch. Besides discussing my Nepal report, I also asked his advice on a job offer from the State Department. Mr. Clayton's response was crisp and to the point: "Return to the firm. We need you in Shanghai, now. How soon can you leave?"

I stepped backward, surprised by the offer. After a discussion with Idie, I accepted the job in Shanghai, China, with Anderson Clayton, beginning in March 1946. While excited about the prospect of going to Shanghai, I was disappointed not to be able to follow through with trade talks between the government of Nepal and the United States.

Preparations for my trip began immediately, with careful thought this time as to how Idie would travel to China on a freighter with fourteen-month-old Harriet. I went to Houston first, to check in with the ACCO office. Idie and Harriet followed, visiting relatives and looking for doctors who would vaccinate them for typhus, cholera, and yellow fever.

Before leaving Houston, in late February, I hugged my girls tightly, then boarded a train for Los Angeles, where I would catch a ship to Shanghai.

March 7, 1946 — *SS Christer Salen* at Sea

Dearest Idie: you know how difficult it was for me to leave you this time. Seeing all those who were reunited with no concern of separation again, it did not seem fair for us to continue ours. Something from within kept driving me on so strongly, I could do nothing but follow where it led. Never have I ever wanted so little to do a thing and yet been driven so resolutely to do it.

That does not seem to show a great deal of consideration for either you or Harriet, but the more I thought in terms of you, the more insistently the quiet voice said *Go*. I have always thought of you as part of me. It is still the same, so know whatever the force behind my leaving, you two were considered. Please come to me soon.

I was feeling more than a little sorry for myself after watching you and others wave goodbye, wondering why it had to be this way. I opened your little testament, the one that has been to so many places with me. Without conscious effort, I turned to my favorite book of John. I opened to chapter 15, verse 27: "And ye also shall bear witness because ye have been with me from the beginning." I remembered the other time you sent me away with the prayer I adopted as my motto: "In all thy ways acknowledge Him, and He shall direct thy paths." (Proverbs 3:6)

I felt better then and am now sure this is the right thing. Soon there will be no regrets. Love you always, Harry

Goodbye!

AFTERWORD

In August 1943, when Harry was especially anxious to go home to Idie, the American Vice Consul in Karachi, Clarence E. Macy, called him indispensable to the war effort. Harry seemed not to believe it, as in letters to Idie he rarely spoke, for security reasons, about his leadership concerning the strategic procurement of war materials or his work with the Lend-Lease program.

After World War II ended and Harry had left India, he received a letter in January 1946 from William Bissell, chief of the India and South Asia Division of the State Department. Bissell praised Harry's superb skills in managing the entire operation of the Indian Affairs division of the Foreign Economic Administration war agency during the last months of the war.

The chief made a point of saying that the letter was his personal expression of appreciation for Harry's efforts, many involving delicate negotiations with the government of India.

The letter is included below, making it clear that the exceptional performance of the erstwhile young country boy from Texas had made a critical difference in the successful procurement of war materials for the United States, thereby contributing to the ultimate Allied victory.

ADDRESS OFFICIAL COMMUNICATIONS TO
THE SECRETARY OF STATE
WASHINGTON 25, D. C.

DEPARTMENT OF STATE
WASHINGTON

THE INTERIM FOREIGN ECONOMIC AND LIQUIDATION SERVICE

January 7, 1946

In reply refer to
BA-1513-WTB
Room 2723 T Bldg.

Mr. Harry W. Witt
2525 North Stone
Tucson, Arizona

Dear Harry,

    To mark the end of our work for the Foreign Economic Administration on Indian affairs, I want to tell you, with something more than a handshake, how satisfactory and stimulating it was to work with you across the distance separating this city from India.

    I first knew of your work after the war-agency merger which took the form of the F.E.A. Your first war assignment was, I believe, with the Metals Reserve Corporation. When I went to India in 1944, you had been doing field work for the U.S.C.C. almost exclusively, in connection with buying and developing sources of strategic materials.

    During absences of the then Special Representative of F.E.A. you were left in charge of the office, and I had a chance to observe your operating ability. Between February, 1945, when the Special Representative left for the United States and the end of August, 1945, when his successor arrived, you had entire charge continuously of a staff of about 40 people, situated in New Delhi, Calcutta, Bombay and Assam.

    During that time, you were responsible for carrying out the Lend-Lease program, procuring strategic materials for the U.S. government, and coordinating the activities of those engaged in enemy intelligence work and air transportation from China. The first of these functions involved delicate negotiations with various departments and high officials of the Government of India to protect the U.S. taxpayers' interest in Lend-Lease and to make sure that India received from us what she needed for fighting the war. These negotiations you carried out decisively and effective-

- 2 -

ly. The procurement function involved equally critical dealings which resulted in the provision of manganese, beryl, burlap and many other war materials in quantities that definitely would not have been available without effective efforts on your part.

You succeeded in maintaining close and friendly relationships with government officials and at the same time a firm stand on U.S. policies which often were questioned or opposed by the Government of India. Throughout, you also kept closely in touch with the American Diplomatic Mission and U.S. Army officers.

Your accomplishments were achieved in an atmosphere of considerable difficulty, due to emergency war demands, changes in U.S. requirements and regulations, trying personnel crises, and the confusion produced by India's sprawling democracy -- and centuries' old red tape.

I am writing this letter of my own initiative to put on record the appreciation felt for the skill and high quality of your work, which I wish to do since I was the individual in Washington most concerned with and affected by your operations.

Sincerely yours,

William T. Bissell, Chief
India and South Asia Division